THE FEMALE
EXPERIENCE
AND THE
NATURE OF
THE DIVINE

THE FEMALE
EXPERIENCE
AND THE
NATURE OF
THE DIVINE

Judith Ochshorn

INDIANA UNIVERSITY PRESS • Bloomington

Manufactured in the United States of America

Library of Congress Cataloging in Publication Data

Ochshorn, Judith, 1928–
The female experience and the nature of the divine.

Includes index.
1. Women and religion.   2. Sex and religion.   3. Sex
in the Bible.   4. Polytheism.   I. Title.
BL458.026   291.1'78344   81-47012
ISBN 0-253-31898-X   AACR2

CONTENTS

ACKNOWLEDGMENTS

A number of people saw portions of the first and revised drafts of this book or read them in their entirety. Among those whose criticisms or support I found most valuable were Juanita Williams, David Horsman, Daniel Bassuk, James Strange, Esther Broner, Rosemary Radford Reuther, and Rabbi Theodore Brod. Obviously, the final version represents only my own judgment and errors in judgment, which are not to be attributed to those who were kind enough to share their time and expertise with me.

Special gratitude is extended to Sharon Eskridge for her intelligence and dedication in typing the manuscript, and for her unfailing friendship and support throughout its long course.

Above all, I thank my children. My daughter, Cathy, with her usual insight and love, first understood the importance of such an inquiry, told me how much it meant to her as a woman, and made it possible by her very presence. Her brothers, Benjamin, Ezra, and Daniel, all provided sustained and affectionate patience, material help, and constant encouragement, enabling their mother to pursue her own search for a better grasp of the meaning of our past, in the hope of contributing to a more humane future for them.

INTRODUCTION

WHY yet another book on women and religion? Why yet another probe into the distant past, into the religious beliefs and visions of ancient, vanished civilizations—to discover what?

I would like to relate how this book came to be—partly to indicate why beliefs about the significance of gender in the ancient Near East are so important for us to understand today, and why current theories about the outlook of these early civilizations seem inadequate; partly to show how the tendency of scholars to inflate women's role in reproduction and to use it as the basis for locating men's activities at the heart of human culture and social change both impoverishes and distorts the historical record; partly to suggest how a feminine-centered analysis of the last might yield a host of rich new insights about a critical turning point in that record; and partly to acknowledge my debt to those whose work helped to direct my own onto a new track.

Like people, books are a product of their own time and place. My interest in comparing the ways in which ancient Near Eastern polytheistic and monotheistic religions viewed female sexuality, the relation of gender to the exercise of power in the divine and secular spheres, and the participation and roles of women and men in cult in their religion-centered communities, was generated by several different but related experiences and shifts in personal consciousness. All were linked in one way or another to the contemporary resurgence of feminism, the movement of some of its concerns into the mainstream of scholarship, and the reciprocal nourishment of the latter and the women's movement. Until feminist scholars began to challenge the accuracy of widely accepted knowledge by demonstrating that traditional methodologies and interpretations of data—indeed sometimes the data themselves—frequently reflected cultural biases toward women, and until terms like "sex roles" and "androgyny" moved into the realm of understood usage in feminist writing and research, it would very likely have been impossible even to conceptualize the argument of this book.

Like many others, in the early seventies I began to teach Women's Studies courses, the academic response to the exclusion of women from serious and systematic study in most disciplines. While my formal training was in history, that field's overriding emphasis on political, military, and diplomatic alliances and conflicts among elite groups of men had long since ceased speaking to me. But the challenge of trying to recover part of the history of women—to formulate the right questions, to use data that might reveal some of what is yet unknown about the female experience—and my long interest in the history of ideas converged to revitalize for me the allure of our past and to restore my sense of its profound continuity with our present and future.

If, as Joan Kelly-Gadol so aptly put it, the goal of women's history is "to restore women to history and to restore our history to women,"[1] then a corollary of this definition is that the denial to women, or any other group of people, of knowledge about their past figures significantly in the etiology of their oppression. Thus, in addition to my intellectual interest, the necessity of reclaiming and redefining our past spoke to me in a deeply personal way.

As I began to piece together information scattered in many sources about the lives of women, I was struck by a recurrent motif, namely the pandemic, if changing, influence of Western religious attitudes toward the sexes throughout history, and the many ways in which religious values often contributed to and became interwoven with social ideology, or provided one (though usually not the sole) rationale for civil practices.

It is a commonplace that religious values frequently have reflected some of the most basic perceptions, aspirations, and values of their own cultures. The importance of this aspect of religion has been matched only by the authority of its tradition in Western thought about the nature of women and men, and by its mediation in helping to shape, legitimize, and sanction social attitudes toward the sexes, social expectations of appropriate gender-based behavior, and social rewards and penalties for conformity and deviance.

However, the connection between religious or social attitudes and practices has been extremely complex. Certainly the status of women or the nature of relations between the sexes in any society cannot be inferred in a simple, linear, causal fashion merely from the content of the society's religious beliefs about femininity and masculinity. Nevertheless, for all its permutations through time (some of which will be traced in this book), the impact of religion, whether overt or covert, has been far-ranging, and when that impact has been restrictive it has, most often, been especially so for women.

This view may seem a bit exaggerated, particularly in times like our own, when we fancy that we live in something like a secular age, in the sense that religious belief (or the lack of it) seems a matter of personal choice. However, it may be precisely in such times that the force of our Judeo-Christian heritage is most influential, since we are not compelled to subject its views about the significance of gender to rational or conscious scrutiny. Witness, for example, today's well-organized political attempts to circumscribe the reproductive free-dom, or very lives, of women—attempts allegedly based on that religious heritage, or, more specifically, on the Bible.

When I first team-taught a course on women and religion, I became exposed to the recent work of feminist scholars who have been engaged in a reassessment of the sources and content of the Judeo-Christian tradition. Their general aim has been to explore the manner and extent to which that tradition, with its heavy masculine overtones, imagery, and orientation, may be reconciled with the inclusion of women as well as men as full persons and participants in religious life. This effort has been broad-based and has begun to raise central ques-tions about the accuracy of biblical translations and interpretations, the intellectual and sociological origins of religious attitudes toward the sexes, and the position of women in just about every phase of doctrine and ritual.

It would be difficult to acknowledge by name my debt to the many people working in this area. There were three who, in different ways, most facilitated my own thinking about the significance of biblical imagery, the systemic ambivalence toward women expressed in early monotheistic literature, and the consequences of our religious tradi-tion for both sexes. Phyllis Trible showed how translations of the Old Testament conveyed the sexual-cultural bias of their authors, who, in their overwhelming use of masculine words and images, excluded original, equally valid allusions to the feminine. Rosemary Radford Ruether analyzed the writings of the early Church Fathers and demon-strated an essential ambivalence in their views on women. And Mary Daly, in her earlier work, evaluated our religious legacy as alienating for both sexes and proposed new ways of apprehending the divine and identifying theological concerns.[2]

But for all their acuity, even brilliance, and despite the fact that they enabled many of us to "see" Judaism and Christianity with new eyes, the analyses of these theologians were for me ultimately problematic. Their arguments and conclusions were somehow dissonant, their final statements somehow too upbeat and hopeful in light of their own discussions and, in the case of Trible, her exegeses somehow too sanguine.

For instance, Trible notes the patriarchal character of the social order described in the Old Testament but chooses to emphasize instead other biblical evidence for what she terms a counterculture, favorably disposed to women, which, she finally concludes, embodies the underlying spiritual message of the Bible.[3] Some of her work on the unwarranted (if not inaccurate) use of solely masculine language and metaphors in biblical translations is of real value, illustrative of the interplay of historic cultural attitudes toward the sexes and what has until now been represented as the authentic rendition of the Bible, and it sensitizes us to the weight of meaning borne by language itself. However, while there is no question of the importance of how language is used, Trible tends to minimize those pejorative and ambivalent views of women which do not seem susceptible to semantic modifications, and they are to be found in both the Bible and later commentaries.

Though Ruether is hardly conciliatory toward the misogynism of the early Church Fathers, she sees their exaltation of Mary as the other and equal face of their deep ambivalence toward women. Ruether grounds the patristic vision of a spirit-matter dichotomy in the dualistic thought of its own time, in which the mind was believed infinitely superior to the body, and she shows how easily this view became linked with feminine and masculine traits, behavior, and valuation. Women became the symbol and embodiment of the flesh, threatening superior masculine reason and spirituality with their dangerous sexuality. However, Ruether apparently fails to see that the adoption by women of virginity, which, from the male-centered stance of the Church Fathers, permitted them to emulate and even attain the spiritual heights of a Mary by liberating them from God's twofold curse—bearing children in sorrow and suffering domination by a husband—rested on the acceptance by these very same women of male theologians' definitions of their feminine nature as inferior, tied more to the life of the body than to that of the spirit, and defined only in relation to the nature and requirements of men.

In other words, women had the capacity for reason and spirituality only if they pursued the monastic life. Men, as "naturally" rational and spiritual persons, might have chosen to enhance and perfect their spirituality (and thereby their masculine nature) through celibacy, but that choice for women meant their liberation from all the "natural" physical and mental shortcomings of their sex, as catalogued by men.

In order to achieve spiritual eminence, women first had to embrace the abhorrence of the feminine shared by the early Church Fathers. They had to mask and reject everything seen as consonant with their feminine natures—including even the one thing that made them in any way superior or even necessary to men, namely their indispensable role in reproducing the species. Therefore, instead of enhancing and perfecting their femininity through virginity, women had to do violence to everything they were (in the patristic view) and become masculinized.

And yet again, despite what Ruether sees as the terrible punishment this early Christian ambivalence toward women inflicted on what she terms "the natural affections of men and the natural humanity of women," she concludes on a note of hope. She finds it possible that the "transcendence and spiritual personhood"[4] (one wonders, whose?) won in that tradition at such an awful cost might somehow be transformed by fitting them into the presumably less dichotomous, more humane Hebrew vision of physical creation in the body.

Before Mary Daly abandoned her belief in the possibility of reforming our religious legacy, her perspective was less optimistic than that of Ruether or Trible. Yet her reading of the Judaic and Christian traditions as only misogynistic seemed, at last, overly simple. It ignored the complexities introduced by early androcentric translations of biblical texts, delineated by Trible, and the pervasive ambivalence toward women in at least part of that tradition, documented by Ruether. But beyond all that, I was left with the feeling that something really important was being overlooked, remaining unsaid by all of them.

Moreover, in the larger picture, in spite of the persuasiveness and acumen of the new scholarship, there seemed to be theoretical shortcomings and gaps everywhere I looked. For example, Simone de Beauvoir's seminal work, *The Second Sex,* as well as more current writings by some feminist anthropologists,[5] contends that even when women in different cultures at different times have enjoyed a measure of power and autonomy, they never lived in equality with men. And though cultures have assigned value to "nature," women have always been consigned to a "nonnecessary" but universal "otherness," a perpetual state of marginality or subordination to men, existentially rooted in their biology as childbearers.

Sophisticated as these arguments are, they overgeneralize. They simply do not square with what we now know about the apparent sexual, personal, economic, political, or intellectual autonomy of various groups of women at different times, relative to the position of men of the same class and time. They disregard, for example, the female lyric poets widely known during the Archaic Age of Greece, or Spartan

women by the fourth century B.C.E., or pre-twelfth-century Lady Abbesses in England, France, and Germany, or, later, the medieval *femme
sole* traders of western Europe, or the wives of artisans in fourteenth-
century Genoa.[6] In short, it is probable that societies as a whole have
never been sexually egalitarian in practice. But those instances we do
have of times in which men, like women, of a particular class within a
society lived under constraints of service to the state, or in which
conditions peculiar to a warrior society enabled upper-class women to
accumulate property, act in the public sphere, and finally limit their
reproduction (e.g., in Sparta and Imperial Rome), mean that we must
refine and somewhat qualify the absolutely universal character of the
sexual dominance-subordination paradigm, and look further.

Likewise, recent books on early "gynocracies," evocative of ancient matriarchies or of civilizations that worshiped "The Great Goddess,"[7] appear to be based, at best, on wishful thinking and unsound
scholarship. At this point, it seems most unlikely that there ever was
a matriarchy (though in my view matriarchy, or the rule of an entire
sex by another purely on the basis of gender, is no more desirable than
patriarchy, since I do not hold with biological reductionism, or the
belief that humaneness resides in one's genes or genitals, or that
possession of a womb totally defines the "nature" of women).

At worst, this kind of reasoning frequently misunderstands the
character and content of *poly*theism. It unaccountably collapses all
female divinities into *the* Great Goddess, while disposing of male deities with an intellectual sleight of hand, or unfailingly sees goddesses
and gods engaged in combat for supremacy along sexual lines (ignor-
ing the struggles of gods among themselves for kingship), or comes to
the unwarranted conclusion that the worship of goddesses inevitably
signifies the ascendant or dominant status of women in those societies
which venerated them. That the elaborate worship of the goddess
Athena during the Classical Period in Athens coincided with the tightly
circumscribed roles and subordinate position of Athenian upper-class
women speaks for itself.

Some scholars, in seeming pursuit of these golden if lost times,
transmute their rejection of the Judeo-Christian heritage as patriarchal
into a focus on the worship of goddesses whose endowments interestingly bear little resemblance to the ones actually attributed to them by
their own cultures.[8] Alternatively, other recent works have emphasized
the *Mother* Goddess aspect of ancient feminine divinities, or strangely
misrepresent the dominant role of powerful goddesses in the widespread Sacred Marriage rites as seductive in a human sense (a concept
alien to the mentality and attitudes toward female sexuality found in
the literature that celebrates those rites). In a singular twist of the

goddesses' function in the Sacred Marriage, which seems to lift the texts out of their cultural milieu, these female deities are portrayed as sex-objects for kings (even as the goddesses ruled over them) or as selfless initiators of fertility for the community. In addition, the sacred rite itself, which glorified the active and beneficent sexuality of goddesses, and for which their sexual unions with kings were viewed as merely instrumental, is equated with the origin of phallic worship![9]

Equally unsatisfactory to me were Jungian attempts to reconstruct our past, via comparative mythology, anthropology, or theology.[10] Though seemingly more benign than traditional approaches because of their assignment of equivalent weight to feminine and masculine archetypes, in their ahistorical assumptions of universal, eternal sameness in the meanings of feminine and masculine, they also seemed to oversimplify and violate the complexity and variety of human experience.

In general, something seemed to be missing in all of these theoretical constructs. More specifically, what occasioned my greatest unease was my growing awareness of the significance of attitudes toward gender, power, and female sexuality in ancient polytheistic literature, and how none of the existent theories took them into account. As noted elsewhere, one's data are only as good as the questions asked, and somewhere along the line there had been a failure to ask some of the right questions.

The decisive catalyst to my own investigation (and here the image of a detective following clues is hardly an overstatement) came from an unexpected quarter—from an issue raised in the early 1970s at an international meeting of Assyriologists in Rome by one whose major contributions, monumental as they are in his own field, have until this decade been only peripheral (though indirectly vital) to feminist scholarship. Samuel Noah Kramer is without doubt one of the most eminent of Sumerian scholars. These days, it is nearly impossible to read anything on ancient Mesopotamia that does not in some fashion bear the mark of his pioneering work, or refer to his original translations of scores of recovered clay tablets describing the many aspects of Sumerian life and culture, or base its information on his many books and articles about ancient Sumer. Kramer is probably responsible for introducing the very name of Sumer—an enormously important but hitherto obscure ancient civilization—to a wide English-speaking audience, comprising laypersons and scholars alike.

Nearly ten years ago, then, Kramer responded to a query posed by feminists in general and feminist theologians in particular about the apparent maleness of God in both Judaism and Christianity. He observed that perhaps scholars have not yet adequately examined the significance of the enduring worship of great goddesses in those ancient Near Eastern polytheistic societies that provided the cultural ambience of monotheistic beliefs and cult, even as the God of the emerging monotheism appears to have been conceived of as overwhelmingly male. Taking up Kramer's challenge, with no preconceptions about what I might find, I encountered in the surviving written records of ancient polytheistic religions attitudes toward gender, power, and female sexuality, and evidence of the wide participation of women as well as men in cult, all of which were, in some ways, not only strikingly different from attitudes found in biblical literature but also suggestive of a religious vision of sexual egalitarianism that has not yet been recognized or assessed.

This discovery was, of course, breathtaking, but especially so since it was based on an abundance of references in translations of ancient documents by scholars who were—by Kramer's admission, and judging by their own published studies of these ancient civilizations—not particularly cognizant of the importance of attitudes toward gender or the implications of those attitudes. Moreover, the research undertaken by traditionalists and feminists alike has assumed a universal, perhaps inevitable, linkage of sex and power, and this outlook seemed conspicuously absent from polytheistic texts. In sum, in the process of exploring the written remains of the highly advanced, religion-centered civilizations in the ancient Near East, what became clear to me was the prevalence of religious beliefs about the significance of gender and female sexuality—persisting across most of these cultures in surprisingly unchanged form for some 3,000 years—which appeared to be radically different from subsequent Western beliefs.

To return to the original question: Why examine ancient polytheistic literature produced by dead civilizations? What possible relevance or meaning can it have for us today? Surely I do not advocate a return to polytheism, nor do I make the claim that what appears to have been sexually egalitarian attitudes in religious life comprises *necessary* proof of sexual equality in every facet of social life at any given time.

However, quite apart from the intrinsic importance of the views expressed in this literature and the need to set the historical record straight, an understanding of these views may be crucial to our understanding of what is humanly possible. And if it is true that people in many societies that regarded divine-human relationships as central to survival and prosperity could conceive of divinity, and of ways of relating to the divine, in a manner that was not particularly contingent on sex, it dramatically alters how we now explain and evaluate the origins of Western monotheism as well as the ethical significance generally attached to its appearance.

Further, if my findings hold up, they would appear to lay to rest forever a variety of theories about our past, for example that it is explicable, in necessary or nonnecessary ways, in terms of women's possession of wombs; or the existence of eternal, historically transmitted feminine and masculine archetypes in the psyche; or the political overthrow of a golden matriarchy by patriarchy; or the view that power has always been a correlative of sex.

Over the years, when confronted for the first time by instances of the impossible, irrational, punitive constraints not infrequently placed on women only because of their sex, many of my students have asked some of the right questions: "But how did it start? How did it come to happen that women as a sex have often been seen as simultaneously inferior and superior to men, or have been regarded in different, disparaging ways as compared to men? Why were women seen as less rational by their nature than men, or as dangerous to men through their sexuality or their exercise of power?"

To them, as always, I can only repeat that, obviously, these are large and complicated questions, and that no single answer (or book) would suffice. What follows will begin to explore some of these issues by examining what appears to have been a critical turning point in Western attitudes toward the significance of gender. This shift in consciousness occurred, in part, during the long course of the passage from polytheism to monotheism in the ancient Near East. Part of the process of restoring women to history and restoring our history to women may well be the provision of new models for alternative modes of thought and life.

PART I

GENDER AND POWER: THEORETICAL ISSUES

CHAPTER 1

Laying the Groundwork

SOME cultural beliefs and attitudes run so deep they may acquire, over time, a potency and momentum of their own that far transcend their original intention. Their very durability and diffusion mark out for them a field of underlying assumptions, and it is anything but easy to make an existential leap out of one's cultural conditioning in order to analyze or challenge them. Often, in fact, our lives must be affected negatively before these assumptions even become visible.

The Problem

One such belief is that power has always been a correlative of gender. Almost irrespective of ideological orientation, most theories about our past have one element in common, namely the view that power relationships, changing power relationships, and even the exercise of power itself, in both the divine and secular spheres, have always been closely linked to membership in sexual groups, and the underlying assumption is that it has never been otherwise.

Whether or not earlier civilizations consciously viewed as important the assignment of roles or attributes to one sex or the other, it seems clear that pervading the character of any culture at a given time —its systems of thought and religious beliefs, its major institutions and their manner of operation, its patterns of acceptable and deviant behavior, its types of artistic expression, its very language—are the implicit and explicit beliefs of that culture about the nature of femininity and masculinity. However, to say that beliefs about gender have been basic to culture is not to say that gender, roles, and power have always and necessarily been intimately linked by culture with equal weight across the board.

Those historians who simply project their own cultural biases about the nature of the sexes backward in time have drawn their analyses along fairly simple lines. They define masculine activities as having always been most important to culture and social change. Therefore, history recounts the achievements of men and a few deviant women, e.g., the fifteenth-century virago Caterina Sforza, admired by her contemporaries as the *prima donna d'Italia* because she had the courage of a man. Even feminist theorists and historians, who do not accept the inevitability or reasonableness of male dominance, have tended to see our past in terms of the almost necessarily close affiliation of power and sex.

For instance, Simone de Beauvoir undertook her analysis of "the second sex" from within just such an intellectual framework. Her contention was that human history, from the very beginning, demonstrates the establishment of whatever was masculine as the norm, embodying those traits that were considered existentially human. Whatever was feminine was relegated to the outsider group (presumably not as fully human), the Other. Women were never autonomous. They were always defined and described by reference to the essentially human—the male—and never the converse. Men were always the essential, women the inessential, and, in fact, "the two sexes have never shared the world in equality."[1]

This is a compelling hypothesis. The location of consciousness and power along sexual lines permits much historical information to fall into place and pattern. But something is askew. If all people knew, from earliest times, that what was most essentially human was masculine and that masculine activities determined human culture, why did ancient, advanced civilizations attribute such far-ranging powers to goddesses as well as gods, and why were both worshiped in their sacred rituals? Why did women as well as men occupy such prominent positions in ancient Near Eastern polytheistic cults? Why the recurrent anger and ambivalence toward women as a group, running like a curious fear throughout Western history? Before monotheistic beliefs took hold, why did Aristotle downgrade the obvious importance of women in reproduction in order to elevate the role of men in the process?[2] In the speech he allegedly made to the Roman Senate in the second century B.C.E., why was Cato so fearful of acceding to the demands of Roman matrons for relief from a luxury tax—not because he deplored the possibility of financial loss to Rome, but because he saw the repeal as only the first step in the usurpation of power by Roman women?[3]

Why the ambivalence, indeed polarity, of attitudes toward women in parts of the Bible, sometimes identifying Wisdom, which informs all of God's creation from the very start and sustains it thereafter, as feminine (Prov. 8, 9; Apocrypha, Wisd. of Sol. 6:12–25, 7–10, 11:1), and sometimes raging against the proud daughters of Zion (Isa. 3:1–5, 12–26, 4), and the Great Whore of Babylon (Rev. 17, 18)? Even the view that parts of the Bible were written at different times by different authors is not sufficient to explain why these contradictory attitudes could be accepted for so long as a fairly coherent whole, nor does it explain the origins of these contradictions.

Later, why the attacks on women's character in medieval literature at the same time that women were visibly so economically productive on the land and in urban guilds?[4] Why the burning of so many women as witches at precisely the same time that the Renaissance and Reformation opened up for men grand new vistas and mobility based on individual excellence and personal access to God?

It is most likely, of course, that in each of these instances there were many reasons why, and that in some cases women were used merely as scapegoats and pawns in the larger political struggles between men, as, for example, when the burning of witches peaked in ferocity in the sixteenth century.[5] And in each case there were certainly real economic, political, and social issues involved, as well as attitudes toward women that were used to justify and lend credibility to such attacks.

But at least one of the reasons for the anger and ambivalence toward women might have been the outcome of tensions surrounding their association with power, and the content of those tensions differed in polytheistic and monotheistic cultures. In the second half of the first millennium, the flourishing Greek and Roman civilizations had been preceded by a very long period of goddess worship and female prominence in cult and, therefore, public life. This religious tradition was juxtaposed with the relative absence of power suffered by most Greek and Roman women at a time when the de facto liberties of those of the upper class were on the increase.[6] Hence, some of the fear and denigration of women expressed by Aristotle and Cato may have represented their response to these changes in the real power of upper-class women.

In contrast, the monotheistic stance on the relation of sex to power stood in rather sharp conflict with older and other notions of relationships between the sexes. Just as the Christianization of Northern Europe was neither rapid nor easy, and people in those countries apparently held on to a number of their older, polytheistic beliefs well into the Middle Ages[7] (which might partly explain the special virulence of Inquisition ideology), so earlier the biblical ambivalence toward and fear of women might have represented reactions to enduring polytheistic conceptions of sex roles, and of power related to sex. Or the expression of this ambivalence and fear might have served as one means of setting monotheism apart from the polytheism in its environment by sanctifying attitudes toward women that were quite different from those of competing religions.

Across cultures, religions have addressed themselves to some of the most profound and universal issues in life, tending both to reflect and to shape part of their culture's response to them. Correspondingly, conceptions of sex roles in the religious views and rituals of any society have reflected and helped to shape some of the deepest beliefs about the nature of each sex. At times when religion has been central to communal life, as in the cultures of the ancient Near East, religious beliefs have exerted an influence on thought and behavior that extended far beyond mere theology.

If a watershed in the development of Western religions is examined, namely the period from around the third millennium B.C.E. through the early centuries of the first millennium C.E., which witnessed in the ancient Near East the emergence of monotheism out of a polytheistic milieu, a radical shift is apparent in attitudes toward sex roles, female sexuality, and the relation of power to gender. Incredibly, our past is so much with us, it is necessary to return to the dominant Near Eastern cultures of thousands of years ago in order to understand some of the sources of assumptions about the importance of sexual identity that have plagued Western thought—many of which are still part of our socialization process today.

Defined in their broadest sense, attitudes toward sex roles involve assessments of worth, autonomy, and potentiality as they relate to gender. These attitudes not only reflect views about femininity and masculinity, i.e., judgments about part of the real experiences of people, but, perhaps more crucial, also express value judgments about what women and men are perceived as capable of doing. Just as they describe normative standards for behavior, so, in myriad ways, they come to affect the institutions and customs of every society. Moreover, beliefs about the nature of femininity and masculinity as applied to the divine—or to women and men and what have been designated as their proper roles in relation to each other and to whatever has been a culture's concept of supra-natural forces in its universe—have not infrequently figured in attempts to establish a rationale for hierarchies of power based on sex.

Obviously, rationales are not hierarchies, and attitudes toward the sexes do not mirror precisely how people live, any more than behavioral norms accepted as good or just at any given time correspond exactly to the realities of people's lives. In class- or caste-stratified societies, sex roles, both normative and real, often vary as a function of membership in social or economic classes and racial or ethnic groups.

Furthermore, the relationship of attitudes to institutions and beliefs to practices is extremely complex. There have been many periods marked by disjunctions in time, characterized by the abrasiveness of the new and the reluctance of the old, which have seen the persistence of older beliefs in the face of concrete, material changes, or the intrusion of new ideas into a social structure that continues to function according to tradition and custom.

Nevertheless, within the general context of conflict, adaptation, and change that we call history, there has been a complicated, imprecise but important reciprocity of influence between beliefs and practices. And it is from this perspective that the following chapters will trace part of the change in attitudes toward the importance of gender and its relation to power during the formative years of Western civilization, by tracing changes in religious beliefs about the nature of femininity and masculinity as monotheism began to appear in the polytheistic ancient Near East.

The Sources

Like that of the early Hebrews and Christians, the social universe of polytheistic societies was dominated by religious beliefs and sacred rites, which frequently served as the matrix of their cultures, economies, and political systems. Both polytheism and monotheism shared a belief in the interpenetration of the divine and the secular in everyday life. While it is, of course, impossible to gauge the depth of personal religious commitment, it is evident that both polytheistic and monotheistic societies saw divine-human relationships as crucial to the survival and prosperity of the community and the individual. Polytheistic religions not only preceded but spread concurrently with the evolution of monotheism. And while biblical authors variously appropriated or altered, reacted against or rejected, some of the tenets and rituals of the polytheistic religions in their environment, apparently there is little doubt that the latter heavily influenced the development of Judaism and Christianity.

The sources of our knowledge about polytheistic religions from the third through the first millennium B.C.E. are varied and often fragmentary. For the period earlier than that under scrutiny here, they are almost exclusively visual representations, e.g., cave paintings, figurines, and other artifacts. In general, we can only guess at their probable significance for the cultures that produced them.

However, by the third millennium our information about many aspects of ancient life expands to include written documents, which have only recently begun to be recovered and deciphered in large numbers. Necessarily incomplete and somewhat random, subject as they are to the vagaries of chance "finds" and the durability of materials used for their inscription, the texts have many lacunae—some are broken off, others are illegible, and still others remain obscure. But despite these inherent limitations, the profusion of firsthand accounts —myths, hymns, epics, lamentations, proverbs, descriptions of rituals —enables the reconstruction of enough of the ancient world to provide us with rich data on the cradle of Western monotheism.

For example, astounding as it may seem, before the nineteenth century nothing was known about the existence of ancient Sumer, and it was as though the Sumerian people had never lived. But it now seems likely that in the long period between 3500 and 2000 B.C.E., Sumer was one of the dominant cultures of the entire Near East. Moreover, with the exception of Egypt (and, it now appears, probably Ebla as well),[8] perhaps no other civilization of that area had such wide-reaching influence on subsequent religious thought and practice.

By the end of the third millennium, this society clustered around the Tigris and Euphrates Rivers was conquered by the Semites of Accad, to the north. Sumer ceased to exist as a political entity and its non-Semitic people disappeared, or, more likely, were assimilated into what was later to become Babylonia. But though it was extinguished as a "living," spoken tongue, Sumerian continued to be used as the religious and literary language of the Semitic conquerors. In addition, the Sumerian pantheon was incorporated into the Babylonian; the study of the Sumerian language and literature continued in schools that trained scribes; and the study of both was pursued in those places that served as the centers of intellectual and spiritual life for the Babylonians, Assyrians, Elamites, Hurrians, Hittites, Canaanites,[9] and, it now seems likely, for the Eblaites as well.

Likewise, as recently as 1964, excavations uncovered the existence of an enormous and hitherto unknown Syrian empire, extending out from its capital city of Ebla, which seems to have been one of the major Near Eastern civilizations in the second half of the third millennium. Preliminary translations of some of the thousands of tablets found, many of them in a new Western Semitic language akin to Ugaritic and Hebrew, indicate that this discovery will probably necessitate the revision of current theories about early political, cultural, and religious history.

Ebla's political boundaries apparently were as far-flung as its vast commercial domain. Evidence of the existence of prosperous, highly advanced urban centers in the Eblaite empire has altered earlier notions that Syria and Palestine were at that time inhabited primarily by nomadic tribes. Ebla's scientific texts may antedate by seven hundred years similar ones found in Babylonia. Its literary texts include myths, hymns to divinities, incantations, and proverbs, many of them written in a newly discovered language, Paleo-canaanite. Others are inscribed in Sumerian and mention Sumerian deities like Enki, Enlil, Inanna, and Utu. In sum, it appears most likely that a reciprocal cultural relationship was maintained between Ebla and Mesopotamia, and the earlier belief that Accad held sway over the entire area in this period has now been supplanted by a picture of two high civilizations, Accad in the east and Ebla in the west.[10]

These excavations may have rather spectacular implications for the history of monotheism. Even now, enough is known about the Eblaite language, social customs, and religion to suggest that Ebla either might have been the place of origin of the ancient Israelites themselves, or at least might have provided the cultural background and religious traditions out of which some of the stories and beliefs in the Old Testament evolved, partly in opposition to those traditions, partly under their influence. If this allegedly close Eblaite-Hebrew affiliation should be demonstrable (and scholars in the field are contending that it appears probable), then current theories about the origin and development of monotheism might require dramatic modifications.[11]

Like the literature of polytheism, biblical texts are of great antiquity and enormous complexity and even yet elude sure dating and certain understanding. It is believed that their composition spanned a period of time approximately as long as the Bible's existence in its present form. Just as the emphases of polytheistic religions altered somewhat over time in order to accommodate changing economic, political, and social realities,[12] so the many parts of the Bible reflect societal changes during the long course of its genesis.

Obviously, there are many beliefs about its origin. Some hold that it was divinely inspired from beginning to end; others that only the Pentateuch, or first five books, was of divine origin; and still others that its different sections were written at different times by men of deep religious sensitivity and convictions. What follows will be based on the last view and, in addition, the probability that its history includes oral traditions and numerous redactions in the process of decision about what to exclude and what to include in the final canon. Also, it should be noted that some speculate that its final form and content were subject to an inordinate shaping influence by the priesthood, always a minority in the community of believers, which may have been especially influential in those years marked by the absence of a unified political state.

The complexity of biblical literature is matched by its heterogeneity: it hardly presents a unified, sequential, uncontradictory line of thought in its entirety. In the Old Testament alone, there are portions that seem of priestly origin; others are characterized as wisdom and prophetic literature, and still others are historical accounts that seem to parallel, with a good degree of accuracy, the several stages of Israel's history. There are books like the Song of Solomon, sometimes interpreted as a symbolic rendition of the union of God and Israel, but, in its explicitly sensual language, reminiscent of Egyptian love poetry and Sumerian accounts of the Sacred Marriage. Thus, the literature is both ideologically and stylistically diverse.

While parts of the Bible may represent a radically new religious vision, others bear signs of continuity with or reactions against contemporaneous religious beliefs and cult. There are references to vestiges of polytheistic beliefs and, more certainly, cultic practices by the Israelites, evidenced, for example, by the prohibitions against worshiping graven images, erecting "Asherahs," and continuing cultic prostitution. There are allusions to what seem to have been alien social patterns, suggestive of matrilineal relationships and matrilocal marriages, as in the Book of Ruth and in the accounts of Jacob's marriages to Leah and Rachel. This non-Hebraic influence was, of course, inescapable, since there was much intermingling and intermarriage of the Hebrews with other peoples already living in the lands where they settled.

Editions familiar to us today were preceded by translations of earlier times, which naturally incorporated a fair number of their own cultural attitudes toward women and men, and some of these are currently being questioned. For instance, the Revised Standard Version of the Old and New Testaments in English is now being reworded in order to eliminate the sexist language of early translators, which seems to have derived more from the antiwoman biases of their own societies than from the wording of the original or early texts. This in itself will probably comprise a significant redaction for English-speaking people.

Complicating matters further, there are references in the Bible to other literature, believed to have been of a similar religious nature and evidently known about in those times, but kept out of the final version. In this century, spectacular archaeological discoveries of such writings —the Nag Hammadi texts, the Dead Sea Scrolls—have greatly enhanced our access to the world of the Bible. Indeed, these texts have presented us with alternative conceptions of divinity and of divine-human relationships—particularly with regard to beliefs about femininity and masculinity—which are sometimes radically different from those found in both testaments.[13] In addition, the forty-seven books of the Pseudepigrapha, originating in the intertestamental period of around 200 B.C.E. to 70 C.E., were consigned to obscurity because of doubts about their authenticity and are only now being recovered and gathered together for publication.[14]

For purposes of comparing polytheistic and monotheistic attitudes toward gender, female sexuality, and power in the religious literature of the ancient Near East, this study shall confine itself only to selected passages from *biblical* literature—passages that seem to lend themselves to such comparisons, or those that were cultically crucial to early monotheism, as representative of the latter's views. In addition to the constraints imposed by length, it seems to me that there are some rather weighty reasons for focusing on the Bible and excluding an analysis of other religious writings of those times.

Simply, while the Bible undoubtedly does not represent the only early monotheistic viewpoint, as finally redacted, its point of view was what won out, prevailed, endured, and influenced social ideology about the sexes for the next two thousand years. For better or worse, it was the Bible and not the Nag Hammadi texts that provided the basis for later exegeses and has been, for countless generations, taught to people as containing the words of God.

At least in the West in historic times, theology, philosophy, art, and popular beliefs have shared some common ground. The impact of biblical literature has been widespread and continuing, and its views have been intertwined on many levels with the development of Western social attitudes.

Rationale for the Use of Biblical Texts

The Old and New Testaments provoked centuries of commentary and interpretation by Talmudic scholars, early Church Fathers, experts on canon law, Protestant dissenters, philosophers, and the like. For a considerable period, universities maintained close ties with the church. From the time of the Renaissance and Reformation, biblical writings were widely disseminated among ordinary people through translations of sacred texts and commentaries into the vernacular; biblical imagery was drawn upon by many artists, and the content of biblical teachings provided fertile soil for the germination of a variety of philosophical beliefs.

The Bible not only explicated a monotheistic conception of divinity but also laid out the proper relationship between God and believers and the specific obligations of members of each sex in their relations to each other in this world as well as to God. Its influence was sometimes felt in specific ways in real life, as in the case of biblical injunctions, which touched at many points the family lives of the middle class in sixteenth-century England through the proliferation of conduct books. Later, the Enlightenment's emphasis on human reason to correct injustice and attain a more perfect society directly confronted the notions of faith and obedience to biblical commands as the basis of a well-ordered state. And this confrontation, along with economic and social factors, helped contribute to the sweeping intellectual and political upheavals of the eighteenth and nineteenth centuries.

Sometimes, controversies were fueled by differing interpretations of God's intentions. In the 1830s the brilliantly reasoned, radical proposals of Sarah Grimké in her *Letters on the Equality of the Sexes,* written in her argument with the clergy of Massachusetts over proper sex roles, are couched in her Christian convictions based, in part, on what she sees as differences between the intentions of God in Scripture and their interpretations by men. Even today, the ordination of women and the possibility of reconciling Judaic and Christian traditions with feminism are very live and emotional issues, often grounded in interpretations of the Bible.[15]

There is yet one more reason why I chose to look only at biblical narratives as expressive of early monotheistic attitudes toward the importance of gender. Certainly, many differing views can be extrapolated from the vast biblical literature, depending on which sections are being discussed, and space permits nothing more than a selective sampling here. However, the apparently greater ease with which many feminist theologians today can confront the sexism or ambivalence toward women in later translations of or commentaries on the scriptures rather than in the Bible itself—the gingerly fashion in which the Bible is approached and, in a variety of ways, "rescued" from its own misogyny or ambivalence toward women—all suggest that it might be timely, once again, to look at some of the biblical passages that set early monotheism apart as most fundamentally different in outlook, in its attitudes toward the importance of gender, from surrounding polytheistic religions. A comparison of these biblical narratives with polytheistic texts may illuminate the extent to which differentiations made on the basis of sex are imbedded in the Bible's view of divine-human encounters and underscore the nature of those sex-linked distinctions.

Since the current revival of feminism, so much has been written in the last decade about women and the Judeo-Christian tradition that it is by now possible to isolate a number of the major positions. Some have rejected Western religions outright as a part of the patriarchal oppression of women.[16] At the other extreme are those who see the vision of parts of the Old or New Testament as originally benign, egalitarian, even feminist, but later distorted, either by translations that masculinized more sexually inclusive imagery, or by attitudinal changes in the Bible rooted in sociological necessities, or by moral decadence.[17] In between these two positions are those who, for example, believe that despite the patriarchal social structure of ancient Israel, or the "domestic codes" of the New Testament, which restricted or subordinated women because of the secular conflict between freedom and order, women either were as highly honored as men in their separate-but-equal roles as mothers or shared with men a spiritual equality in Christ.[18]

Some have explored other religious writings, produced during the several hundred years when the Bible was compiled in its final form but excluded from the canon, and they have found descriptions of a much stronger female presence than in the Bible. Others have reinterpreted the canon and uncovered what they see as an unacknowledged, almost suppressed, motif of female involvement and importance.[19] With respect to later commentaries, some maintain that they introduced a more humane view and ethical treatment of women, or expressed a basic ambivalence toward women, which represented a departure from the biblical view of creation, or incorporated an attitude toward women as equals of men in a spiritual sense, but not in this world.[20]

Except for the opinions of those who have given up altogether on the relevance of organized religion to the liberation of women to full personhood, the many examples culled from biblical or later writings to support one or another of these arguments all seem to rest on a fundamentally optimistic assessment of the Bible. In this view, whatever part can be shown to be reflective of past cultural biases or historical circumstances in its denigration of women ultimately may be de-emphasized or abandoned by being "understood," in favor of those parts that seem to have a more universal moral or spiritual applicability to both women and men. Often at the heart of this stance is the attitude that biblical literature is susceptible to an almost incredible diversity of interpretations, and the more underlying belief that the advent of monotheism represented for women and men alike a seminal moral and spiritual advance over polytheism. It is the last assumption that needs reexamination.

In the development of Western religions, one of the revolutionary changes was the movement in religious belief from polytheism to monotheism. In this shift, transpiring over the course of several millennia and radiating its effects widely up to the present, many of the fundamental preoccupations remained essentially the same—the nature of people and the universe as illuminated by their beliefs about the nature and purpose of their creation; the manner in which the universe continued to function; anxieties over dangers and calamities in this life and the felt need to assume or delegate control or direction over them; the visible facts of generation and death, and the inability to explain these facts of life and death by merely visible phenomena —in short, the range of cosmological and ontological problems that have formed the basis of myth, religion, and ritual in any age.

But during this passage from polytheism to monotheism, ideas about the nature of divinity and people's relationship to it underwent some substantial modifications. Accompanying them was the emergence of somewhat different perceptions of divine immanence and transcendence, marked by changing conceptions of sex roles in both the divine and secular spheres and changing attitudes toward female sexuality.

The Argument, and More on Methodology

The argument of this book is that what has been taken as a near-universal outlook in all cultures, namely the tight linkage of power and powerlessness to gender, originated in Western culture rather late, in a specific area and time coincident with the origins and flowering of monotheism. For a few thousand years prior to the birth of Jesus, the polytheistic literature of the ancient Near East is replete with suggestions of a vision that we might today call androgynous, one that did not blur sexual distinctions so much as render them relatively less important than other social or individual concerns, or that emphasized, valued, feared, or despised attributes common to both women and men more than the differences between the sexes.

Usually, the exercise of divine power was not seen as the exclusive prerogative of either sex, and the ascription of power to deities of one sex was rarely associated with the inferiority of the other. Most often, female and male divinities were seen as engaged in a wide range of activities indispensable to the human community, and they not uncommonly shared broad and equivalent powers. On earth, while some cultic rites were exclusively restricted to members of one sex or the other, very often both women and men participated in cult as initiates, celebrants, and priests. And most conspicuously absent in the polytheistic view were expressions of fear of female biology and sexuality.

In time, this androgynous outlook gave way to the radically new vision of monotheism, which encompassed an association of power and powerlessness with gender in a manner quite foreign to the polytheistic mentality. This association has helped influence the ways in which we have understood our past. Specifically, our beliefs about the characteristics of women and men and how we have understood their roles in the historical scenario have corresponded, in part, to biblical portrayals of power, or the lack of it, as almost always associated with sexual identity. Thus, for example, for all the enormous importance rightly attached to the existence and recovery of literature like the Nag Hammadi texts, and for all they reveal about the ideological conflicts and varieties of opinions among early Christians, it was the Bible's attitudes toward femininity and masculinity, sex roles and sexuality— and not those of the Christian gnostic texts—that so mightily influenced Western thought.

Most Jews maintain that the Torah cannot be fully understood without a knowledge of the Talmud, and Catholics tend to lean heavily in their doctrine on the writings of the Church Fathers and on canon law. Nevertheless, later commentaries on the Bible will also be excluded from consideration, in order to maintain a structural parallelism with polytheistic texts, which record the attributes, powers, and "words" of divinities. In other words, while both the Bible and later commentaries on it were written by men (as distinct from the polytheistic texts, some of which were written by women, e.g., *The Exaltation of Inanna*), it seems appropriate to compare with the polytheistic texts only what was purported and believed to convey the direct messages or commands of God (i.e., the Bible) rather than human interpretations of those messages (i.e., the Talmudic and Patristic writings), however great their continuing authority.

Likewise, liberties will be taken with the knowledge of modern biblical scholarship, which we have, after all, been graced with for only a fairly short time. Passages from the entire New Testament will be examined, and the Synoptic Gospels will not be looked at as fairly distinct from, say, the probably later Gospel of John. My primary concern is not with what Inanna, Osiris, Yahweh, or Jesus *really* said, or with what scholars say they said, or with when they probably said it.

My interest is in the content of polytheistic and biblical literature as it might have reflected or helped to shape prevalent social ideologies about the importance of gender and the roles of the sexes. And for most of the last two millennia, the vast majority of Christians probably perceived all of the gospels as equally authentic, particularly those passages which directly quote Jesus. In like fashion, even if some of the writings attributed to Paul may *really* be later additions,[21] that is irrelevant to the historical fact that during the Reformation mainstream Protestantism tended to incline rather precipitously toward those sections of the Pauline literature which kept women in their place —subordinate to men and once-removed from Christ, at least in this life. Similarly, notwithstanding current re-readings of the serpent-woman scene in Genesis,[22] the long litany of the sins of Eve and all the daughters of Eve, recited throughout Western history, cannot be so easily silenced. It is, irrevocably, a part of our past. If it now will not stand up to sophisticated biblical critiques, who knew that then?

One final note on methodology. There is a basic asymmetry between ancient polytheistic and monotheistic literature.[23] As already mentioned, most polytheistic texts deal with the attributes and activities of goddesses and gods as they interact with each other and with the human community. While they also describe the ritual observances required of worshipers, whose individual and communal fortunes were portrayed as dependent on the nature and quality of their relationships to divinities, they rarely contain references to laws of divine origin designed to regulate intersexual or family life, inheritance of property, and the like. In general, such matters were relegated to civil jurisdiction, to statutes clearly of human origin, e.g., the Code of Hammurabi.

By way of contrast, the Bible contains many references to laws, presumably emanating directly from God, that do regulate relationships between the sexes, and they establish a host of rules governing family life and sexuality, which are violated, people are warned, only under threat of divine punishment. Hence, for example, while one may infer some things about the social structure of ancient Israel from the Pentateuch, one cannot as simply elicit the same kind of information from the religious literature of ancient Sumer, and indeed it would be a mistake to do so without the greatest caution, or lacking other corroborating evidence.

If, then, polytheistic texts exhibit more sexually egalitarian attitudes than those found in the Bible one cannot, on that basis along, conclude that polytheistic societies at the times those texts were probably written were *necessarily* more sexually egalitarian than monotheistic communities during the periods that likely produced the many parts of the Bible. That kind of claim must, of course, rest on detailed comparative analyses of customs, legal systems, and social structures, polytheistic culture by culture, in which gender is added as a decisive category to other variables such as class or caste, and this remains to be done.

Nevertheless, in the absence of such research, and however tentatively, some of what we already know is provocative. The public roles of women as well as men in cult at a time when religion appeared to exert a powerful influence on society both ideologically and institutionally—in areas of political, economic, and social organization—along with evidence of neutral or favorable attitudes or practices relating to female sexuality, all suggest at least the possibility that relatively greater sexual egalitarianism might have prevailed within some classes or castes of polytheistic societies as compared with contemporaneous monotheistic societies. Even given the frequent disjunctions in time of beliefs and practices, it does not seem extreme to presume as a working hypothesis that at some points in time, religious views about the sexes might have been suggested by social realities. But again, at this point it must remain only conjecture.

In short, a comparison of civil laws in polytheistic societies with divine commandments and laws in biblical literature is clearly inappropriate. However, since I shall be comparing attitudes toward the significance of gender in the religious literature of polytheistic societies with those in biblical texts, it does seem appropriate to use passages containing divine laws and commands in the latter that directly bear on the beliefs of its authors about the moral capacities of women as compared to men; the extent to which women were recipients of divine judgment and grace as compared to men; and the extent to which women shared with men in the divine covenant.

The following chapters are not a review of the latest scholarly literature on ancient religions. Instead, for purposes of comparison and contrast, I shall use primary sources in English translation, i.e., polytheistic myths, hymns, descriptions of rituals, incantations, and selections from the Bible, except when secondary sources tend to enhance my argument or when I differ with their conclusions. It is hoped that an analysis of these primary materials from a woman-centered perspective will raise a host of new issues and questions.

Among them is the need to explore further the general relation of goddess-worship and the widespread and important public activities of women in cult to the secular roles and status of women in different cultures. What is the relation of class membership to this issue in specific, class-stratified societies? Since the existence of sexually egalitarian concepts in religious belief and even in religious practice does not necessarily signify the existence of sexual equality in social structure, what is the relation, if any, between the beliefs and the reality, and what are the conditions necessary for their coincidence? These questions need further investigation.

Also, in light of my findings, what is the usefulness of feminine/ masculine archetypes (or the Jungian approach) as a conceptual tool in analyzing our past? What does the polytheistic outlook toward sexual identity tell us about the "nature" of femininity and masculinity? What can in reveal about the relation, if any, of women's biology to the fulfillment of women's potential as full persons in the public arena?

Further, how integral a part is ambivalence toward women, not only in subsequent commentaries (as Ruether demonstrates in the writings of the early Church Fathers), but in the Bible as well, or is it possible to reconcile our biblical heritage with feminist values, as feminist theologians maintain? Did biblical monotheism, as many claim, indeed represent an ethical advance for women *as well as* men? Is it possible to determine how the shift from prominence in polytheistic cult to far more restricted and lesser roles in monotheistic cult affected the consciousness of women? Do we have any means of inferring how women accommodated themselves to or resisted this shift? Is that what we shall find in the Pseudepigrapha as, for example, parts of the recovered gnostic texts seem to suggest for a later period?

More generally, if my reading of polytheistic literature is valid there is a need to reassess the view most commonly held, namely that for all the variety and complexity of the historical record, gender has always been regarded or functioned as a correlative of power. All these issues obviously cannot be dealt with in what follows, but it seems to me that the questions themselves are critical.

PART II

POLYTHEISTIC ATTITUDES TOWARD GENDER

CHAPTER 2

Gender and
the Nature of the Divine:
The Polytheistic View

A NY attempt to assess the importance of gender to polytheistic
conceptions of the divine in the ancient Near East from the third
through the first millennium immediately confronts what seems, at
first, an almost insuperable barrier, namely the variety in the religious
outlook of its many civilizations and the shifts in religious concerns
over time. Therefore, before examining those aspects of polytheistic
beliefs and practices which strongly suggest the existence of similarities in cross-cultural approaches to the divine, and particularly similarities in the significance attached to gender, it may be well to outline
briefly some of the basic differences in the views of the major centers
of civilization.

Egypt, Mesopotamia, Canaan: Some Differences

The disparate ways in which human life and endeavors were seen as
linked to the operation of divine forces appear to have been based in
part on the different experiences of worshipers in their natural environment.[1] For example, in Egypt the experience of regularity in nature
—the overflow of the Nile at predictable intervals to irrigate the land,
the sun, which could be trusted to rise over Egypt every day, and the
physical compactness of the country—seems to have contributed to a
feeling among Egyptians of continuity, safety, and durability. Their
outlook was marked by pride in the power and achievements of human
effort, reinforced by their appraisal of divinities as operating in their
lives with reliable beneficence.

Egyptians tended to see life as part of the unfolding of destiny,
preordained from the beginning by mighty but essentially nonviolent

21

goddesses and gods. As part of the divine plan, a harmonious regularity and order obtaining between nature and society was guaranteed by the presence of a god sitting as pharaoh, or at least consubstantive with him, on the throne of Egypt. Thus, despite variations in specific content, Egyptian cosmological beliefs generally assumed a benign purpose in creation and, not unexpectedly, were paired with the development of a view of life after death as possibly benign as well.

Very early, Egyptian myth and theology became absorbed with mapping out the nature of life after death and developed the idea of a connection between the moral qualities of one's life on earth and the kinds of rewards and punishments anticipated in the afterlife.[2] Moreover, the assignment of some of their chief goddesses and gods to the task of "weighing" the virtues of each person's heart after death in order to determine the eternal "residence" of the deceased; the belief that the pharaoh as the incarnate god Horus became the god Osiris at death; and the preoccupation of their myth, religion, and art with funerary arrangements and rites all attest to the seriousness with which the Egyptians viewed divinities as dependable, and human life on earth as fundamentally reasonable in origin and character.

In Mesopotamia, despite the acknowledgment of order and cosmic rhythms in the universe, the experience of unpredictability, even devastation in nature—the Tigris and Euphrates bursting their bounds without warning, destroying dikes, inundating crops and threatening the food supply, and the vulnerability of the area to scorching winds, terrifying thunderstorms and torrential rains that swept across the land—seems to have influenced Sumerian and Babylonian beliefs in rather dramatic ways.

The universe came to be seen as the outward face of gigantic contests among powerful, potentially divergent, and conflicting forces, personified as deities who were viewed as exercising their powers in more arbitrary, violent fashion than Egyptian goddesses and gods. In contrast to the relatively confident, static world view of the Egyptians, the people of Sumer and Babylonia tended to understand their role in the world as fairly insignificant and subject to change, and they saw themselves as virtual slaves to tremendous and threatening cosmic forces. They appeared to feel that their only options were servitude and obedience to goddesses and gods, and their only hope for deliverance from adversity was recourse to prayer, propitiation, and sacrifice.

Though rulers of Mesopotamia identified themselves closely with deities, and the greatest of them claimed divine descent, they were after all regarded as mortals, not gods, with the possible exception of those who "married" goddesses in the Sacred Marriage rite. But in any

event, the "bride" was understood to be the initiator and active partner in the ceremony, and divine favor might be withdrawn from the
rulers at any time. Therefore, society as a whole was seen as fairly helpless before divine decisions it could neither predict nor influence.

For instance, the "Lamentation Over the Destruction of Sumer
and Ur"[3] recounts the wholesale and terrible religious, economic, and
social ravage of Sumer and its people through conquest and natural
disasters. This catastrophe is not shown as a consequence of any particular wrongdoing on the part of the king or the people, but is portrayed as being arbitrarily decreed by the nation's four leading deities
at that time—An, Enlil, Enki, and Ninhursag. After the destruction the
tutelary god of Ur, Nanna-Sin, relents and pleads with his father, Enlil,
for the restoration of that city and nation.

Nanna's plea follows a long, detailed description of the wasting of
Sumer when its goddesses and gods abandon it, but does not hinge
solely on the loss to them of ritual tribute:

> Oh Enlil, gaze upon your city *full* of desolation,
> Gaze upon your city Nippur, *full* of desolation,
> Ur—(even) its dogs *snuff* not at the base of its walls.[4]

As executor of the decisions of the divine assembly, Enlil replies:

> The verdict of the assembly cannot be turned back,
> The word commanded by Enlil knows no overturning,
> Ur was granted kingship, it was not granted an eternal reign,
> Since days of yore when the land was founded to (now) when people have
>   multiplied,
> Who has (ever) seen a reign of kingship that is everlasting![5]

Enlil's response, therefore, refers not only to the intransigence of
divine edicts and the impermanence of secular rule but also, in light
of the "desolation" of Nippur, to the transitoriness and potential dangers of life itself for the whole community.

Consistent with the experience of impermanence and caprice in
their surroundings, some of the Mesopotamian myths of origins describe the creation of people as an afterthought of divinities, intended
to free them from menial labor. In a version current in Sumer during
the third millennium, people (many of them defective) were created by
a goddess and god for the sole benefit of deities, to serve and feed
them,[6] and the later Babylonian myths of creation echoed this senti-
ment.

In line with an appraisal of human creation as almost accidental on the part of less than always benign deities, Sumerian and Babylonian conceptions of life after death saw the latter as sombre and fearsome. Though there is some reference to judgment of the dead, implying the possibility of differential treatment, for the most part the Netherworld was characterized as a Place of No Return, where virtuous and evil people alike were doomed to reside forever in dismal, grey, shadowy subservience to the ancient and awful goddesses and gods of death.

In sum, while the mythic visions of both civilizations reflect the beliefs that each individual is part of a social group, that human society is part of nature, and that nature represents the visible form of divine and cosmic forces, dissimilarities in the natural environments of Egypt and Mesopotamia helped to shape quite dissimilar beliefs in each culture about the nature of divinity and divine-human relationships.

The geography and climate of Canaan likewise colored its conceptions of divinity, though undoubtedly some of that area's religious views by the second millennium also stemmed from its long history of foreign incursions and dominance and its ethnic pluralism and fragmentation. Canaanite myths are notable for their sense of the community's vulnerability to a fluctuating and precarious food supply, a result of fairly regular but prolonged cycles of drought and fertility.[7]

Many figurines of Astarte, the Canaanite version of the goddess Ishtar and one of the consorts of the god Baal, have been unearthed in this area. Their exaggerated female sexual characteristics, together with mythical accounts of Baal's periodic death and resurrection, which ushered in periods of drought and abundance, would seem to fix the securing and maintenance of fertility as paramount motifs in Canaanite religion. However, a similar emphasis may be detected in other parts of the Near East as well.

Intersections of Outlook: Cultural Diffusion

The proliferation of accounts of the Sacred Marriage rite, the celebration of the annual death and resurrection of young vegetation gods in Mesopotamia, and the belief that the Egyptian pharaoh at his death became Osiris and would, from his physical burial-site, continue to provide for the fertility of the land all indicate the preeminence of fertility as a basic concern of polytheistic myth and ritual. Also, the Canaanite belief in the involvement of both goddesses and gods in guaranteeing the provision of an abundant food supply after the season of drought is replicated in other cultures.

Sacred prostitution and human sacrifice are often considered typical of Canaanite religion, but, apparently, both were also practiced in Egypt and Mesopotamia, and perhaps the difference, if at all, may have been only of degree. For example, there are references to several classes of temple prostitutes in both Egypt and Mesopotamia. High priestesses, avatars of the goddesses Inanna and Ishtar, participated in the Sacred Marriage, just as priestly surrogates for Egyptian queens and princesses served as "brides" of the god Amon-Rē. With regard to human sacrifice, Sir Leonard Woolley excavated royal tombs in Sumer that contained the retinues of deceased kings, who were buried along with their masters, even as female and male slaves are thought to have been interred in the tombs of Egyptian nobles in order to protect them. And the burial of implements and valuables along with the deceased, which characterized the Canaanite cult of the dead, was not confined to Canaan alone.

In short, the myths and sacred rites of Canaan seem to have centered on fertility and apparently paid scant attention to divine involvement in the origin of the universe or the nature of life after death. However, and there is not general agreement on this,[8] while the relative absence of etiological and eschatological myths might have been distinctively Canaanite, it would appear that the overriding importance attached to fertility was not, in itself, unique to Canaan, and there were other points of resemblance to Egyptian and Mesopotamian religious practices as well.

Thus, despite real material and traditional differences in approaches to the divine that may be noted among the various geographic locales, tribes, and nations, and despite the emergence of different religious concerns and emphases at different periods of time, some distinctive common elements appear to have been shared by most of their religions.

This should come as no great surprise, since none of these civilizations developed in total isolation from one another, and there seems to have been a pattern of genuine cultural diffusion for a few thousand years throughout the ancient Near East. Graphic evidence of the magnitude of this pattern is to be found on a stele retrieved from the Golden Age of Phoenicia (ca. 1150–853 B.C.E.). Its characteristics are a blend of those found in the art of the ancient Babylonians, Egyptians, North Syrians, Cappadocians and Hurrians.[9]

To cite but a few examples of the historical basis for this process of cultural impingement and cross-fertilization, Egypt was in control of Palestine for a few hundred years after the expulsion of the Hyksos conquerors from both countries in the second millennium; Amorites and Elamites invaded Babylonia after it had controlled Elam for the first half of the second millennium, and the Elamite conquest of five Hebrew tribes in Canaan is documented in Gen. 14; Assyria came to incorporate much of Mesopotamia under its dominion; Myceneans moved southward and came to dominate many Eastern Mediterranean areas; and Phoenicia became the center of north-south and east-west trade routes and extended its influence deep into the Mediterranean, as far west as Carthage.

Accompanying the movement of armies, trade, and peoples throughout the Near East was the movement of culture, ideas, and religious beliefs and rituals. The dissemination of the last was facilitated by the organization of priests into guilds, whose members crossed national boundaries to find employment in many lands.[10] Thus a fair number of similar views and rites are encountered in many places.

This claim may be documented in a number of ways. As one instance, the recurrent use of the same mythological motifs argues for the probability that like religious beliefs and practices were diffused among the societies of Crete, Canaan, and Israel until some time after 1500 B.C.E. The tale of the king or patriarch who must redeem his "true wife" in order to rule—found in the *Iliad*, in which King Menelaus must reclaim Helen in Troy; in the Ugaritic *Epic of Kret*, in which King Danel must reclaim his "destined bride," Hurrai;[11] and in Gen. 12:10–20 and 20:1–18, in which the royal husband Abraham must reclaim Sarah from the palaces of the pharaoh and Abimelech—all suggest the possibility, when joined with other kinds of evidence, that these three ancient societies might have belonged to the same international, Eastern Mediterranean network, in which the most important linguistic and cultural elements were Phoenician, and therefore Semitic.[12]

There are many other, more general instances. For thousands of years, the efficacy of oracles, omens, and incantations was everywhere acknowledged; first-millennium mystery cults bent on personal salvation spread with great rapidity throughout the Graeco-Roman world; religious attitudes toward sexuality—especially female sexuality—with only some exceptions showed little variation from culture to culture; and Samuel Noah Kramer surmises that the Song of Songs in the Old Testament may be based on the widely practiced Sacred Marriage rite.[13] Therefore, while taking cultural differences into account, it seems fitting to consider certain aspects of ancient Near Eastern polytheistic religions as based on shared conceptions of divinity, and to explore the manner and extent to which these shared views accorded significance to gender.

Religion-Centered Communities and Views of the Divine

As noted, it is impossible to ascertain the depth of individual attachments to religious precepts and rituals. However, one of the most striking cross-cultural similarities appears to have been a belief in the potency of magic and the reality of divine intervention in daily life. In contrast with the more modern perception of a cleavage between the divine and the secular, the role of religion in the ancient world was both pervasive and profound.

Societies were characterized by the integration of religious assumptions and rites into almost every facet of individual and community life. One recent description of ancient Egypt, for example, traces the development of culture itself—art, literature, drama, science, philosophy, government and the like—to its roots in Egyptian religious beliefs, cultic rites, and the practice of magic,[14] just as in ancient Mesopotamia intellectual life was grounded in religious beliefs, and both flourished in schools subsumed by temples in the Euphrates Valley.[15]

Perhaps the most fundamental of shared polytheistic beliefs was a pluralistic conception of divinity. It rested on the ascription of a wide variety of supernatural powers to many goddesses and gods, each of whom was regarded as the possessor of one or, more often, several special attributes and powers, which might or might not reside exclusively in that particular deity. Polytheism prevailed even in Egypt, side by side with the existence of what some have termed "solar monotheism," embodied in the figure of the sun-god Rā.[16]

From the perspective of communities of worshipers, the endowment of their goddesses and gods with an array of powers that could effect both good and evil in every portion of their lives probably served the people of those times with a means of rescuing the workings of their natural and social universe from a realm of happenstance and unpredictability. In a world in which deities were active agents, at least an aura of comprehensive, sequential, rational order might be anticipated, conditional on the performance of prescribed rites. Furthermore, participation in repeated sacred rituals joined to familiar myths most likely engendered in the worshipers impressions of continuity in their personal lives and in the relation of their community and environment, as well as feelings of a measure of engagement in and control over the creation of their own future.

The beneficent exercise of divine power or, in other cases, the triumph of the power for good, assigned to some deities, over the power for evil, attributed to others, was viewed as enabling individuals and societies to negotiate a safe passage through the difficult course of birth, life, and death. In addition, they could do so with some assurance that their natural surroundings would not assume an adversary role, that basic social needs might be met, and that possibilities lay open for divine intervention to ward off predictable or unforeseen dangers. Flowing from this activist cosmology, several other early and common features of ancient Near Eastern polytheism may be distinguished.

One was a sense of human society's physical proximity to divine forces, or what was envisioned as divine immanence, manifested in many ways and apprehended by worshipers as an integral part of their immediate environment. Sometimes the place of birth, area of activity, or habitation of deities was geographically designated with meticulous particularity. Thus Isis gave birth to Horus, the prototype of all future pharaohs, in the marshy delta of lower Egypt after the dead body of his father Osiris floated in a coffin up the Nile to Phoenicia and was reclaimed there by his sister-wife; grieving Demeter was rejoined by her daughter in the Greek city of Eleusis after Korè's abduction and rape by Pluto and her enthronement as Persephone, Queen of the Dead. These careful locations of geographical origins and itineraries probably helped to make goddesses and gods seem more accessible to practical human concerns, as well as serving to establish the sites of cultic worship.

At times, objects and animals were personified and deified, as were processes, or the natural world was rationalized through the residence of individual deities in its specific components, as in the case of Yamm, the Canaanite sea-god. Sometimes essential, life-giving phenomena were explained by abstractions that connected concrete, visible occurrences with the permanent presence of divinities. For example, the Egyptians devised the mythic construct of the Boat of a Million Years, inhabited by the supreme sun-god and other chief goddesses and gods, travelling as the sun in its daily passage through the sky over Egypt.

At other times, divine immanence was portrayed as a more generalized omnipresence, but nevertheless still operational in the destinies of individuals, nations, and even deities, as in the personification of truth, justice, right, and civil and cosmic order in the Egyptian goddess Maat. The actions of deities as well as pharaohs were governed by Maat; because of her, what was right and just occurred in nature as well as in society, and the absence of Maat from Egypt denoted chaos. And at still other times, the immanence of divinity was experienced through the projection of sacred qualities onto the worshipers' natural surroundings. Groves, forests, trees, and mountains assumed magical and sacred powers, insofar as they were believed to be inhabited by in-dwelling divinities. In Canaanite mythology (and this same motif was to be repeated later in Ps. 19:2–5 by the Israelites), nature itself was seen as animate; segments of the heavens and earth communicated the glory and mystery of the god(s) and creation to the initiated.

If divinity was early conceived of as interventionist, resident in specific locales, and immanent in nature, its character was portrayed as overwhelmingly anthropomorphic. Though in possession of tre-mendous power, goddesses and gods, like mortals, were born, ate, drank, loved, married, had children, hated, fought, conquered or were themselves vanquished, suffered jealousy and bereavement, and, while most were believed to be immortal, even died.

Deities were often seen as acting to advance human welfare, but they also behaved capriciously, and in either case their motives were by no means always clear to people. Some were usually identified as the source of good or evil events, but others were like the god An, forefather of the Sumerian pantheon, who was associated with su-preme authority and even beneficence and simultaneously came to be seen as the parent of evil spirits, or sickness and death.

Gender and the Character of the Divine

In these multifaceted ways in which the divine was encountered and defined, both goddesses and gods were seen as interventionist in hu-man destiny and immanent in nature. Both were appealed to in order to preserve the stability and prosperity of communities. Neither god-desses nor gods were seen as the sole sources of cosmic or social beneficence or malevolence to the exclusion of deities of the other sex. In divine-human interactions, the prerogatives and characteristics of deities, anthropomorphic as they were, did not cluster along sexual lines, or gender was not viewed as the most important locus of divine behavior. Among the host of greater and lesser deities in each pan-theon, no single goddess or god was to emerge as the sole creator and sustainer of life, source of fertility, social order, wisdom and justice, champion of battle, and final judge in the afterlife, and none of these powers was attributed only to deities of one sex.

One of the misconceptions dispelled by a comparative analysis of ancient Near Eastern myth and cult is that the gender of deities animat-ing nature or representing its functioning somehow reflected what was then understood as the sexual "nature" of people, and therefore their natural sex roles on earth. Projecting more recent ideologies backward into antiquity, this view of ancient polytheism is often only part of a more general theory about the nature of the essential differences between the sexes. Grounded in the archetypal "content" of the feminine and masculine, this theory is based on a belief in the natural complementarity of women and men, ahistorically determined by their sex.[17]

From this perspective, the moon in its periodic phases and the earth with its seasonal, abundant yield, for instance, were usually represented mythologically as goddesses because their dark, mysterious, cyclical functioning and fecundity were identified with the periodicity of women's menstrual and birth cycles, and with their awesome ability to bear life. And darkness, mystery, and periodicity are equated with femaleness. Likewise, solar and weather deities are often assumed to have been masculine because they represented supremacy over the fertility and life of the earth, actively providing sunlight and warmth or aggressively threatening destruction through devastating weather. And supremacy, activity, and aggression are equated with maleness.

While it is true that Artemis in one of her many aspects stood for the moon, just as Apollo in one of his represented the sun, these two are by no means typical of the universal designations of lunar and solar deities. On the contrary, from the third through the first millennium, myths and sacred rites most frequently portrayed both female and male divinities as personifications of identical cosmic phenomena.

In Sumer, both the sun and moon were symbolized by the male gods Utu and Nanna. In Canaan, Shapsh was the goddess of the sun. Among the Hattic and Hittite peoples of Anatolia, both the storm-god and the sun-god were male, but the sun-goddess of Arinna was the principal figure in the Hittite pantheon, overshadowing in importance all the other goddesses and gods, and was regarded as the chief protector of the Hittite state and monarchy.[18] In Assyrian nature hymns, the god Sin personified the moon and the goddess Sarpanitum the stars. And in Egypt, where the god Rā was a solar deity, texts inscribed on shrines and royal tombs from about the fourteenth to the twelfth century B.C.E., but most probably based on originals composed at a much earlier time, attest that the god of wisdom, Thoth, was assigned responsibility for the moon as a "placetaker" for the sun.[19]

In some cultures, the sky was indeed identified with male gods, such as the Sumerian-Accadian An/Anu, but in Egypt the reverse was true. Seb (or Geb), son of the god Shu, and titled the "hereditary chief" of the gods and the "father of the gods" (i.e., Osiris, Isis, Nephthys, and Seth), was originally designated as the god of the earth. Later, he also became the god of the dead, signifying the earth in which the deceased was laid. Seb's consort, Nut, initially was the personification of the sky, represented the active feminine principle at the creation of the universe, and was considered the mother of the gods and of all living things. Along with her husband, Seb, she was regarded as the provider of food to the living as well as the dead, shared with him the responsibility of providing physical space for the dead in the after-life, and was worshiped as protector of the dead. Though exact loca-tions varied with different schools of religious thought, all assigned some portion of the heavens, or the domain of Nut, as the final and eternal resting-place of the righteous deceased.[20]

Conversely, in many early cultures the earth was represented as a goddess, an obvious extension of the female ability to reproduce, as in the instances of the Sumerian goddesses Ninti/Ninhursag and the Greek goddess Gaia. Though it is by no means certain, for many epochs prior to the third millennium—before the domestication of animals made visible the male involvement necessary to reproduction, and when the significance of human paternity was very likely uncertain —the worship of fertility goddesses was apparently prevalent in the ancient Near East.

Based on an apparent reverence for the life-giving abilities pro-jected onto female divinities as exemplars of "The Great Mother," the latter seems to have been considered the most sacred figure of those early times. Under different names, her rule extended over all of life and death, and it is believed she was worshiped simultaneously as mother goddess, mistress of animals, and recipient of the dead.[21] Even later, after the development of fairly sophisticated levels of agriculture, commerce, and political organization, a Sumerian myth of origins refers to the goddess Nammu, associated with the primeval sea and reproducing parthenogenetically, as "the mother, who gave birth to heaven and earth."[22]

Gender and the Attributes of the Divine

However, even very early a male son-consort seems to have been acknowledged, though he was of far lesser status than the dominant goddess,[23] and by the third millennium mythic literature begins to reveal a number of new attitudes toward the relation of gender to divine attributes. Many of these attitudes suggest the existence of rather widely held beliefs in a kind of equivalence of power exercised by both female and male divinities.

By that time most of the major fertility goddesses were hardly viewed as mere breeders. Their association with the earth and fertility had come to expand beyond the bearing and nurturing of life, and its reception after death back into the womb of the earth, to an important measure of participation not only in the creation of the universe but also in its organization and maintenance at a civilized stage of development. And just as gods had come to assume important functions as divine embodiments and sources of fertility and vegetation, and as divine overseers of the dead, roles formerly ascribed to goddesses alone, so the latter came to be portrayed as extremely active in many areas and were endowed with attributes like martial prowess, often also associated with male divinities, that ranged far beyond their older and continuing roles as fertility and chthonic deities. Indeed, by the third millennium the religious vision of the Near East, for the most part, accorded only slight importance to the sex of its deities. There are even instances of a measure of fluidity in the sexual designation of divinities, and at times the same divine power was envisaged under both a female and male aspect.

For example, in a Mesopotamian hymn to the moon-god Nanna, which commemorates his role as a source of fertility and abundance, he is alluded to as bisexual. First he is identified: "Father Nanna, lord, conspicuously crowned, prince of the gods."[24] Then the imagery shifts to his male power to engender life: ". . . fierce young bull, thick of horns, perfect of limbs, / with lapis lazuli beard, full of beauty."[25] And this passage is immediately followed by the delineation of his other sexual side, the female power to give birth: "womb, giving birth to all, who has settled down / in a holy abode."[26]

In like fashion, the Sumerian-Accadian An/Anu(m) was conceived of as supreme among the gods and the male deity of the sky, but as the last he was sometimes represented as both female and male, since rain was believed to flow from the breasts or udder of his consort, Antum, or from the clouds.[27] And in one version of the Babylonian myth of creation, *Enuma Elish,* the creator-god Mardúk battles with the mother-goddess Tiamat, who is described as a male monster:

> Who was the [great] dragon?
> Tiāmat was the [great] dragon!
> Bēl in heaven has formed [his image].[28]

In two Assyrian hymns, the gods Marduk and Sin are referred to as both female and male. In one, Marduk is addressed: "Thou art lord, as Father and mother [among men] art thou."[29] In the other, Sin is described as:

> Father, begetter of lords and men,
> Who dost build dwellings and establishest offerings
> . . . .
> Father, begetter of all living things,

and also as:

> Mother womb begetter of all things
> Who has taken up his exalted habitation among living creatures.[30]

There is a papyrus of Nesi-Amsu, inscribed rather late but based on Egyptian myths and traditions that date back to the Old Kingdom and predynastic times. It refers to the god Nuna, the deity of the primordial mass of slime or water out of which the universe was parthenogenetically created by divine masturbation, as a hermaphrodite or bisexual, though he had a female counterpart, Nunet or Nunit. Moreover, there is evidence in Egyptian myth that the self-created and creator deities and their progeny of both sexes were regarded as bisexual, e.g., Tem, the son of Nuna; Seb or Geb, the earth-god; Osiris, lord of the underworld; and the goddess Amenet, a form of the goddess Neith of Saïs.[31] Likewise, in an Old Kingdom text from "The Memphite Theology," there is an allusion to the possible bisexuality of the creator-god Ptah:

> Ptah-Nun, the father who [made] Atum.
> Ptah-Naunet, the mother who bore Atum.
> . . . Ptah—who bore the gods.[32]

Gender, Divine Power, and Sexuality

While divinities were not usually both female and male in most polytheistic pantheons, the fact that they sometimes were underscores the seemingly lesser importance assigned to sex than to other divine characterics. It suggests the slight degree to which gender figured as a determining ground of divine power, except in those cases in which the sex of the deity was related to its specific attributes. Moreover, apparently in no sense was divinity itself conceived of as solely female or male.

As shall be seen, in the major myths both goddesses and gods were viewed as extremely powerful, whether dependent on each other or acting in tandem, operating in concert with deities of the same sex, or acting autonomously. But in any case, both their level of activity and scope of power were not seen as contingent on their sex. Threaded through ancient polytheism was the belief that divine activities most essential to human prosperity or most threatening to human survival —e.g., those involving fertility, wisdom, justice, social order, drought, and war—were engaged in by goddesses and gods alike.

The specific characteristics of divinities became explicit to worshipers through their many relationships, celebrated in sacred rites, literature, and art. Both divine relationships—illustrative of their sometimes complementary, sometimes interfacing, sometimes conflicting powers—and relationships among goddesses, gods, heroic characters, and ordinary mortals were considered significant in illuminating the nature of the divine. And in both divine and divine-human interactions, the sex of deities and humans figured only minimally.

In the divine sphere, the primary affiliations of females and males were multiple, often based on blood ties as well as marriage. For the most part, these relationships were portrayed as more comprehensive than any familiar to most people, frequently including liaisons between mother and son/lover/husband/brother and, less frequently, between father and the corresponding female figures. Sexual unions occurred either in or out of wedlock, and the concepts of divine illegitimacy or incest were foreign to the ancient mind. Both goddesses and gods were shown as sexually active, and if their behavior was subject to any moral judgments the latter were made irrespective of sex.

There was no dichotomy between divine "body" and "spirit," nor was there any association of impurity or sin with the reproductive functions of deities of either sex. Sexuality was seen as a normal and positive part of natural/supernatural functioning, and it was undoubtedly regarded as important for both goddesses and gods. But, as shall be more fully documented later, the particular manner in which divine female sexuality was linked in most instances to the benefit of the human community spilled over into expansive attitudes toward the sexuality of real women.

In the secular sphere there were, of course, some times and places in which sexual activity, male or female, was prohibited. But these prohibitions were often of a temporary nature, immediately tied to the performance of specific sacred rites. On the whole, the neutral or favorable disposition toward female sexuality in polytheistic religions came to comprise one of their fundamental differences from monotheism.

Gender and Official Religion

Individuals and groups related to the divine in two basic ways. One was through the medium of "official" religion, the other through the many facets of "popular" religion. Both were enormously important, and some conjecture that one of the functions of the former was to systematize and incorporate the beliefs of older folk-religions into official theologies.[33] Though a more substantive consideration of their respective pertinence to the issue of gender must be reserved for a later discussion of polytheistic cult, some general observations may be made at this point.

In official religion, kingship was widely associated with divine provenance, and the fate and welfare of the community were identified in many ways with the fortunes of the ruler. Indeed, most frequently the well-being of society was seen to rest on that of the king; e.g., when the latter committed an act of sacrilege, the whole community was put in jeopardy. For example, "The Curse of Agade," dating from around 2000 B.C.E., describes the destruction of the city when its king, Naram-Sin, refuses to passively accept Agade's abandonment by some of its goddesses and gods and therefore brings about its consequent debilitation. Naram-Sin finally defies divine authority by ordering the desecration of the Ekur, the sanctuary of Enlil. This, in turn, provokes a terrible divine curse, which renders Agade totally unfit for any kind of life.[34]

In early Mesopotamia, as well as in Egypt throughout most of its recorded history, rulers were often viewed as intercessors between the community and the divine, or were themselves designated as divine. If the former, they were either believed to be direct descendants of divinities, created by them to occupy the throne, or were seen as divine agents. In all these roles, both female and male deities were invoked for the protection of the king and his people. In an inscription left by King Sargon, who acceded to the throne around 2350 B.C.E., he identifies himself as: "Sargon, King of Accad, overseer for the goddess Ishtar, king of Kish, anointed priest of the God Anum, king of the land, the exalted *ensi* of the god Enlil."[35]

The Accadian form of the name of Assyria's King Assurnasirpal, who ruled from 883 to 859 B.C.E., means: "The God Assur protects his son and heir."[36] The king gave a huge banquet to celebrate the construction of his palace at Kalah, and after listing his military conquests and civil accomplishments, he wrote: "I presented the city to Assur, my lord."[37] However, as part of the inaugural of his new royal capital there, he founded and lavishly adorned temples dedicated to both female and male deities. As he recorded it:

> . . . the temple of Enlil and Ninurta, the temple for Gula, the temple for Sin, the temple for Nabu, the temple for Ishtar, mistress of the land, the temple for the Sibitti gods, the temple for Ishtar-Kitmuri, the temple for the great gods I founded anew in the city and established the oath of the great gods, my lords, in them.[38]

In a similar reliance on the powers of divinities of both sexes, and in a fashion apparently typical of the genre, a treaty concluded between

Esarhaddon and Ramataia in 672 B.C.E. states that if the latter were to abrogate its provisions, the wrath of the major goddesses and gods of Assyria, Babylonia, and Sumer would be visited in concrete ways on the violators.[39]

In the later years of the Babylonian and Assyrian empires, kings could still offer sacrifices—always the special prerogative of priests—and during the millennia they ruled over the area, from earliest to latest times, they counted among their titles that of "priest." It was only in later ages, concurrent with the expansion and increasing complexity of civil and religious life, that a differentiation of functions took place, and the priests moved from their positions as royal attendants in the palace to those of servants of the goddesses and gods in the temple.

In Egypt, the same process of differentiation and specialization may be discerned from earlier to later times. It seems most likely that the earliest priesthood was merely an incidental responsibility of local nobles, who were considered head priests in their own communities. In the course of time, as the nation developed and the pharaoh came to be exalted as the literal incarnation of the god Horus, he was seen as the sole official servant of the gods. However, this position was more theoretical than real. In the evolution of a state religion, coincident with the very beginning of the nation's history, in theory the pharaoh alone worshiped the goddesses and gods, but in fact he was represented in each of the many temples in the country by a high priest who offered prayers, sacrifices, and libations "for the sake of the life, prosperity and health" of the pharaoh.[40]

In general, for much of this long period in Mesopotamia and Egypt, both women and men were to be found in the priesthood; persons of both sexes mediated between mortals and goddesses and gods; and in ritual interactions between the human community and the divine, apparently neither women nor men were regarded as standing in a closer or more distant relation to divinity on account of their sex. Indeed, the consolidation of political hegemony by some rulers (e.g., Sargon the Great) was accomplished, in part, through the placement of women from their families in commanding positions in the temple hierarchy. And paralleling this was the practice, among ordinary people, of currying favor with one's deity by dedicating a daughter to its service in the temple.

The gradual separation of the functions of king and priest went along with the accumulation, over time, of retinues, land, and wealth by both the royal and ecclesiastical centers of power, which often, but not always, supplemented each other. Not infrequently, women as well as men attached to the temples were involved in and benefitted by this process. In short, for most of this period, persons of both sexes participated in many of the most important cultic rituals, which constituted one level of human interaction with the divine, and in the long reach of the temple into community life.

Personal and Popular Religion

There is abundant evidence that the worship of household goddesses and gods coexisted with the official cultic worship of tutelary deities of cities and, later, more national divinities. For example, there is a Sumerian proverb that describes how if one's personal god is alienated, there is no one to intercede on behalf of the worshiper before the assembly of the gods.[41] In a recent work that traces the evolution of religious thought in Mesopotamia over the course of several millennia, Thorkild Jacobsen identifies the rise of "personal religion," or the sense that an individual's fortunes or misfortunes were of supreme importance to one's personal divinity, as the dominant religious metaphor by the beginning of the second millennium. In appeals to personal deities for intervention in human lives, both goddesses and gods were seen as sources of relief from affliction. One prayer to Ishtar reads:

> I have cried to thee, (I) thy suffering, wearied, distressed servant.
> See me, O my lady, accept my prayers!
> Faithfully look upon me and hear my supplication!
> Say "A pity!" about me, and let thy mood be eased.[42]

Later:

> What have I done, O my god and goddess?
> As one not fearing my god and my goddess I am treated![43]

And in another prayer:

> . . . I am afflicted, covered over, cannot see.
> "O my merciful god, turn unto me" I entreat thee,
> I kiss the foot of my goddess; before thee I crawl![44]

There were a number of other forms of worship that seem to have been layered between private family rites and official sacred rites. For instance, in Mesopotamia several unpretentious chapels modelled on normal temples have been excavated in a small residential section of Ur. Cuneiform tablets discovered in them reveal that they had been set up and maintained by private, voluntary contributions from ordinary citizens. They were dedicated to minor deities, probably representative of a host of lesser goddesses and gods who were above all accessible to lay persons, and who might have been relied upon to serve the needs and provide protection to ordinary people of both sexes in an environment characterized, and sometimes threatened, by divine immanence and intervention.[45]

Likewise, the employment of magical omens, incantations, and oracles was widespread throughout the ancient Near East for thousands of years. These practices were engaged in by both women and men, and divine interest was solicited on behalf of persons of both sexes. Furthermore, in the first millennium Orphic, Dionysian, Eleusinian, and Isaic mystery cults, which centered on the worship of either female or male deities, both women and men were initiates, participants, and priests, or gender was not in itself a matter of prime religious concern or a basis for access to the divine. And, as appears to have been true elsewhere, the long history of Egyptian religion was marked by a continuous and relatively easy coexistence of personal piety and official cult, in which individuals worshiped goddesses and gods at domestic altars as well as in temples, and no apparent conflict existed between the lay and official priesthood.[46]

Gender and the Ethical Dimensions of the Divine

There was yet another dimension of divinity that might have answered to the needs of individuals and communities when they moved beyond an overwhelming concern for an adequate food supply. By the third millennium, though deities were by no means considered always merciful or just, and divine justice sometimes seemed incomprehensible by human standards, a number of goddesses and gods began to be viewed as compassionate, righteous, or wise, and were seen as dispensers of both judgment and mercy.

For example, in an inscription found on the inside of a coffin used for the burial of a wealthy Egyptian during the Middle Kingdom, the goddess Isis is referred to as "Lady of Goodness."[47] During the Nineteenth Dynasty, a hymn of thanks was written to the god Amon-Rē, who is described as:

> ... he who hears the prayer, who comes at the voice of the poor and distressed, who gives breath (to) him who is weak. . . . Thou art Amon, the lord of the silent[48] man, who comes at the voice of the poor man. If I call to thee when I am distressed, thou comest and thou rescuest me. Thou givest breath to him who is weak; thou rescuest him who is imprisoned.[49]

Prior to the Amarna period, a hymn addressed to Amon-Rē refers to him as the deity of truth, righteousness, mercy, and judgment. He is called:

> ... The lord of truth
> ... Who extends his arms to him whom he loves.
> (But) his enemy is consumed by a flame.[50]
> ... Who hears the prayer of him who is in captivity,
> Gracious of heart in the face of an appeal to him.
> SAVING THE FEARFUL FROM THE TERRIBLE OF HEART,
> Judging the weak and the injured.[51]
> ... Lord of truth
> the righteous one, Lord of Karnak,
> In this thy name of Maker of Righteousness.[52]

And toward the end of the ancient Egyptian Empire, a hymn to the goddess Meresger, the "Peak of the West," portrays her as at once judge of transgression and source of mercy:

> I knew not good or evil. When I did the deed of transgression against the Peak, she punished me, and I was in her hand by night as well as day.... "she smites with the smiting of a savage lion. She pursues him who transgresses against her."
> (But) when I called to my mistress, I found her coming to me with sweet breezes. She showed mercy unto me.... She turned about to me in mercy.[53]

This conception of divinity as an ethical force was also present in other parts of the Near East. In one hymn to the Sumerian goddess Nanshe, she is referred to as the deity

> Who knows the orphan, who knows the widow,
> Knows the oppression of man over man, is the orphan's mother,
> Nanshe, who cares for the widow,
> Who seeks out (?) justice (?) for the poorest (?).
> The queen brings the refugee to her lap,
> Finds shelter for the weak.[54]

The goddess's concern for morality is indicated when her role is described as:

> To comfort the orphan, to make disappear the widow,
> To set up a place of destruction for the mighty,
> To turn over the mighty to the weak ... ,
> Nanshe searches the heart of the people.[55]

In like fashion, the Sumerian god Utu, who functions as judge of the living and the dead and executor of divine justice to deities and mortals, is also shown as dispensing divine mercy. After the ruler Dumuzi's Sacred Marriage to the goddess Inanna and her ascent from the Netherworld, Dumuzi is first judged by Inanna for his failure to pay her proper homage and then is chosen by the goddess as her replacement in the realm of the dead. When Dumuzi flees, terrified, from the demons of that realm who pursue him, he appeals three times to Utu to change his shape so that he might elude them. Three times this god mercifully complies:

> Utu took his tears as a gift,
> Like a man of mercy, he showed him mercy,
> He turned his hands into the hands of a gazelle,
> He turned his feet into the feet of a gazelle. . . .[56]

And in *The Exaltation of Inanna,* that great goddess is referred to as judge and punisher of humanity:

> When mankind   comes before you
> In fear and trembling   at (your) tempestuous radiance,
> They receive from you   their just deserts.[57]

A sampling of Assyrian hymns evidences a belief in the same kind of divine concern for mercy, righteousness, and judgment. The sun-god Shamash is addressed as "judge of the world," "Merciful God, who raisest up the lowly, who protectest the weak,"[58] and as "lofty Judge of heaven and earth."[59] A hymn to the moon-god Sin reads: "Thy word causest truth and righteousness to arise, / that men may speak the truth."[60] The creator-god Marduk is described as "Merciful one among the gods,"[61] and another hymn to Marduk says:

> Thou liftest up the weak, thou increasest the small;
> Thou raisest up the powerless, thou protectest the weak.
> Marduk, unto the fallen thou grantest mercy.[62]

The warrior-goddess Belit proclaims, "Him who is bowed down I lift up, the aged one I lift up."[63] Like Shamash, the goddess Ishtar is also referred to as "Judge of heaven and earth,"[64] while another hymn says of Ishtar, "The wicked and the violent man thou correctest, proclaimest their condemnation."[65]

The same ethical attributes of divinity are found in Canaanite myth. El, father of the gods and head of the pantheon, is variously described as "God of mercy,"[66] "wise," and "kindly,"[67] "Beneficent El Benign,"[68] and as a judge.[69]

That these projections of moral and judgmental qualities onto goddesses and gods were in earnest is evidenced by references in the literature of many societies to what appear to have been consensual views of morality and immorality. For example, in the instructions Marduk was believed to have given to people after their creation, the god says:

The fear of god begets mercy,
. . . And prayer absolves from sin.
. . . Against friend and neighbor thou shalt not speak [evil].
Speak not of things that are hidden, [practice] mercy.
When thou makest a promise (to give), give and [hold] not [back].[70]

In Egypt, as early as the third millennium during the Old Kingdom, didactic literature described the nature of moral behavior in terms of qualities like generosity, justice, kindness, modesty, self-discipline, truthfulness, and the like.[71] These normative virtues were to form the basis of an individual's relationships with all people and were articulated in specific ways, as, for example, when the official Harkhuf wrote in his autobiography:

I gave bread to the hungry,
Clothing to the naked,
I brought the boatless to land.
. . . Never did I judge between two [contenders]
In a manner which deprived a son of his father's legacy.[72]

Later, on the Rosetta Stone, which lists the virtuous deeds of King Ptolemy, it says: ". . . in return for these things the gods and goddesses have given him victory, and power, and life, and strength, and health, and every beautiful thing of every kind whatsoever."[73]

"Equality of Opportunity" . . . Female and Male Alike

By the beginning of the Middle Kingdom (ca. 2040–1730 B.C.E.), there had emerged in Egypt a new religious emphasis on the equality before divinities of all people, regardless of rank or wealth. ". . . the gods delighted more in good character than in elaborate offerings; the poor man could thus have as good a title to god's interest as the rich. 'More acceptable is the character of a man just of heart than the ox of the evil doer.' "[74] A striking passage from the Coffin Texts of this period, not yet found repeated elsewhere, presents the notion that all were created with "equality in opportunity." The god considered supreme at that time sets forth the purposes of creation:

> I relate to you the four good deeds which my own heart did for me . . .
> in order to silence evil. I did four good things within the portal of the
> horizon.
> I made the four winds that every man might breathe thereof like his fellow
> in his time. That is (the first) of the deeds.
> I made the great flood waters that the poor man might have rights in them
> like the great man. That is (the second) of the deeds.
> I made every man like his fellow. I did not command that they might do
> evil, (but) it was their hearts that violated what I had said. That is (the
> third) of the deeds.
> I made that their hearts should cease from forgetting the west, in order
> that divine offerings might be made to the gods of the provinces. That
> is (the fourth) of the deeds.[75]

In a country where position and wealth might well have depended
on access to water and favorable climate, the second and third passages assure the god's support of equality of opportunity. The fourth
passage, which refers to the west or the region of eternal life, urges all
people to piously serve their local deities in order to attain immortality. It was now possible for commoners of either sex to become Osiris
at their death, just as the king at death became Osiris. Thus, Egyptian
religion was clearly based on the involvement of people of all classes
in the community. It exhibited a remarkable degree of fusion of popular and official religion. And the participation of women and men from
every stratum of society in cultic rites and celebrations is well attested.

Indeed, insofar as deities were depicted as acting in judgment of
human behavior, a consensual view of morality is implicit, and this
suggests several things about the relation of gender to polytheistic
conceptions of the divine. Not only were both goddesses and gods
endowed by their worshipers with an ethical sense, but also there is
evidence that, to the ancient mind, neither divine judgments about
people's virtue and transgressions nor divine extensions of compassion made substantive distinctions based on sex. Instead, if goddesses
and gods judged, punished, and showed mercy, they seem to have
done so to women and men alike because of their commission and
omission of specific moral or ritual acts. Women as well as men were
recipients of divine favor and displeasure and were the beneficiaries of
rituals conducted on their behalf. In sum, gender was not usually a
decisive factor in divine-human interactions.

CHAPTER 3

Sex Roles and the Relation of Power to Gender:
Polytheistic Texts

BEGINNING with the third millennium, perhaps the most obvious changes in conceptions of divine sex roles may be found in the expanding responsibilities of the great fertility goddesses. Most of them are not shown as incessantly bearing offspring in order to populate heaven and earth; rather, for the most part, they produce a limited number of unique and immensely important progeny.

Mother-Goddesses as Active Agents

The Sumerian mother-goddess Nammu had only two children, An and Ki, but they were heaven and earth. The Babylonian mother-goddess Ishtar was prayed to by her earthly "children" for relief from affliction and was moved to pity by their suffering. But there is no reference by name to her own children, if, indeed, she had any, except for her "son"-consort, Tammuz, whose death and resurrection each year provided for the fertility of the earth.

Isis, who with her brother-husband, Osiris, came to be the most extensively worshiped goddess of Egypt, later was to eclipse him as the powerful and widely worshiped syncretistic goddess of the Mediterranean world in the age of Imperial Rome. Linked with, among many other things, the feminine, producing, and procreative principle in nature, Isis bore but one son, Horus. However, he established the patterns of kingship in Egypt, and with his mother was at the center of the recurrent and monumental struggle with and victory over the forces of cosmological evil, personified by the god Seth.

Demeter, one of the most ancient and enduring of the Greek fertility goddesses, was worshiped in folk-religions throughout the

Olympian period and even up to fairly recent times around the Mediterranean and into Northern Europe. She had three children, Korè, Iacchus, and Plutus, but only the first was to assume a central position along with her mother in one of the more important ancient sacred rituals, the Eleusinian Mysteries.[1]

It is only the venerable goddesses, elevated almost solely by virtue of their fecundity at the orgin of the universe, which, of course, required a population, who are depicted as reproducers without peer. The Canaanite goddess Asherah, who mothers seventy deities as the consort of El, the ancient head of the pantheon, and the Greek goddess Gaia, who, without a consort, gives birth to her son-husband, Ouranos, and then to a host of Titans, Giants, Nymphs, and Furies,[2] are both personifications and deifications of the principle of fertility. But, though their children are vital to the functioning of life, their maternal role in no way limits or even necessarily defines their sphere of activity and power, and they are noteworthy for more than their contributions as breeders.

Gaia intervenes to protect her children, who are to animate the universe and assume responsibility for its continuance, by actively opposing their incarceration by Ouranos. It is she who assures the right ordering of nature by encouraging her son Kronus to castrate his father with a sharp sickle she designs and provides.[3] Later, both Gaia and Ouranos foretell the future to their son Kronus and his sister-wife, Rheia. They both inform Kronus that he shall be vanquished by one of his children, and he therefore swallows each of them at birth. They both respond to Rheia's grief and anxiety when she is about to bear Zeus, and to her desire to conceal the baby and revenge herself on Kronus for all the others he swallowed. And they both advise Rheia to give birth and hide Zeus in Crete.[4]

But it is Gaia, the earth, who finally and alone secretes Zeus, keeps him alive, raises him, and presents a counterfeit child (a swaddled stone) for Kronus to swallow. And ultimately Kronus, "fooled by the resourceful promptings of Gaia,"[5] disgorges the stone, along with the other primal deities of Greece, once Zeus, father of the gods and men, matures and overthrows his father.[6] Thus, this fertility goddess preserves and restores to life and their functions those divinities who keep the universe operating in its customary fashion and are to assume responsibility for its operation at a civilized level.

In like fashion, Asherah is pictured as an active agent. After Baal's triumph over the sea-god Yamm, Baal and his sister-wife, Anath, beg Asherah to intercede with El in order to secure Baal's status among the gods, or obtain El's permission for Baal to have his own palace, and this Asherah does. Perhaps more significant, as the aged El's consort,

Asherah is at first Baal's enemy and tries to further the interests of one of her other sons in his stead.[7] But when the vegetation theme becomes dominant in Canaanite mythology, around 1400–1350 B.C.E., and Baal supplants El as the more prominent and dynamic young god, personifying storms, wind, rainfall, and nourishment for crops, Asherah transfers her allegiance to Baal, and both she and the younger goddess Anath apparently compete to become his consort.[8] In other words, Asherah's role as breeder does not impinge upon her desire for power, nor, since Baal and Anath are presumably her children, does her role as mother diminish her active sexuality.

The Active Sexuality of Goddesses

Furthermore, in their frequently concurrent designations as goddesses of fertility or love and war, female divinities were not only worshiped as patrons of those in love or those at war, under whose auspices people went about the usual business of their lives, but they were also shown to be actively engaged in love and war on their own behalf. In *The Epic of Gilgamesh* (most of which was probably written by the first centuries of the second millennium but was based on much earlier Sumerian sources that were probably substantially the same), "glorious Ishtar, Queen of Heaven," entranced by the "beauty of Gilgamesh,"[9] proposes that he be her bridegroom. Later, in the Egyptian "Hymn to Osiris" (ca. 1550 B.C.E.), Isis is described as so sexually active that after the death of Osiris and her retrieval of his body, in the form of a falconlike bird, "She overshadowed him with her feathers, she made air (*or* wind) with her wings, and she uttered cries at the burial of her brother. She raised up the prostrate form of him whose heart was still, she took from him of his essence, she conceived and brought forth a child."[10] Or their son, Horus, divine prototype of all the pharaohs, is posthumously sired by Osiris through the sexual activity of Isis, who impregnates herself from his corpse.

This view of Isis as the sexually active partner in the conception of Horus is not universally accepted. For example, in pointing out some of the differences between the vegetation gods Adonis and Tammuz on the one hand and Osiris on the other, Henri Frankfort offers a curiously androcentric interpretation of these lines when he confuses the *relationship* between Osiris and his sister-wife Isis with the specific *activity* described, and assumes the goddess's subordination in both:

> We touch here upon a fundamental contrast between Osiris and the Asiatic gods. Osiris is emphatically not dependent, and is not a child of the goddess who succors him. Osiris is the son of Nut, an aspect which

is stressed in the funerary texts, since it contains a promise of rebirth through the mother to eternal life. But in the myth Osiris is sought and found by Isis, his sister and wife, who in this respect resembles the Asiatic mother-goddess. But she differs from them in her total dependence upon the god; Osiris dominates Isis. When she conceived Horus after Osiris' death, when she had 'erected the tiredness of the powerless one,' *the mystery of unquenched vitality was evidently not in the goddess but in the god who begot Horus.* (Italics mine.)[11]

This assumption of a superordinate-subordinate relationship between Osiris and Isis is particularly curious, because a stele that recounts one version of the impregnation of Isis locates the basis for this event in the initiative, power, and sexuality of Isis:

"Thy sister ISIS acted as a protectress to thee. She drove thine enemies away. She averted seasons [of calamity], she recited formulae with the magical power of her mouth, [being] skilled of tongue and never halting for a word, being perfect in command and word. ISIS the magician avenged her brother. She went about seeking him untiringly. She flew round and round over the earth uttering wailing cries of grief, and she did not alight on the ground until she had found him. She produced light from her feathers, she made air to come into being by means of her two wings, and she cried the death cry for her brother. She made to rise up the inert members of him whose heart was at rest. She drew from him his essence, and she made therefrom an heir."[12]

The Isis-Osiris relationship does not resemble the Asiatic mother-goddess/son-consort model. Isis does indeed "succor" Osiris, who is "sought" and "found" by the goddess, but it is as a brother and husband, not as a son. In many texts, theirs is depicted as a lateral relationship, in which each divinity possesses great and comparable power, and Horus is the only son of the goddess. Hence, her active role in assuring vengeance for the death of her husband and stability for the Egyptian throne via the birth of Horus certainly involves Osiris, but it all finally rests on Isis's initiative alone, sexual and otherwise. Moreover, in contrast to his earlier active kingship and his later active role in presiding over the dead, this intermediate portion of the god's history is marked by his passivity. Osiris's heart was, in fact, "at rest," and it is Isis who *enables* his vitality to work.

The Martial Aspects of Fertility Goddesses

Likewise, the warlike attributes of fertility goddesses were neither merely symbolic of their power nor used as a literary device to further the action in myths, but were seen as very real and terrible. For instance, *The Exaltation of Inanna*[13] is one of the earliest extant Accadian hymns from the end of the third millennium, part of a great cycle of hymns to the temples of Sumer and Accad and an important contribution to Mesopotamian theology. Written by Enheduanna, princess, poet, and high priestess of the moon-god Nanna, it extols the power of the Sumerian fertility-goddess Inanna; describes the transfer of the *me's*, "the divine norms, duties, and powers, assigned to all cosmic and cultural entities at the time of creation, in order to keep them operating harmoniously and perpetually,"[14] from the great god Nanna to Inanna, and along with them supremacy among the gods; recounts Inanna's role among civilized people in general; and then concludes with a splendid celebration of her cultic primacy in the city-states of Ur and Erech, the ancient centers of Sumerian religion.

The beginning of the hymn establishes Inanna's position among the deities by describing her as possessor and guardian of the *me's:*

1. Lady of all the me's,
       resplendent light,
2. Righteous woman clothed in radiance,
       beloved of Heaven and Earth,
3. Hierodule of An
       (you) of all the great ornaments
4. Enamored of the appropriate tiara,
       Suitable for the high priesthood
5. Whose hand has attained
       (all) the "seven" me's,
6. Oh my lady, you are the guardian
       of all the great me's!
7. You have picked up the me's,
       you have hung the me's on your hand,
8. You have gathered up the me's
       you have clasped the me's to your breast.[15]

"Hierodule of An," a phrase used to describe other goddesses as well, is most often used in reference to Inanna. Its theological significance may derive from the appearance of this phrase in the earliest Sumerian inscriptions as a high title or throne-name of the queen consort. The hymn seems to imply the elevation of Inanna to equal rank with An, son of Nammu, the earliest and most potent god of the sky,[16] though it is not made clear just how and why this transfer of the *me's* to Inanna has been effected.

"(You) of all the great ornaments / Enamored of the appropriate tiara" probably refers to the outward symbols of Inanna's divinity and power. The importance of the "ornaments" and "tiara" may be inferred from a Sumerian myth, "Inanna's Descent to the Nether World," in which her preparation for the journey is described. In addition to arraying herself "in the seven ordinances,"[17] (the divine *me's*), she also adorns herself with:

> ... the *sŭgurra,* the crown of the plain,
>   she put upon her head,
> . . . .
> The measuring rod (and) line of lapis lazuli
>   she gripped in her hand,
> Small lapis lazuli stones she tied
>   around her neck,
> *Sparkling. . .* stones she *fastened* to
>   her breast,
> A gold ring she *put about* her hand,
> A breastplate *which. . .,* she *tightened*
>   about her breast,
> With the *pala*-garment, the garment
>   of ladyship, she covered her body,. . .[18]

As Inanna passes through the seven gates of the Netherworld, she is compelled, according to its rites, to divest herself, one by one, of "the sŭgurra, the crown of the plain," "The measuring rod (and) line of lapis lazuli," the "small lapis lazuli stones" of her neck, the "sparkling . . . stones" of her breast, etc.[19] After being shorn of the external symbols of her divine authority, she is ushered, naked and powerless, into the presence of her sister and enemy, Ereshkigal, goddess of the dead, and is turned into a corpse.[20]

The Exaltation of Inanna, then, opens by depicting the goddess as possessing the great divine attributes and all of the visible signs of her power, and being of equal stature with An. In contrast with her role elsewhere as the sexual source of fertility and of royal success through her Sacred "Marriage" with the king, Inanna is here shown as autonomous, the terrible goddess of war, the judge and punisher of humanity, and the personification and deification of the raging and destructive forces in nature that neither people nor deities can withstand.

>   9. Like a dragon you have deposited venom on the land
> 10. When you roar at the earth like Thunder, no vegetation can stand
>   up to you.
> 11. A flood descending from its mountain,
> 12. Oh foremost one, you are the Inanna of heaven and earth![21]
> 13. Raining the fanned fire
>   Down upon the nation,
> . . . .
> 17. Devastatrix of the lands,
>   you are lent wings by the storm.

18. Beloved of Enlil,
       you fly about in the nation.

. . . .

20. Oh my lady, at the sound of you
       the lands bow down.
21. When mankind
       comes before you
22. In fear and trembling
       at (your) tempestuous radiance,
23. They receive from you
       their just deserts.
24. Proferring a song of lamentation,
       they weep before you,
25. They walk toward you along the path
       of the house of all the great sighs.
26. In the van of battle
       everything is struck down by you.
27. Oh my lady, (propelled) on your own wings,
       you peck away (at the land)[22]
28. In the guise of a charging storm,
       you charge.
29. With the roaring storm
       you roar.
30. With thunder
       you continually thunder.
31. With all the evil winds
       you snort.

. . . .

34. Oh my lady, the Anunna,
       the great gods,
35. Fluttering like bats
       fly off from before you to the clefts,
36. They who dare not walk (?)
       in your terrible glance,
37. Who dare not proceed
       before your terrible countenance.
38. Who can temper
       your raging heart?
39. Your malevolent heart
       is beyond tempering.[23]

When humanity withholds its worship of Inanna as a vegetation and fertility-goddess, she is awful in her reprisals:

43. In the mountain where homage is withheld from you vegetation is
    accursed.
44. Its grand entrance
       you have reduced to ashes.

45. Blood rises in its rivers for you, its people have nought to drink
46. It leads its army captive before you of its own accord.

. . . .

55. Its woman no longer speaks of love
    with her husband.
56. At night they no longer
    have intercourse.
57. She no longer reveals to him
    her inmost treasures.[24]

In the final section of the poem, the full power and fury of Inanna are recapitulated:

121. That one has not recited as a "Known! Be it Known!" of Nanna,
     that one has recited as a " 'Tis Thine!'":
122. "That you are lofty as Heaven (An)—
     be it Known!
123. That you are broad as the earth—
     be it Known!
124. That you devastate the rebellious land—
     be it Known!
125. That you roar at the land—
     be it Known!
126. That you smite the heads—
     be it Known!
127. That you devour cadavers like a dog—
     be it Known!
128. That your glance is terrible—
     be it Known!
129. That you lift your terrible glance—
     be it Known!
130. That your glance is flashing—
     be it Known![25]
131. That you are ill-disposed toward the. . . —
     be it Known!
132. That you attain victory—
     be it Known!
133. That one has not recited (this) of Nanna,
     that one has recited it as a " 'Tis Thine!'"—
134. Oh my lady beloved of An,
     I have verily recounted your fury![26]

This account of Inanna as the supreme goddess of fertility and war is similar to subsequent descriptions of her Babylonian counterpart, Ishtar, in "The Hymn to Ishtar," written during the First Dynasty of Babylon (ca. 1600 B.C.E.), and in the "Prayer of Lamentation to Ishtar."[27] Inanna's ferocity is also matched in a later description of Hathor, one of the oldest fertility goddesses of Egypt. There is a mythological tale that accompanies pictures of the heavenly cow Nut (the sky-goddess) carved into the stone walls of a number of royal Egyptian tombs between 1350 and 1100 B.C.E. Part of the myth tells of Hathor's descent to earth as the Eye of Rā, as his active agent, in order to annihilate the human race after the sun-god discovers that people are plotting against him. In the evening Hathor returns, jubilant at having completed part of her mission. By the next morning, when Rā relents and decides to spare the rest of the people on earth, the only way he can prevent the bloodthirsty Hathor from completing her task is to arrange for red beer to be poured out on the fields before Hathor's arrival so that she might mistake it for human blood, become intoxicated, and desist.[28]

In like fashion, Canaanite mythology pictures the warlike attributes of Baal's sister-consort, Anath. For example, when confronted by "troops" in front of her house, Anath, goddess of the hunt and battle, slays everyone:

> And lo Anath fights violently
> She slays the sons of the two cities
> She fights the people of the seashore
> Annihilates mankind of the sunrise.[29]

The violent Anath exults as their severed heads and hands fly through the air:

> Under her (flew) heads like vultures
> Over her (flew) hands like locusts.[30]

Like Hathor, she sloshes around in the blood of her victims:

> She plunges knee-deep in the blood of heroes
> Neck-high in the gore of troops.[31]

Anath is victorious and overjoyed at the massacre:

> Much she fights, and looks;
> Slays, and views
> Anath swells her liver with laughter
> Her heart is filled with joy.
> For in the hand of Anath is victory.
> For she plunged knee-deep in the blood of soldiers
> Neck-high in the gore of troops.
> Until she is sated
> She fights in the house
> Battles between the tables.[32]

The Goddesses and Gods of Fertility: Anath and Baal

After her second furious battle and victory Anath shows her other face, that of fertility goddess. The blessings of peace after war parallel the renewal of the land after a long seasonal drought:

> She draws water and washes:
> Dew of heaven
>   Fat of earth
>   Rain of the Rider of Clouds.[33]

The response of nature to Anath's lapse from brutality is to bless the earth and people with fertility and an abundance of game. Her alternating activities as brutal goddess and fertility goddess call forth from nature, when Anath is in her peaceful phase:

> Dew that the heavens pour
>   Rain that the stars pour.[34]

Thus, the myth the "Baal and Anath Cycle" describes Canaan's periodic fertility and drought, symbolized by the death and resurrection of the fertility-god Baal. But when Baal is recurrently slain by Mot, the god of sterility and death, the drought can terminate and the season of fertility begin again only after Anath's intervention. Baal's resurrection is dependent on Anath, who confronts Mot about her brother-consort, Baal. After Mot's admission that he has murdered Baal:

> She seizes the God Mot
> With a sword she cleaves him
> With a fan she winnows him
>   With fire she burns him
>   In the millstone she grinds him
>   In the field she plants him.[35]

Since Mot has swallowed Baal, his planting in the earth signals the rebirth of Baal out of the interred corpse of Mot and the commencement of a seven-year cycle of fertility. The gods rejoice at Baal's resurrection and the world prospers. After seven years Shapsh, the omniscient sun-goddess, is sent to find Baal and she sees him once again battling Mot. The latter accuses Baal of having forced him from the throne for seven years, annihilating him, and Mot's words refer to what Anath made him suffer in order to avenge Baal:

"On account of thee, O Baal, I have seen shame
  On account of thee I have seen scattering by the sword
On account of thee I have seen burning by fire
  On account of thee I have seen grinding in the millstones...."[36]

Mot's complaint about his treatment by Anath attests to the importance of her intercession to guarantee the return of fertility to Canaan. Along with Baal, she is intimately involved in assuring benevolence and regularity in nature. Mot's litany of the "shame," "scattering," "burning," and "grinding" he suffered at the hands of Anath suggests her part in the triumph over sterility and in the subsequent planting and processing of grain. The courage of Anath in facilitating the renewal of fertility in nature contrasts sharply with Baal's behavior at one point in his cyclical confrontation with his most prominent adversary, death. In text #67, after Baal kills the seven-headed Leviathan, he is summoned into Mot's presence. Quaking with fear, Baal submits himself to Mot in eternal slavery, and in consequence all nature becomes barren:

Aliyan Baal feared him
  The Rider of Clouds dreaded him.
Word went back to the god Mot,
  Was relayed to the Hero, El's beloved:
"The message of Aliyan Baal
  The reply of the Mighty Warrior:
'Hail, O god Mot!
I am thy slave, e'en forever.' "
. . . .
The deity Mot rejoiced.[37]

The great power and autonomy of Anath are also portrayed in other sections of the myth. For instance, despite Baal's newly won ascendancy over the gods (procured in large measure through Anath's conquest of his enemies), he remains the only major deity without a palace of his own, that is, without the external trappings of his status. Baal therefore sends messengers to Anath, urging her to cease her warfare, establish peace, and visit him in his mountain home. To entice her, Baal promises to reveal to Anath the secrets of nature. In exchange, he wants Anath to convince Asherah to intervene in his behalf with El, her father, and win the latter's permission for the construction of Baal's palace. Anath tells Baal she will compel El to agree to his request by threatening him with violence if necessary:

And the Virgin Anath declared:
"The Bull, God of my father, will yield

> He will yield for my sake and his own
> For I shall trample him like a sheep on the ground
> Make his gray hair flow with blood
>   The gray of his beard with gore
> Unless he grants Baal a house like the gods
>   Yea a court like the sons of Asherah!"[38]

Anath then travels to her father's palace, and in fear of the fury of his daughter, El hides from her and says:

> "I know thee to be impetuous, O my daughter,
>   For there is no restraint among goddesses.
> What dost thou desire, O Virgin Anath?"[39]

Once El capitulates to her threat of violence, Anath adopts the tone of a reverent daughter:

> "Thy word, O El, is wise
>   Thy wisdom, unto eternity
>   Lucky life is thy word.
> "Our King is Aliyan Baal
>   Our judge, above whom there is none."[40]

Anath's appeal is shrewd, for it is timed to coincide with the support of Asherah and her progeny for Baal's palace, and against those two goddesses El has no recourse but to yield.

These Canaanite myths recounting the periodic death and resurrection of the male weather-deity Baal, whose life and death symbolically represent and elicit similar patterns in the flow and ebb of nature and the life and death of vegetation, stress equally the indispensability of Anath's activities, which are linked with the return of fertility. Throughout, she exercises her power against the cosmic forces of sterility and death, assures the elevation of Baal to the kingship of the gods, and thus assumes corresponding and equivalent status with Baal as a fertility deity.

Likewise, the association of this female divinity with war and violence is mirrored by the roles of the male divinities Baal and Mot in their periodic and mortal struggle for supremacy:

> They tangle like hippopotamuses
>   Mot is strong, Baal is strong.
> They gore like buffaloes
>   Mot is strong, Baal is strong.
> They bite like serpents
>   Mot is strong, Baal is strong.
> They kick like *racers*
>   Mot is down, Baal is down.[41]

Once Baal's palace is completed, he celebrates by inviting the seventy sons of Asherah and other special deities to a great feast. This latter group of goddesses and gods, personified and deified animals and objects of the anthropomorphic type common to many Near Eastern myths, honor the event in sexual pairs:

(Baal) caused the ram gods to drink wine;
  Caused the ewe goddesses to drink wine.
He caused the bull gods to drink wine;
  Caused the cow goddesses to drink wine.
He caused the chair gods to drink wine;
  Caused the throne goddesses to drink wine.
He caused the pithos gods to drink wine;
  Caused the jar goddesses to drink wine.[42]

Cyrus Gordon, one of the more important translators and interpreters of Canaanite mythology, comments on the above: "Note how each category comes in parallel pairs, male and female, giving poetic form to what would otherwise be a prosaic list."[43] However, quite apart from poetic considerations, it may be that the sexual pairing signifies an acknowledgment by Baal at his accession to the kingship of the gods (i.e., the acquisition of his own palace), that female and male divinities share responsibility for the workings of nature and civilization. Certainly it would reflect his own interdependence with Anath, Asherah, and Shapsh in the most crucial phases of his life, death, and resurrection and would reflect the more general concern of Canaanite myths with the guarantee of fertility. Moreover, the public, sacramental setting in which Baal causes these parallel deities of both sexes to celebrate his ascension to primary rank, witnessed by the major deities of the Canaanite pantheon, would seem to lend credence to this possibility.

The conception of divine sex roles in the Baal and Anath myth, in which enormously important and equivalent powers are exercised and sometimes shared by female and male divinities, recurs as a dominant motif in the mythic literature of this period. Perhaps one of the most striking examples is the designation of male divinities as gods of vegetation or fertility who share the generative powers formerly held by fertility goddesses alone.

Isis and Osiris

Baal's role as the lord of fertility, operating as a force of nature with his sister-consort, Anath, is replicated in Egypt in the figure of the god Osiris. Overarching all the differences among local cults, he was worshiped almost universally as the god of resurrection and immortality after death. By around 2500 B.C.E., he began to incorporate many of the attributes of the greatest gods, was worshiped as the equal of Rā, and came to be regarded not only as the god and judge of the dead but also as the creator of the world and of everything in it. In one of his aspects Osiris was identified with the Nile River and the fertility of the earth in general; i.e., the grain or plants growing from seemingly dead seeds in the earth and the life-giving water of the Nile River were seen as manifestations of the vitality of Osiris as chthonic deity.

The "Memphite Theology," a text probably dating back to the early years of the Old Kingdom, describes how the death of Osiris transforms him into a center of vitalizing or generative energy. The extraordinary fertility of Memphis, referred to as the "granary. . . where the sustenance of the Two Lands is taken care of,"[44] is attributed to its choice as the site of Osiris's burial, and he literally becomes its earth. "Thus Osiris became earth in the Royal Castle on the north side of this land which he had reached."[45] Similarly, the Nile, particularly when its annual inundation of the land provided for the fertility of Egypt, also came to be a manifestation of Osiris. In a hymn to Osiris dating from around 1600 B.C.E., the god is identified as the source of the river and hence the fertility of Egypt: "Homage to thee, O thou who art within thy boat, thou bringest Hāpi (i.e., the Nile) forth from his source."[46]

This mythic association of Osiris with fertility was reinforced by the conviction that the pharaoh was at once divine (as the incarnation of Horus) and the intermediary between humanity and nature. At their death, each of the pharaohs "became" Osiris, evident from all the things the earth produced afterward, and it was believed that their power continued to work for the benefit of the people. The potency of the king buried in the earth was seen as the vital force that made plants sprout, the Nile flood, and the moon rise, and it was considered a never-ending process, part of the eternal order of the universe.[47]

Therefore, Osiris in death emerges as the male counterpart of the "feminine, reproducing" force in nature, the mother-goddess Isis. She came to absorb many of the attributes of the earlier Egyptian mother-goddesses Hathor, Neith, and Nut and later, as "the Goddess of many names," was equated with every major fertility goddess of Western Asia, Greece, and Rome.[48] By the second century B.C.E. Isis would overshadow Osiris and be worshiped as the supreme goddess with universal powers at the center of one of the most widespread mystery religions of the Mediterranean world. But for a couple of thousand years prior to that, both Osiris and Isis, in some of their aspects, embodied for Egyptians the most pervasive and benevolent powers of fertility.

Other male divinities also shared responsibility for fertility with goddesses. The most well known in the popular religions of Syria and Mesopotamia were Adonis, Dumuzi, and Tammuz. Fundamental to the myths and rituals commemorating their periodic descent to the Netherworld and their subsequent rebirth, in all the local cultic variations, was the association of these gods in death and resurrection with the seasonal "death" and revival of vegetation.

Zeus and Dionysus

One of the most specific representations of the sharing of generative powers by female and male deities may be found in the mythic portrayal of Zeus. From the beginning, he was the principal deity of the immigrating Greeks, who assimilated into their own pantheon the native divinities of the people they conquered and others from adjoining areas, e.g., Asiatic divinities they came into contact with through trade and population movements. Originally the Indo-European god of the sky and weather, in time Zeus became identified with the ancient male god of fertility cults in Crete, whose presence and worship was believed to guarantee an abundance of crops and game.[49] Impregnating and/or marrying every major fertility goddess of the older indigenous religions as the Indo-Europeans consolidated their political hold over the islands, Zeus finally assumed the one power that male fertility gods could not until then share with their divine female counterparts, namely, the indispensable ability to bear offspring.

It has been conjectured that mythic accounts of the birth of the goddess Athena from the head of Zeus and the birth of the god Dionysus from his thigh may well be both symbolic and literal expressions of male envy and resentment of women's role in childbirth.[50] But they are also physical statements of the extent to which those powers of reproduction, formerly ascribed exclusively to female divinities, had come to be seen as shared by male gods of fertility as well. And just as Athena in some of her aspects was linked with the protection of agriculture and the harvest, so Dionysus in some of his was identified as the god of luxuriant vegetation and was himself a composite of Thracian and Phrygian male gods of fertility.[51]

The Broad and Equivalent Powers of Goddesses and Gods

Throughout the ancient Near East from the third through the first millennium, the mythological depiction of the exercise of power by divinities of both sexes, in which both goddesses and gods are shown as endowed with many of the same attributes, was not restricted to the province of insuring fertility but ranged over a broad and varied spectrum of activity, which affected human and divine functioning on many levels. Even as the martial prowess of the female deity Anath, crucial to fertility, had its sexual counterpart in the life-and-death struggle between the male deities Baal and Mot, the issue of which assured the reemergence of vegetation in Canaan, so the violence of the fertility goddess Hathor was matched by the recurrent violence of the male divinities Horus and Seth.

A text dating from the 20th dynasty (ca. 1200 B.C.E.), "The Contest of Horus and Seth For the Rule," describes the intermittent, hard-fought contest between these two gods to inherit the kingship of Egypt at the death of the pharaoh, who had become Osiris, or to establish which deity was the rightful heir of Osiris. Their monumental struggle and the reconciliation of their claims to rule, resolved by the Ennead or assembly of Egyptian deities, was viewed as restoring unity, peace, and stability in both the divine and secular realms. Seth is mollified by his inclusion as a powerful god by Rā in his celestial Boat of a Million Years. Upper and Lower Egypt are peacefully united by the coronation of a single pharaoh as the incarnate Horus,[52] and orderly royal succession is assured.

Enlil and Ishtar

In Mesopotamia, a sexual counterpart to the violence attributed to Inanna-Ishtar may be found in the activities of male divinities, particularly Enlil, in *The Epic of Gilgamesh*. The latter provides some significant information about the beliefs of this period, because it was one of the most enduring and widely proliferated pieces of literature common to the area, fragments of which have been recovered from Sumerian, Babylonian, Hittite, Hurrian, Accadian, and Assyrian centers of civilization. The most complete account is an Assyrian version from the palace library at Ninevah (ca. 700 B.C.E.),[53] which includes a section on a deluge, not unlike the biblical flood in Noah's time, precipitated by the advice of the active male head of the Sumerian pantheon, the "warrior Enlil," who was "counsellor" to the gods.[54]

As told to Gilgamesh by Utnapishtim the Faraway, who alone, like Noah, is able to survive along with his family, animals, and craftsmen by building a stout ship under the direction of the god of wisdom, Ea:

> In those days the world teemed, the people multiplied, the world bellowed like a wild bull, and the great god was aroused by the clamour. Enlil heard the clamour and he said to the gods in council, "The uproar of mankind

is intolerable and sleep is no longer possible by reason of the babel." So the gods in their hearts were moved to let loose the deluge.[55]

Recalling the fury unleashed by the goddess in *The Exaltation of Inanna:*

> With the first light of dawn a black cloud came from the horizon; it thundered within where Adad, lord of the storm was riding. In front over hill and plain Shullat and Hanish, heralds of the storm, led on. Then the gods of the abyss rose up; Nergal pullled out the dams of the nether waters, Ninurta the war-lord threw down the dykes, and the seven judges of hell, the Anunnaki, raised their torches, lighting the land with their livid flame. A stupor of despair went up to heaven when the god of the storm turned daylight to darkness, when he smashed the land like a cup. One whole day the tempest raged gathering fury as it went, it poured over the people like the tides of battle; a man could not see his brother nor the people be seen from heaven. Even the gods were terrified at the flood, they fled to the highest heaven, the firmament of Anu; they crouched against the walls, cowering like curs. Then Ishtar the sweet-voiced Queen of Heaven cried out like a woman in travail: "Alas the days of old are turned to dust because I commanded evil; why did I command this evil in the council of all the gods? I commanded wars to destroy the people, but are they not my people, for I brought them forth? Now like the spawn of fish they float in the ocean." The great gods of heaven and of hell wept, they covered their mouths.[56]

When the flood recedes on the seventh day, Utnapishtim offers a sacrifice and libation to the gods who crowd around. Finally, the goddess Ishtar appears and lays the responsibility for the destruction of humanity on the presumably unrepentant Enlil:

> Then, at last, Ishtar also came, she lifted her necklace with the jewels of heaven that once Anu had made to please her. "O you gods here present, by the Lapis Lazuli round my neck I shall remember these days as I remember the jewels of my throat; these last days I shall not forget. Let all the gods gather round the sacrifice, except Enlil. He shall not approach this offering, for without reflection he brought the flood; he consigned my people to destruciton."[57]

Enlil, Ninlil, and Ninurta

Other evidence that strongly suggests an equivalence of power exercised by goddesses and gods, and the ease with which divine attributes could as readily be associated with deities of either sex, or with deities of both sexes simultaneously, may be found in a group of Sumerian hymns dedicated to the gods Enlil and Ninurta.

A long, devotional "Hymn to Enlil, the All-Beneficent," probably composed by a temple poet of Nippur, describes how the god established his residence in the Ekur, the temple complex of that city; how the latter guards humanity's highest ethical and spiritual values, and therefore is an appropriate home for Enlil; and how the priesthood faithfully executes the holy rites of his shrine. It glorifies Enlil as the architect of the awe-inspiring Ekur, to which mighty lords and princes bring their prayers and sacrifices, and identifies him as the source of all procreation, fertility, and culture. The hymn concludes first with an exaltation of the mystery, grandeur, and finality of Enlil's "word," which produces fruition and life for people, and then with an exaltation of his consort Ninlil, who decrees the fates.[58]

A number of things are especially noteworthy about this hymn. In contrast to Enlil's portrayal in *The Epic of Gilgamesh* as the uncaring, violent destroyer of humanity in the deluge, he is here presented in his other guise, as the benevolent fountainhead of fertility, civilization, and religious order. Indeed, he is the sexual counterpart of the Sumero-Babylonian goddesses Inanna and Ishtar, who are pictured in myth as, alternately, compassionate fertility and mother-goddesses (as, for example, when Ishtar mourns for her children after the deluge), associated with the maintenance of society at a civilized level,[59] and raging destroyers.

In his eulogy of the fertility-god Enlil and the power of his word, the poet writes:

> ... Without Enlil, the Great Mountain,
> No cities would be built, no settlements founded,
> No stalls would be built, no sheepfold erected,
> No king would be raised high, no *en* born,
>
> . . . .
> The fish of the sea would lay no eggs in the canebrake,
> The birds of heaven would not spread (their) nests over the wide earth,
> In heaven the rain-laden clouds would not open their mouths,
> The fields (and) meadows are not filled with rich grain,
> In the steppe grass (and) herbs, its delight would not grow,
> In the garden, the wide mountain-trees would bear no fruit.
> Without Enlil, the Great Mountain,
>
> . . . .
> The cow would not "throw" its calf in the stall,
> The ewe would not bring forth the ... lamb in its sheepfold,
> Mankind, the teeming multitude,
> Would not lie down in their ... ,
> The beasts, the four-legged would bring forth no offspring, would not
>   mount to copulate.
>
> . . . .

You, lord Enlil, who are lord, god, (and) king,
Who are the judge (and) decision-maker of the universe
Your noble word is as weighty as heaven, you know no opposition,
At your word, all the Anunna-gods are *hushed,*
Your word—heavenwards it is a (foundation) platform,
Heavenwards it is a tall *pillar* reaching to the sky,
Earthwards it is a platform that cannot be overturned....[60]

The other striking element in this 170-line paean to Enlil is that it concludes with an exaltation of both the god and his consort Ninlil, similar to the "pairing" of male and female divinities at the elevation of Baal to the kingship of the gods. Significantly, this fertility-goddess is described not merely as the ceremonial spouse of the chief male god, but as the eloquent one who "decrees the fates" or determines the "unalterable" destiny of the universe:

She who has sweet graciousness, the *star-covered*,
Mother Ninlil, the holy wife, whose word is gracious,
[Garbed] in the holy *ma*-garment... ,
The faithful woman—having lifted (your) eyes (upon her) you took her in marriage,
The attraction of the Ekur, the queen who knows what is seemly,
The eloquent one who is elegant of speech,
Whose words are sweet to the flesh,
Has seated herself by your side on the holy dais, on the pure dais,
Speaks eloquently with you, whispers (tender words) by your side,
Decrees the fates in the "place where the sun rises."
Ninlil, the queen of the universe,
Cherished in the (songs of) praise of the Great Mountain,
The lofty one, whose words are firmly grounded,
Whose command and favor are unalterable,
Whose pronouncements is all enduring,
Whose plans "confirm the word"—
Oh Great Mountain Enlil, exalted is your praise.[61]

Ninlil then not only shares the "holy dais" with the great god, but the structure of the poem, devoted almost entirely to praise of Enlil's awesome power, suggests that she shares that same power. In the text, the absolute authority of Enlil's "word" is established. That the penultimate line of the poem, written in praise of Enlil, should say of Ninlil that her "plans 'confirm the word' " of her consort, may indicate the equivalence of her "plans" and his "word." Furthermore, reinforcing the concept of sexual "pairing" of powers among divinities, earlier in the poem Enlil, like Ninlil in the passage just cited, also is described as he who "decrees the fates":

Heaven—he alone is its prince, earth—he alone is its great one,
The Anunna—he is their exalted god,
When in his awesomeness he decrees the fates,
No god dares look at him, . . .[62]

In like fashion, two hymns to the male deity Ninurta mirror the dual aspects of Hathor, Anath, Inanna, and Ishtar, and provide still another instance of a sexual counterpart to the nature and powers of these goddesses. In the "Hymn to Ninurta as God of Vegetation," he is shown in his beneficent role as a potent fertility- and vegetation-deity, "the farmer of Enlil," who is worshiped as the source of richness in the land and sea and is responsible for the generation of animals. In the "Hymn to Ninurta as a God of Wrath," he is prayed to in his fearsome role as the god of battle, who subdues the rebellious country-side by destroying the contentious and disobedient, and whose anger and verdicts as a judge are terrifying.[63]

The Deities of Wisdom, Justice, and Social Order: Inanna and Enki

Those divine powers relating to the provision of wisdom, justice, and social order—seen as fundamental to the stable functioning of societies—were again shown as being dispensed by both goddesses and gods, most often within the same pantheon.

"Inanna and Enki: The Transfer of the Arts of Civilization from Eridu to Erech"[64] is a Sumerian myth inscribed as early as 2000 B.C.E., but based on concepts believed to have been current centuries earlier. It tells how Inanna, queen of heaven and tutelary goddess of Erech, is anxious to increase the prosperity of her city, make it the center of Sumerian culture, and thus enhance her own position. She therefore decides to journey to Eridu, the ancient seat of Sumerian civilization and the residence of Enki, the god of wisdom, who has in his possession all the divine decrees basic to the pattern of Sumerian civilization. Inanna's intention is to procure these decrees by any means available, transfer them to Erech, and thereby make both its status and her own unsurpassed.

Enki receives Inanna with a huge banquet, and while he is drunk he turns more than a hundred of these decrees over to Inanna, one by one. The enormity of this transaction may be inferred from their content, for among them are those which refer to:

lordship, godship, the exalted and enduring crown, the throne of king-ship, the exalted scepter, the exalted shrine, shepherdship, kingship, the numerous priestly offices, truth, descent into the nether world and ascent from it, the "standard," the flood, sexual intercourse and prostitution, the *legal* tongue and the *libellous* tongue, art, the holy cult chambers, the "hierodule of heaven," music, eldership, heroship and power, enmity, straightforwardness, the destruction of cities and lamentation, rejoicing of the heart, falsehood, the rebel land, goodness and justice, the craft of the carpenter, metal worker, scribe, smith, leather worker, mason, and basket weaver, wisdom and understanding, purification, fear and *outcry,* the kindling flame and the *consuming* flame, weariness, the shout of victory, counsel, the troubled heart, judgment and decision, exuberance, musical instruments.[65]

Inanna is delighted with these gifts, loads them on her heavenly boat, and sails off to Erech. When Enki recovers his sobriety, notices that the decrees are gone, and is told that he himself gave them to Inanna, he is greatly upset by his generosity and attempts to prevent her valuable cargo from reaching Erech at all costs. He dispatches his messenger and sea monsters, who are instructed to seize the "boat of heaven" from Inanna without harming her or preventing her return to Erech.

At each of the seven stops on her way from Eridu to Erech, Enki's messenger and the sea monsters try to recapture the decrees, but they are forestalled by Inanna. When Enki's messenger informs her that his master wants the "boat of heaven" back and wishes Inanna to return to Erech without the decrees, she accuses Enki of having "broken" and "defiled his great words" to her, of having spoken "falsehood" to her. Seven times the sea monsters seize "the boat of heaven," and seven times Inanna instructs her own messenger to "save the 'boat of heaven,' and Inanna's presented decrees."[66] Her messenger obeys; Inanna arrives at Erech with the divine decrees and unloads them as the overjoyed inhabitants of the city feast and celebrate, and the poem ends with a speech by Enki to Inanna. However, the text at this point is so damaged it is unclear whether Enki is threatening revenge or offering reconciliation.

While the guardianship of the divine decrees originally resides with Enki as the god of wisdom, the circumstances surrounding their transfer to Inanna would seem to indicate that the matter of *who* has the guardianship is rather arbitrary. If Enki had not drunk too much, or if he had and had chosen to show his pleasure with Inanna in another way, her attempts would have proven unsuccessful. The decrees were in Enki's possession because he happened to be the god of wisdom, and they came into Inanna's possession because she happened to be clever enough to induce him to present them to her. At no point in the narrative is there any suggestion of who has the greater right to them, nor is there any implication that it is somehow more fitting that these all-important decrees should be under the protector-ship of a deity of one sex or the other.

Moreover, if the imposition of rewards and penalties for certain types of behavior indicates anything about how a culture views sex roles, Enki's solicitude for Inanna's safe arrival in Erech would seem to indicate that the passage of possession of the arts of civilization from a male to a female deity was not considered particularly heinous in Sumer during the third millennium. On the contrary, while Enki is disturbed at having been duped out of his guardianship of the decrees by Inanna, she in turn accuses him of breaking his word by requesting the return of his gifts. The extent to which these two major deities were seen as exercising equivalent power may be gauged by the fact that Enki does not initiate a direct confrontation with Inanna; instead their conflict is resolved through intermediaries. And in the end, while Enki remains the great Sumerian god of wisdom, the goddess Inanna pos-sesses all the knowledge of Sumerian civilization. By virtue of her stewardship over all the divine decrees, Inanna becomes, in fact, the sexual counterpart in wisdom of the great god Enki. And this is, of course, reflected in Enheduanna's *The Exaltation of Inanna*.

Anath, Baal, Shapsh

Elsewhere, female and male divinities seem to have shared responsibil-ity for a wide range of socially indispensable functions without regard to sex. As noted earlier, in Canaanite myth Baal knows the secrets of nature, but he is willing to share them with Anath in exchange for her help in securing his palace. Like Anath and the male protagonists, the omniscient sun-goddess Shapsh also plays a crucial part in the Ca-naanite fertility drama. She assists Anath in the burial of the corpse and the offering of ritual sacrifices in honor of Baal after he is killed by Mot; she is sent to find Baal after the news of his rebirth reaches El; she discovers Baal once again fighting with Mot, and when the battle is fought to a stand-off she forces Mot into submission for a while by warning him of El's punishment if he should harm Baal.[67]

Maat

In Egypt, as political and theological dominance passed from one area to another over a very long period of time, the evolution of religious beliefs was marked by the incorporation of characteristics of many local deities into the figures of the paramount gods and goddesses; or a claim was made for the primacy of local divinities who, not surpris-ingly, exhibited the attributes of the reigning ones; or there was an assignment of similar powers to very many deities. This resulted in a profusion of myths and rites peopled by scores of deities who were highly syncretistic. Together they constituted a theology that was at once extremely conservative, in that no deities or mythic accounts were discarded, and extraordinarily tolerant and untroubled by any apparent inconsistencies in its manifold descriptions of divine functioning and human obligations. However, a number of integrative beliefs provided continuity, among them a vision of both nature and human society being ruled by Maat and therefore following congenial courses.

For thousands of years the goddess Maat was seen as the personification and deification of law, truth, and justice. Very early, it was believed that all people, the king, and even deities, had to submit to an examination of their moral qualities in a celestial court before a supreme judge. Righteous and just, the latter's every action was guided by Maat:

> The fundamental idea underlying this word seems to be 'straight,' 'straightness,' and hence what is straight, what is right, rectitude, integrity, uprightness, genuineness, true, truth, righteousness, law, both moral and physical. The divine or heavenly judge lived, reigned, ruled, and judged by MAAT, who was the equivalent of our 'JUSTICE.'[68]

Maat then was considered the foundation for the moral behavior of deities and the existence of a just social order on earth. From earliest times, the goddesses Isis and Nephthys were designated as the Maati because they symbolized integrity, righteousness, and truth. Further, it was believed that the divinity of the pharaoh was manifested by his control of the natural and social forces of the world for the good of humanity, and, in this role, he maintained the divinely ordained nature of society and championed justice, or Maat.

Another seminal preoccupation of Egyptian religion is referred to in the Pyramid Texts, the Coffin Texts, and the Book of the Dead, namely, the requirements for resurrection in the body after death—for royalty by around 2500 B.C.E., and for worthy nonroyal persons as well by around 2100 B.C.E. After death, the deceased was judged before Osiris, addressed by the former as "Lord of the Maat goddesses," and the dead person said, ". . . the Lord of the city of Maati is thy name. Verily I have come to thee, and I have brought Maat unto thee, and I have destroyed wickedness."[69] At the time of judgment, in the presence of forty-two deities in the Hall of Maat, and after the recitation of the Negative Confession of sins not committed by the supplicant, the dead person's heart was often shown on one side of a balance scale, weighed against a feather, symbolic of Maat, on the other, and his/her eternal fate was decided.

In the Pyramid Texts and elsewhere, Maat was considered a primeval entity associated with the creation of the universe. She was most closely related to the sun-god Rā, the creator-god Ptah, and the earthly king, all three of whom were most regularly called "Lords of Maat." By the middle of the third millennium, the highest judge bore the title "Priest of Maat."[70] In short, the goddess Maat was conceived of as embodying the all-embracing principles of order, law, justice, individual righteousness, and truth, for divinities and people alike, in life and after death.

Thoth

There is an Egyptian god Thoth, who, in his antiquity and in the pervasiveness of his influence over those aspects of their existence which most engrossed the people of Egypt, seems to parallel the goddess Maat. He was not listed as one of the chief gods of Heliopolis or among those who belonged to the cycle of Osiris. But neither was Horus, and some scholars believe that both omissions may be due to errors by the scribes.[71] However, Thoth's presence was noted in some of the most important endeavors of Egyptian people in this life; he played a pivotal role in their most serious conceptions of the afterlife; and he was connected in myth and rite with some of the central functions of the greatest divinities.

He was one of a group of deities whose worship, in modified form, is believed to have originated in prehistoric times. In those early ages, it is likely that shifting numbers of family, local, and national divinities, and those seen as animating nature, were served and propitiated, along with a number of animals who were considered sacred to goddesses and gods and therefore "divine." Among the last, the dog-headed ape was revered for his wisdom, intelligence, and craftiness, and this animal was the first emblem of Thoth. It was assumed that these apes, heard chattering at sunrise and sunset, were in some ways holding conversations with the sun. By dynastic times, dog-headed apes were described as "the transformed openers of the portals of heaven,"[72] and formed a virtual company of gods.

At the time when Egypt was at the height of its power (around the middle of the second millennium), references to these apes can be found scattered in the *Book of the Dead* and on papyri; they are also represented in statues of the period. It was held that they transmitted their cunning in words to the god Thoth, who, in turn, communicated them to Osiris. And it was supposed that these words of power enabled

Osiris to be "true of voice,"[73] or triumph over his enemies. The assistance these potent words rendered to the dead Osiris in his struggle against his enemies resulted in the dog-headed ape's being considered the friend of the dead in general. Thoth's importance as the associate of these apes can be most fully appreciated in the context of the Egyptians' intense and lasting preoccupation with rituals that might assure immortality and bliss in the afterlife. For example, in the papyrus of Ani (ca. 1500 B.C.E.), this ape is shown sitting next to or on the standard of the balance scale that weighs the heart of the deceased against the feather of Maat.[74]

In later times, after Thoth came to be represented as the Ibis bird, he acquired many more attributes. He was worshiped as the god of letters, science, and mathematics, or knowledge. At the creation of the universe, he was credited with playing the part of something like "wisdom." For instance, in one version of creation related in "The Theology of Memphis," a document dating back to only 700 B.C.E. but regarded as conclusively derived from an original source more than two millennia older, the "Speech" of Ptah—who thought of and created by speech the creator-god Atum and therefore all the other divinities—is deified as Thoth.[75] The latter, in time, came to be worshiped as the god of wisdom, and, consistent with the continuing Egyptian concern with life after death, as late as the Ptolemaic period (ca. 323–30 B.C.E.), the Turin Papyrus shows Thoth as the scribe of the gods, holding a reed in his hand with which he records the result of the weighing of the heart, and then addressing the forty-two divinities assembled in the Hall of Maat. When the deities hear from Thoth that the heart of the deceased has weighed out as true, the latter is granted a home forever in the Field of Peace.[76]

Isis

If Thoth was the god of wisdom, his sexual counterpart in many ways was the goddess Isis. In one of her aspects, as a goddess of nature, she probably represented the dawn in the boat of the sun at the time of creation. Well before the first millennium, like Thoth, Isis was described as having great power in her words. Reflective of the enduring preoccupation of Egyptians with assuring their immortality, both Isis and Thoth know magical formulas that heal and overcome the enemies of the dead. However, in some early renditions of the Isis-Osiris myth, her knowledge of magic is attributed to Thoth, and it was only in later times that she came to be seen as autonomous in her wisdom.

For example, according to the theology of Heliopolis, gleaned from funeral texts inscribed on royal monuments from around 2340–

2180 B.C.E., Isis succeeds in raising Osiris from the dead after his dismemberment by his brother Seth through the use of magical formulas supplied to her by Thoth. She was able to resurrect Osiris and conceive Horus by uttering these formulas with "boldness," "understanding," and "without fault in her pronunciation."[77] And great value was placed on Isis' perfect use of this magical power in the Egyptian quest for immortality and resurrection. By analogy, what Isis did for Osiris might be repeated for other Egyptians at their death through the exact execution of appropriate incantations and rituals.

Because of her role in resolving the conflict between her brother Seth and son, Horus, and especially because of her success in using magical formulas to bring her husband, Osiris, back to life after his death at the hands of Seth, she is variously described in Egyptian mythology as the "lady of enchantments," "an especially powerful magician," "a sorceress," and "resourceful."[78] In the "Hymn to Osiris" (ca. 1550 B.C.E.), she is referred to as the active protector of Osiris, whose powerful words defeat his enemies:

> His sister protected him, she who repelled the enemies and who caused
>   the deeds of the mischief-maker to retreat by the power of her mouth,
> she who is excellent of tongue, whose words do not fail, who is clear of
>   command,
> Isis, the mighty....[79]

Still later, the same kind of access to magic and to power over life and death is attributed to Isis, only by then she is portrayed as the sole source of this knowledge and power. "The God and His Unknown Name of Power"[80] (ca. 1350–1200 B.C.E.), which provides the mythical background of a ritual used to overcome the effects of a scorpion bite, describes an encounter between the supreme god Rā and Isis. In those days, one's name was conceived of as a component of both personality and power, and deities used their names in several ways. A name might be so potent that it could not be pronounced aloud. Or a deity might retain a secret name, known to no one else, and use it as a source of power over all other gods and people. The myth relates how Rā had many names, including a secret one that accounted for his supremacy among the gods. When Rā is old, Isis plans to learn his secret name and thus obtain power for herself:

> Now Isis was a clever woman. Her heart was craftier than a million men;
> she was choicer than a million gods; she was more discerning than a
> million of the noble dead. There was nothing which she did not know in
> heaven and earth, like Rā, who made the content of the earth. The god-
> dess purposed in her heart to learn the name of the august god.[81]

Isis fashions a snake out of Rā's spittle to bite the god and fill him with venom. After Rā is bitten and poisoned, he cries out in anguish to the other gods and goddesses:

> "Come to me, ye who came into being in my body, ye gods who came forth from me, that I may make known to you what has happened! Something painful has stabbed me. My heart does [not] recognize it, my eyes have not seen it, my hand did not make it, and I do not recognize it in all that I have made. I have not tasted a pain like unto it, and there is nothing more painful than it. . . . I am abounding in names and abounding in forms. My forms exist as every god; I am called Atum and Horus-of-Praise. My father and my mother told me my name, (but) it was hidden in my body before I was born, in order that the power of a male or female magician might not be made to play against me. . . .
>
> "Let the children of the gods be brought to me, the beneficent of speech, who know their (magic) spells, whose wisdom reaches the heavens."
>
> So the children of the gods came, every one of them having his mourning, (but) Isis came with her skill, her speech having the breath of life, her utterances expelling pain, and her words reviving him whose throat was constricted. She said: "What is it, what is it, my divine father? What—a snake *stabbed* weakness into thee? One of thy children lifted up his head against thee? Then I shall cast it down with effective magic. . . ."[82]

Isis offers to cure Rā if he reveals his secret name to her. He attempts to fool her, and she refuses to heal him. Then "The great god divulged his name to Isis, the Great of Magic."[83] Isis keeps her part of the bargain. She causes the poison to leave Rā's body, saves his life, and by a process of substitution for the name of Rā in the concluding paragraph, Isis permits any Egyptian suffering from a scorpion bite to invoke her great magic and recover. After Rā tells her his secret name, Isis says:

> "Flow forth, scorpion poison! Come forth from Re, O Eye of Horus! Come forth from the burning god at my spell! It is I who acts; it is I who sends (the message). Come upon the ground, O mighty poison! Behold, the great god has divulged his name, and Re is living, the poison is dead. So-and-so, the [son] of So-and-so,[84] is living, and the poison is dead, through the speech of Isis the Great, the Mistress of the Gods, who knows Re (by) his own name."[85]

At least in this myth (and certainly in her later evolution), she is "clever," "discerning," exhibits "craftiness," and "there was nothing which she did not know in heaven and earth, like Rā, who made the content of the earth." Thus, she has become the sexual counterpart of Thoth in his wisdom, functions here independently of Thoth, Osiris, and Horus, and engages the great Rā in a life-and-death contest, which implies an equivalence of power between them.

The Sumerian Myth of Origins: Divine Sex Roles, Sexuality, and Childbirth

This notion of goddesses and gods exercising great and equivalent power had implications for beliefs about the relation of gender to divine roles, sexuality, childbirth, and sin. For example, there is a Sumerian myth of origins, "Enki and Ninhursag: A Paradise Myth,"[86] inscribed some time in the first half of the second millennium, although the date of its original composition is unknown. Suggestive of the Garden of Eden in Genesis, it describes the creation of Dilmun, a Mesopotamian paradise—a clean, pure, bright place in which there is no sickness or death[87]—by the god Enki and the goddess Ninhursag. Enki, the god of water and wisdom, provides Dilmun with sweet water to make things grow in abundance. Ninhursag, one of the Sumerian mother-goddesses, through her own impregnation by Enki and the subsequent impregnations by him of her daughter, granddaughter, and great-granddaughter, the goddesses Ninmu, Ninkurra, and Uttu, is ultimately responsible for the sprouting of eight very special plants in this garden of abundance.

When Enki notices the eight plants and very likely decides to determine their fates, he commits a sinful act by first wanting to "know" them or taste them. Ninhursag, who creates these plants from the semen of Enki when he has intercourse with Uttu, is angry when he eats the plants and:

> (Thereupon) Ninhursag cursed Enki's name:
> "Until he is dead I shall not look upon him with the 'eye of life.' "[88]

Whereupon Ninhursag leaves in anger, Enki begins to waste away, and the Anunnaki, the great though nameless Sumerian deities, "sat in the dust"[89] with grief.

At this point, the fox offers to bring Ninhursag back to the ailing Enki if Enlil will reward him, and, with their negotiations completed, he somehow locates the goddess and returns her to Dilmun. Ninhursag seats Enki by (or in) her vulva, asks her brother what ails him, and (recalling the powerful magic of Isis) for each of his eight ailments she gives birth to a goddess or god to cure it.

There is some interesting information in this myth about conceptions of divine sex roles. Enki, as the god of wisdom, supplies Dilmun with the water necessary for life and intends to decree the fates of the eight special plants. But Ninhursag, as the deity responsible for their creation, exercises great and equivalent power with Enki when she curses him and decrees his death. Furthermore, just as he is undisputedly the god of life-giving water in his wisdom, she is undisputedly wise in her knowledge of healing, being the only deity who can restore Enki to vigor and life. Not even Enlil or any of the great Anunnaki has this healing power. Also, the particular form the healing process takes is reminiscent of the sexual pairing of divinities on important occasions encountered elsewhere, in other myths. In order to revivify Enki and cure the ailments in specific parts of his body, Ninhursag gives birth to the gods Abu, Nintulla, Nazi, and Enshag, and to the goddesses Ninsutu, Ninkasi, Azimua, and Ninti.[90]

Finally, repeating what is found in many of the myths of the ancient Near East during this period, sexuality and the consequences of sexuality are seen as good. It has already been noted how the sexual activity of Isis, impregnating herself from Osiris when she "erected the tiredness of the powerless one" and bore Horus, was viewed as only beneficial. This act greatly elevated her status to that of "a powerful magician," provided a means (Horus) of avenging the death of Osiris, assuring his immortality and high place among the deities, and established the pattern of peaceful succession in Egypt. In like fashion, in this Sumerian myth of paradise, intercourse is seen as free of shame or sin, and its results are benevolent. Enki waters the dikes and submerges the reeds with his "phallus."[91] The goddesses who are born from the sexual intercourse of Enki and Ninhursag, and who themselves, in turn, have intercourse with Enki to bear yet another goddess, all serve humanity in one way or another. The goddesses Ninmu and Ninsig seem to have been originally connected with vegetation, the goddess Ninkurra's activities were related to stone working or the civilizing arts, and the goddess Uttu's province seems to have been involved with the provision of clothing, all beneficial to people.[92] Moreover, the healing of Enki is accomplished in an explicitly sexual way when Ninhursag seats him by (or in) her vulva and proceeds to give birth to eight deities.

Perhaps most striking of all in this myth is the description of divine childbirth itself as experienced by Ninhursag (and later, in identical language, by the other goddesses), after being impregnated by Enki:

> She took the semen into the womb, the semen of Enki.
> One day being her one month,
> Two days being her two months,
> Three days being her three months,

Four days being her four months,
Five days (being her five months),
Six days (being her six months),
Seven days (being her seven months),
Eight [days] (being her eight months),
Nine [days] being her nine months, the months of "womanhood,"
L[ike... fat], like ... fat, like good princely fat,
[Nintu], [93] the mother of the land, like [... fat], (like... fat, like good princely fat),
Gave birth to [Ninmu].[94]

It is noteworthy that although the period of gestation is condensed for the goddesses, the biological process is identical to that experienced by human women. In contrast to its treatment in later biblical literature, where labor, sorrow, and pain in childbirth are related to divine punishment for Eve's transgression in the Garden of Eden, associated by God with subordination to her husband[95] and requiring atonement for sin by all women after delivery,[96] in this myth childbirth for goddesses is portrayed as rapid, painless, and "good." Furthermore, there is no suggestion of transgression, subordination, sin, or ritual impurity associated with divine female reproductive processes. On the contrary, it is the male god Enki who transgresses or sins in paradise, and he almost dies for it. In fact, Ninhursag's ability to reproduce healing deities saves his life.

If, by the third millennium, no inferiority was ascribed to female divinities as a group because of their role in reproduction, it seems as though their generative powers did not afford them superiority as a group over male divinities either. Instead, their ability to conceive and bear offspring apparently was one of their many attributes that helped to establish a kind of equivalence of power between them and male divinities. For instance, in an account of what was then understood as the divine source of all life and fertility in the various forms of the Sumerian mother-goddess, Thorkild Jacobsen writes:

> As the active principle in birth and fertility, in the continual renewal of vegetation, the growth of crops, the increase of flocks, the perpetuation of the human race, she holds with right her position as a dominant power, takes her seat with Anu and Enlil in the assembly of the gods, the ruling body of the universe. She is *Ninmah*, 'the exalted queen;' she is 'queen of the gods,' 'queen of kings and lords,' the 'lady who makes decisions concerning (all) heaven and earth.'[97]

However, just as the Sumerian cosmology pictures the earth as personified by an active mother/fertility-goddess who "holds with right her position as a dominant power," so it is *along with* Anu and

Enlil, the chief male divinities, that she "takes her seat ... in the assembly of the gods, the ruling body of the universe," "determines fates," and is the "lady who makes decisions concerning (all) heaven and earth." Moreover, Anu and Enlil are worshiped for exercising precisely the same kind of power over "(all) heaven and earth," and Enlil too decrees the fates and operates as a powerful source of fertility.

The Sharing of Power: Greek Goddesses and Gods

Greek myths provide yet other examples of the prevalence of this vision of shared powers between goddesses and gods. In the period that immediately preceded or coincided with the early written formulation of monotheistic beliefs, Greek mythology and ritual came to represent an even more widespread polytheistic outlook, since their content and form were based on a partial incorporation and refashioning of Minoan-Mycenean and Asiatic influences.[98] And, by the time of the Archaic Period (ca. 700–400 B.C.E.), even the most cursory examination of the attributes of major Greek goddesses and gods, in both mythology and popular religion, reveals the relative unimportance of gender as the source of divine power.

Athena was by then viewed, along with Zeus and Apollo, as one of the primary agents of divine power. "When solemn oaths were to be taken, they joined her name with those of Zeus and Apollo, in a way which shows that the three deities represent the embodiment of all divine authority."[99] Her functions were broad, encompassing among others responsibility for those products of human wisdom essential to war and peace.

Like her father, Zeus, Athena was seen as the initiator of storms and bad weather, critical for a seafaring and agricultural society. She controlled thunder and lightning and carried the aegis with the Gorgon's head, symbol of the awful tempest. In many commanding statues, she was, accordingly, the only deity other than Zeus shown hurling the thunderbolt from heaven. Like the male god Ares she was the deity of war. But in her measured wisdom she usually triumphed over his blundering rashness, and was worshiped in Athens mainly as a protector, defender and champion, guardian of the state, and goddess of victory.

However, her central activities revolved around the manifold occupations of peace. Each year, two of the three sacred observances that marked the beginning of the ploughing season in Attica were devoted to Athena as the inventor of the plough and yoke. Along with Poseidon, she was credited with the invention of shipbuilding and the taming of horses. She was believed to have introduced the cultivation of olive trees and was also portrayed as the patron of all women's indispensable handiwork and arts like spinning and weaving, acknowledged in the format of the elaborate rites that celebrated her annually at the Panathenaea and quadrennially at the Greater Panathenaea, for which only girls and women wove and spun special garments.[100] Indeed, in her association with human wit and cleverness, she presided over the whole moral and intellectual aspect of life, and it is this last attribute which perhaps most explicitly illustrates the ancient polytheistic view of divine power as shared with considerable equivalence by goddesses and gods.

Athena's mother, Metis, the first wife of Zeus, is described by Hesiod as knowing "more than all the gods / or mortal people."[101] Gaia and Ouranos inform Zeus that from Metis, "children surpassing in wisdom / should be born." The first is to be Athena, and she is to be "the equal of her father in wise counsel / and strength," and in these aspects exemplifies the slight extent to which ancient conceptions of divine sex roles regarded specific kinds of divine power as contingent on sex. It is predicted that the second child is to be a son, destined to be "King over gods and mortals," whose "heart would be overmastering." And in order to counter the threat of being supplanted by his own son just as he had supplanted his father, and "so that this goddess should think for him, for good and for evil,"[102] Zeus swallows Metis. After her incarceration, Metis not only "thinks" for Zeus, or is the source of his wisdom, but has by then also conceived Athena and is the source of her wisdom and prowess:

> But Metis herself, hidden away
>   under the vitals of Zeus,
> stayed there; she was Athene's mother;
>   worker of right actions,
> beyond all the gods
>   and beyond all mortal people in knowledge;
> and there Athene had given to her hands
>   what made her supreme
> over all other immortals who have
>   their homes on Olympos;
> for Metis made the armor of Athene,
>   terror of armies,
> in which Athene was born
>   with her panoply of war upon her.[103]

Athena, "the equal of her father in wise counsel," shared her role as goddess of wisdom with the third major deity of the triumvirate,

Apollo. He not only was the god of wisdom, but also shared other of his attributes with his twin sister, Artemis, who was frequently worshiped along with him. Like Artemis, Apollo had the power to cause sudden death as well as to heal. Similarly, Zeus ruled the world, ordained its course, and preserved its order, but his reign exhibited the same pattern of power shared with goddesses. In conjunction with the goddess Themis, the divinity of law and order who represented divine justice in all its relations to people, and the goddesses Dike and Nemesis, Zeus was the guardian of justice and truth, the basis of human society. Indeed, in this light, it seems no accident that among the progeny of Gaia and Ouranos at the inception of the universe were the original Titans, six female and six male, parents of all of the deified cosmic forces responsible for the divine, natural, and social order.

Taken together, Zeus, Themis, Athena, Apollo, Dike, and Nemesis seem to embody among them those attributes ascribed to the Egyptian goddesses Maat and Isis, the Egyptian god Thoth, the Sumerian god Enki, and the Sumerian goddess Inanna when she transfers the arts of civilization from Eridu to Erech. The sex of the particular deities involved was apparently of minor significance, so long as the important functions required for the maintenance of nature and society were performed. As has been seen, by the second millennium in Canaan, it was the god Baal who knew the secrets of nature and offered to share them with his sister-consort, the goddess Anath. However, in Egypt, according to the genealogy of Heliopolis, it was the goddess Isis who taught the secrets of agriculture to her brother-consort, Osiris.[104] But even this fails to do justice to the complex multiplicity of powers that often accrued to divinities in polytheistic religions, and that bore such slight relation to their sex. Though Isis was later to be portrayed in many paintings and statues as the mother of the infant Horus, she was certainly not regarded initially or thereafter as only a goddess of fertility or agriculture. In fact, the name Isis translates as "the throne," and her early and continuing designation as the mystical and vital source of kingship was quite different from and additional to her subsequent assimilation of the qualities of mother-goddesses.

Goddesses and Gods as Chthonic Deities:
Ereshkigal and Nergal

There was still another field of power that shifted from the exclusive province of divinities of a single sex to that of both sexes. As noted earlier, prior to the third millennium it seems likely that fertility goddesses were worshiped as chthonic deities in one of their aspects. But in later times it is evident that both goddesses and gods assume power over the realm of the dead. The Mesopotamian myth "Nergal and

Ereshkigal," dating from an Accadian fragment of the fourteenth century B.C.E. and a later, more complete neo-Assyrian version, describes how the god Nergal came to share dominion with the goddess of the dead, Ereshkigal.

In the first version,[105] Ereshkigal is invited to a banquet of the gods in heaven, but since she cannot leave the Netherworld she sends her vizier Namtar in her place. Among all the deities, only Nergal fails to show proper respect to Ereshkigal by not rising at her messenger's appearance. Enraged, Ereshkigal instructs Namtar to return and bring back with him the disrespectful god so that she might kill him. Terrified at the awful power of the Queen of the Dead, Nergal goes weeping to the god Ea, who sends fourteen accomplices along to assist him in the battle for his life in the Land of No Return. Only when her own life is threatened by Nergal does Ereshkigal become reconciled with him and offer to share her power:

> "Be thou my husband and I will be
>   thy wife. I will let thee hold
> Dominion over the wide nether world. I
>   will place the tablet
> Of wisdom in thy hand. Thou shalt
>   be master,
> I will be mistress!" When Nergal
>   heard this her speech,
> He took hold of her and kissed her wiping
>   away her tears:
> "Whatever thou has wished of me
>   since months past,
> So be it now!"[106]

The transition from power over the dead held by the goddess alone to power shared with a male consort is portrayed somewhat differently in the neo-Assyrian version.[107] The essential difference in this telling of the myth is that Nergal becomes Ereshkigal's consort and coruler of the dead not because of his threat but because of her own volition and power. At the banquet of the gods, after Nergal fails to bow to Namtar, who is to take Ereshkigal's portion or dish back to the Netherworld for his mistress, it is decided that Nergal must himself descend to the Land of No Return in order to apologize to Ereshkigal for the insult. The god Ea gives him detailed instructions on how to survive the journey. He is told to cut down special kinds of trees to make a proper staff and is instructed how to adorn himself, presumably for his protection. Nergal is cautioned against accepting any kind of hospitality from Ereshkigal—a throne to sit on, meat and drink, water to bathe with. Finally, he is warned against having intercourse with Ereshkigal when she goes to bathe and uncovers her body before him.

Nergal descends to the Land of No Return, goes through the rites of passage required for entry through the seven gates, and follows the advice of his mentor Ea until Ereshkigal gets ready for her bath. Then, disregarding Ea's warning, "They [both] embraced [one another], / Pas[sionately they got into] bed." And for seven days they lay together, after which Nergal goes back to heaven with a promise to return to the Netherworld. Ereshkigal, who has not been satisfied sexually, grieves for her absent lover and sends her messenger once more to Anu, Enlil, and Ea. In the first part of her message, she is a supplicant:

Since I, thy daughter, was young,
I have not known the play of maidens,
I have not kn[own] the frolic of young girls.
[That god whom] thou didst send and
    who had intercourse with me,
Let him lie with me,
Send [that god] to me that he might be my husband,
    That he might lodge with me.[108]

She concludes with the fearsome threats that she will stop doing her job and will reverse the order of life and death, both measures of her immense power, if she does not get her way:

I am sexually defiled, I *am* not *pure,*
    I cannot determine the verdicts of the great gods,
The great gods who dwell in Irkalla.
If [thou dost not] send t[hat] god,
According [to the *ordinances* of *Irkall*]a
    and the great underworld,
I shall send up the dead that they
    might devour the living,
I shall make the dead more numerous
    than the living.[109]

Her sexual defilement or impurity does not seem to refer to her loss of virginity, or to the act of intercourse itself as being defiling by its very nature. On the contrary, just before this passage Ereshkigal complains to Namtar, "O Erra, my voluptuous mate! / I was not sated with his charms (and) he has left me." And Namtar replies, "I will seize that god, / [. . . that he might k]iss thee."[110]

Ereshkigal's sense of having been sexually defiled and made impure possibly refers to the fact that Nergal, in the first instance, disobeyed Ea's instructions (with her willing cooperation), and thus might have violated the laws of the Netherworld. Or it might have resulted from a feeling that she was "used" by her lost lover, since the Netherworld is literally a Land of No Return or one that cannot be entered and left at will. But what is important here is Ereshkigal's autonomy, for her protest does not use a frame of reference established by Anu, Enlil, Ea, or Nergal. Instead, she is the one who defines the nature of her sexual defilement and impurity, threatens punishment for the whole universe if they are not countered, and lays down the conditions for their amelioration.

In any event, when Namtar delivers Ereshkigal's message and threat to the three ruling gods, Anu, Enlil, and Ea, they apparently take the measure of her power and say: "Namtar, come into the courtyard of Anu, / Seek (redress) from him for (his) *offences* against thee. / T[ake] him!"[111] Thereupon Nergal returns to the Netherworld, he and Ereshkigal passionately embrace once again and lie together for seven more days, and Anu sends a message to Ereshkigal (not Nergal): " '*That god* whom I sent to thee, / [*He shall dwell with thee* for]ever.' "[112] This rendition of the myth, then, would seem to indicate a more peaceful transition from female sovereignty over the dead to shared sovereignty by a female and male deity at the initiative, even command, of the former, and also offers still another example of the even-handed attitude toward female and male sexuality.

Osiris and the Goddesses

In like fashion, in Egypt, while the god Osiris judges the dead with the god Thoth in attendance, the goddesses Maat, Isis, and Nephthys are present as well, the first as an active participant in weighing the heart of the deceased. The last two are ultimately responsible for the whole ritual, because it is they, and particularly Isis, who make possible the resurrection of Osiris after his dismemberment, protect him from his enemies after his death, and thus ensure his place as divine judge in the afterlife. Also conspicuously present at the ceremony of the weighing of the heart, while the beast Ām-mit, the "Eater of the Dead," waits to devour the heart of the deceased should it prove light when weighed against the feather of Maat, are the goddesses Meshkenet and Renenet, or Destiny and Fortune.[113] Hence, concomitant with the Osirianization of Egyptian religion, which apparently was persistent and enduring for those periods of ancient Egyptian history accessible to us, was the assumption of essential roles as chthonic deities by goddesses who participated with Osiris and Thoth in the most significant rituals related to death and the afterlife.

By the first millennium, Greek myths provide a rather interesting contrast to both Egyptian and Mesopotamian views of goddesses and gods in their roles as chthonic deities. Whereas Egyptians apparently felt it appropriate, and perhaps even meaningful, to involve both female and male divinities in their most sacred rites surrounding mortal passage into the afterlife, and Mesopotamians apparently saw the joint rule of the dead by a divinity of each sex as a consequence of the use of force by the god or the invitation of the goddess, Greeks seemed to conceive of governance of the underworld in quite different ways.

Demeter and Zeus

The Olympian period was ushered in by Zeus's overthrow of the old order, which had rested so heavily on the relationship between the goddesses Gaia and Rheia and their offspring, and its replacement by a more patriarchally ordered divine hierarchy. Although the transition to a male-dominant pantheon was by no means complete, as evidenced by the considerable sharing of equivalent attributes and powers by goddesses and gods and by what is known about the sacred rites devoted to them in popular worship, nevertheless the new divine order in fact exhibited some new characteristics.

For example, it was one in which the male gods Zeus, Poseidon, and Hades divided among themselves sovereignty over the sky, sea, and underworld. The power of prophecy passed from the goddesses Earth, Themis, and Phoebe to the male god Apollo at Delphi. The gods consorted freely with goddesses, mortal women, and occasionally, as in the case of Apollo, mortal men as well, and there are no male counterparts to the three great goddesses, Athena, Artemis, and Hestia, who were in this period described as perpetual virgins. (In earlier times and other places, Athena and Artemis seem to have been identified with fertility and mother-goddesses.)[114] And the widely worshiped, indigenous fertility-goddess Hera was reduced to a nag bent on monogamy.

Within this context, it seems curious that with the host of possible consorts for Hades, Zeus should have chosen to bear the results of Demeter's wrath—i.e., the barrenness of the earth—by consenting to Hades' abduction and rape of her daughter Korè, and his installation of her as his queen, the august Persephone. Of course, the kidnap and rape of Korè served as a means of setting the drama of Demeter's mourning into motion, thereby rationalizing the seasonal changes. But, in addition, having at his side the daughter of the powerful Demeter may have been necessary to Hades in order that he might more effectively or legitimately rule the province of the dead. Once again, what is found in this period, even in the androcentric Olympian myths, is not a sex-related designation of role as chthonic deity but a sharing of power by divinities of both sexes.

Goddesses, Gods and the Creation of the Universe

If polytheistic religions did not ground supreme and exclusive authority over the afterlife in the sex of the presiding chthonic deities, so they apparently did not consider that the sex of creator-deities was closely linked to the value of the act of creation itself. In general, while the creation of the universe was seen as extremely important, and the source of life was duly honored and reverently worshiped, the multiplicity of personal and social needs understood as served by a multiplicity of goddesses and gods established some special conditions in the relationship of the worshiper to the worshiped and bore heavily on how gender was perceived as relating to divine power.

Polytheism tended to be fairly pragmatic. Life was seen pretty much as an ongoing process whose continuity and stability had to be attended to, and toward this end the original creator or creator-deities were sometimes relegated to positions as honorific heads of pantheons, while more dynamic, often younger deities, viewed as less remote and more intimately engaged in the everyday concerns of life and death, became the central figures or objects of worship and supplication in sacred rites. Thus, regardless of the sex of the original divine source of life, over time Enlil supplants An, Baal supplants El, Osiris supplants Rā, and Zeus supplants the older deities. Indeed, one of the meanings of the struggle for the kingship of the gods, which runs like a leitmotif through much of Near Eastern mythology, is that responsibility for creation is not an assurance of supreme power eternally enjoyed. Therefore, because the creator-deity had a fairly tenuous hold on his or her absolute power, in the polytheistic view the sex of a divinity, even one seen as the source of life, had a fairly tenuous relation to divine power.

In addition, polytheistic myths of origins everywhere in the Near East include important roles for female and male divinities either at the creation of life or shortly thereafter. Hence, while Sumerians attributed the original creation of the universe to the goddess Nammu, her first act was to reproduce parthenogenetically the male deity An, the sky, and the female deity Ki, the earth. Likewise, Egyptians who attributed the creation of the universe to the god Ptah believed that he immediately and parthenogenetically spawned goddesses and gods essential to life, or that he was bisexual. And the Babylonian story of creation begins with the presence of the original divine couple in Chaos, the goddess Tiamat and her consort Apsu.

In Egypt, no one story of creation may be denoted as characteristically Egyptian. Popular belief identified the first creation with the rising of the sun on the first day, which was then repeated every day afterward. In addition, many localities forwarded their own paramount deity as the original creator, and various schools of theology developed their own scenario of creation. For instance, at Heliopolis the solar deity Atum emerged as the creator of the first dry land in the midst of primeval waters, the Primeval Hill. At Memphis the chthonic deity Ptah, as resident in the earth, was worshiped as the Primeval Hill itself. But there is a consistent thread running through the variant myths of creation, and that is the explicit involvement of divinities of both sexes, even when the initial act of creation itself is attributed to a male deity.

Despite the retention of a strong affinity for solar phenomena and imagery in myths of origins, the land Egyptians lived on and cultivated also assumed significance. Sometimes, the act of creation was portrayed as the rising of land out of the waters of chaos, personified in the god Nun, which continued to surround the earth afterward as an infinite source of life and fertility. Thus the Nile flood was believed to originate from Nun, and the waters of Nun surrounding the Primeval Hill were seen as dividing the land of the living from the land of the dead. The best-preserved story of creation is associated with Hermopolis in middle Egypt. In it chaos was personified as eight bizarre creatures who resided in the primeval slime. Four were snakes, four were toads or frogs. Four were male, four were female, and together they brought forth or created the sun, a male deity.

There were other stories of creation as well. Some, in typical Egyptian fashion, were contradictory but apparently given credence at one and the same time. If the sun is not seen as the creator but as one of the heavenly bodies, then its daily appearance and disappearance must be explained. It was told how the sky, in the form of a woman, bent over the earth and brought forth the sun and stars each morning and evening, or the sky-goddess Nut "bore" the heavenly bodies when they appeared. In other versions, the sun and stars were thought to pass through her body when they were invisible.

As early as the Fourth Dynasty (ca. 2600–2500 B.C.E.), the goddess Neith, as both the mother and daughter of Rā, was believed to give birth to the sun-god every day.[115] Just as Ptah in the "Memphite Theology" is described as creating all things parthenogenetically, by thinking and commanding as the "heart" and the "tongue," or as the First Creative Principle who preceded all other creator-gods, so Neith, as mother of the gods, was believed to have delivered the supreme sun-god Rā without a male consort, and to have given birth to Atum in primeval times before anything else was created. And as late as the second half of the first millennium, she was worshiped as the mother of the gods in her temple at Saïs by the Persian ruler Cambyses.[116]

In the myth "The Repulsing of the Dragon and the Creation" (dated from ca. 310 B.C.E., but whose basic material is believed to derive from a fairly early period), one of the first acts of Rā was to spit out of his mouth parthenogenetically the male and female deities Shu and Tefnut, who then parented the other deities in a more natural manner.[117] And similar to the pattern found elsewhere, the close involvement of female as well as male personifications of divinity shortly after creation can also be detected in the "Memphite Theology," in which the crowning act of the creation of deities and all living things by the god Ptah is described as follows: "The Great Seat, which *rejoices* the heart of the gods, which is in the House of Ptah, the mistress of all life, is the Granary of the God, through which the sustenance of the Two Lands is prepared, because of the fact that Osiris drowned in his water, while Isis and Nephthys watched."[118]

Goddesses, Gods, and the Organization of the Universe: Inanna and Ishtar

Indeed, in ancient myths at least as much emphasis is placed on the organization of the universe after creation as on the act of creation itself, and in this organization the broader roles of fertility goddesses are evident by the third millennium. The Sumerian fragment "Inanna's Descent to the Nether World"[119] is fairly typical. Inscribed in the first half of the second millennium, the date of its first composition is unknown, and it was to serve as the partial basis for an Accadian myth a thousand years later, "Ishtar's Descent to the Nether World."

Inanna, queen of heaven, goddess of life, light, and love, and one of the original great deities of the Sumerian pantheon, for unknown reasons determines to visit the Netherworld, the realm of the dead ruled by her sister and apparent enemy, Ereshkigal. In fear that her sister might put her to death, Inanna insures her survival in the Land of No Return by instructing her divine messenger, Ninshubur, to go to the assembly of the gods, raise a commotion, and plead for her rescue if she should fail to return within three days. Specifically, she is to appeal in turn to the gods Enlil, Nanna, and Enki.

Inanna's fears are realized. As described above, after adorning herself with the relevant divine decrees, royal clothing, and jewelry, she is compelled by order of Ereshkigal to discard part of her queenly apparel successively at each of the seven gates of the Netherworld. She arrives, naked and kneeling, before her sister and the Anunnaki, the dread judges of the underworld. The latter pronounce judgment on Inanna, "fasten" her with "the eyes of death,"[120] and she is turned into a corpse and hung from a stake.

After three days have elapsed, Ninshubur begins to plead for the gods to save Inanna's life. Two peculiarities of style in Sumerian poetry ought to be noted here. The first is that when a poet wants to repeat something specific, as when a deity or hero orders her or his messenger to deliver a message, the latter, despite its length, appears twice in identical form in the text, once when the messenger receives the message, and once when it is actually delivered. The second stylistic feature is that Sumerian poets use two dialects in their epic and mythic compositions, or what have been termed by Sumerologists as the *main* dialect and the very similar *Emesal* dialect. The latter is used in rendering the direct speech of female, not male deities and, for example, is regularly used for the speeches of Inanna.[121] Therefore, when Ninshubur delivers her message to each of the three gods, they know that (a) it is verbatim, and (b) its source is indeed Inanna.

Her message to each of the gods conveys a solid notion of Inanna's power. In identical words, Ninshubur relays the following first to Enlil, the god of the air and by then the active head of the Sumerian pantheon, then to Nanna, the ancient and powerful moon-god, and then to Enki, the god of wisdom and of water:

> O father Enlil,[122] let not thy daughter be *put to death* in the nether world,
> Let not thy good metal be covered with the dust of the nether world,
> Let not thy good lapis lazuli be broken up into the stone of the stone-
> worker,
> Let not thy *boxwood* be cut up into the wood of the woodworker,
> Let not the maid Inanna be *put to death* in the nether world.[123]

The meaning of this passage has remained obscure to some of the translators. For instance, Samuel Noah Kramer writes of these lines:

> It is difficult to see what "thy good metal," "thy good lapis lazuli," "thy *boxwood*," are intended to refer to; on the surface it might seem that they refer to the jewels and ornaments carried by Inanna, but if so, what does "thy *boxwood*" refer to? Falkenstein ... suggests that these phrases are figurative descriptions of Inanna's body; *such usage, however, is as yet without parallel in Sumerian literature.* [124] (Italics in last line are mine.)

Now it may be that Kramer and Falkenstein had difficulty with the passage because they overlooked the possibility that Inanna's message is not a *plea* for divine intervention on her behalf but a *threat,* or that they failed to recognize the scope of Inanna's power. In effect, she may

be telling the gods that if she is put to death the fruits of civilized effort
will be destroyed, or the progress of civilization will be reversed. She
threatens that if she dies, "thy good metal" will be "covered with the
dust of the nether world," or removed from the land of the living and
no longer available for use by human society; "thy good" decorative,
valuable, sacred "lapis lazuli," used to decorate the bodies of divinities
and their residences, will be "broken up into the stone of the stone-
worker," or reduced to its primitive form before it was made ornamen-
tal; and the "*boxwood,*" possibly precious, will be "cut up into the wood
of the woodworker," perhaps back to a state before it has been shaped
for human use, or converted into any kind of wood. There is actually
a precedent for this last interpretation. Apparently some types of wood
were so highly valued for building walls and temples in Sumer that the
heroes Gilgamesh and Enkidu risk their lives in battle with Humbaba,
the Evil One, in order to cut down cedar trees in his forest and bring
them back to Uruk, the city Gilgamesh rules as king,[125] and thus
achieve fame for themselves.

In addition, it was by no means uncommon for goddesses to
threaten the greatest gods with the most awful retribution if they did
not get what they wanted. For example, as has already been seen,
Anath threatens El with violence if he does not grant Baal a palace of
his own; Isis threatens Rā with death if he does not reveal to her his
secret name of power; Ereshkigal threatens to raise the dead so they
might devour the living if the gods deny her the possession of her lover
Nergal; and as shall be seen subsequently, Ishtar also threatens Anu
with raising the dead to outnumber the living if he denies her the right
to execute vengeance against Gilgamesh.[126]

It seems significant that Inanna's instructions to Ninshubur at the
conclusion of her message are different for Enlil and Nanna and for
Enki. In the first two instances, she says to her messenger, "If Enlil
stands not by thee in this matter, go to Ur"[127] (the city of Nanna), and
"If Nanna stands not by thee in this matter, go to Eridu"[128] (the city
of Enki). She knows beforehand that the first two gods may indeed not
stand by her. However, at the end of the identical message Ninshubur
was to repeat to Enki, Inanna says:

> Father Enki, the lord of *wisdom,*
> Who knows the food of life, who knows the water of life,
> *He will surely bring me to life.*[129]

It may be argued that Enki, as the god of wisdom, is perhaps the
only one of the three deities who knew "the food of life, the water of
life," and therefore the only one who *could* restore Inanna to life. It

could be that Inanna wanted to give weight to her threat by informing Enlil and Nanna as well, so that they must, in a sense, share responsibility for her fate, and therefore the fate of civilization. At any rate, Inanna identifies Enlil and Nanna by name only, but refers to Enki by his title "lord of wisdom," which is especially curious because he held a dual title, god of wisdom and of water.

In his wisdom, Enki is deeply troubled by the danger to Inanna (and presumably to the civilized arts). He responds to her message by fashioning out of dirt the *Kurgarru* and *Kalaturru*, two sexless creatures to whom he gives the food of life and the water of life to sprinkle on the corpse of Inanna. They descend to the Netherworld, restore Inanna to life through the magic of Enki, and Inanna ascends to earth, retrieving all the trappings of her majesty and power as she passes through each of the seven gates. The magnitude of Enki's intercession to save Inanna, in contravention of the Anunnaki's decrees, and therefore the implicit magnitude of its cause, namely the threat of Inanna, may be gauged by the power of the Anunnaki. And their power is dealt with directly in three Sumerian myths of origins dating back to the third millennium.

The first, "Enlil and Ninlil: The Begetting of Nanna,"[130] describes the birth of the moon-god Nanna through the union of Enlil and Ninlil, and the successive births after Nanna of three of their other children, the Netherworld deities Nergal, Ninazu, and a third whose name is as yet illegible. In other words, the existence of the underworld, its deities and its rules, is as old as time itself, for the ancient calendars, like the Hebrew one, were lunar, not solar like our own. And Nanna the lunar-deity is so ancient he is created, presumably, prior to the creation of people.

The second myth, "Enki and Sumer: The Organization of the Earth and Its Cultural Processes,"[131] describes the establishment of law and order by Enki and relates how he decrees the fate of Sumer. With regard to the last, the Anunnaki are referred to by Enki as follows:

> The Anunnaki, the great gods
> In thy midst have taken up their
>   dwelling place,
> In thy large *groves* they *consume*
>   (their) food.
> O house of Sumer, may thy stables be
>   many, may thy cows multiply
> May thy sheepfolds be many, may
>   thy sheep be myriad,
> . . . May the Anunnaki decree the
>   fates in thy midst.[132]

The third myth, "Enki and Eridu: The Journey of the Water-God to Nippur,"[133] describes the building of Enki's "sea-house" in Nippur, one of the most ancient and revered cities of Sumer and the spiritual center of the country in the third millennium. When Enki arrives in Nippur, he prepares all sorts of food and drinks for the gods, especially for Enlil, who was then the leading deity of the pantheon:

> Enki in the shrine of Nippur,
> Gives his father Enlil bread to eat,
> In the first place he seated An (the heaven-god),
> Next to An he seated Enlil,
> Nintu he seated at the "big side,"
> The Anunnaki seated themselves one after the other.[134]

After the gods finish banqueting, Enlil is ready to bless his son's creation, and the very first words of praise and consecration are addressed to the Anunnaki:

> Enlil says to the Anunnaki:
> Ye great gods who are standing
>   about,
> My son has built a house, the King
>   Enki;. . .[135]

The Anunnaki, then, the nameless attendant deities, are primeval in origin and rank among the highest and most ancient gods, even in a culture that named literally hundreds of deities in the third millennium. They are portrayed by Enki as "the great gods" who will "decree the fates" of Sumer, are seated alongside the greatest Sumerian deities, An, Enlil, and Nintu, and are spoken to first by Enlil when he blesses his son's house in the most holy of Sumer's cities. As attendant deities of Ereshkigal, they wield great power, and this is attested to by Enlil and Nanna when, in their identical responses to Ninshubur's message, they both refer to "The ordinances of the nether world."[136] Therefore, it is not inconceivable that both Enlil and Nanna were merely bowing to the force of the Anunnaki's decrees, even when they were directed against "the queen of heaven." And it may be surmised that when Enki, a deity known as friendly to humanity (as different from some other Sumerian divinities), understands Inanna's threat that the outcome of her death will be the decline of Sumerian civilization, he acts to neutralize the decrees of the remorseless Anunnaki.

The decrees of the Netherworld are so potent that though Inanna is permitted to reascend to earth, even she must abide by the inviolable rules of the Land of No Return. Anyone who enters its gates may not return to the land of the living unless a substitute is found to take her/his place. Accompanied by heartless demons who have been instructed to return her to the land of the dead if she fails to locate another deity to replace her, she visits first the two Sumerian cities of Umma and Badtibira. Their deities, appalled at her ghoulish companions, "Sat in the dust" and "dressed in sack cloth."[137] Since they show her proper respect, Inanna restrains the demons from seizing them. But when they all approach the city of Inanna's consort Dumuzi, he neither shows signs of mourning nor pays her proper homage. Inanna therefore turns him over to the demons, probably as her surrogate in the Netherworld.[138]

A millennium later, in the Accadian version, "Descent of Ishtar to the Nether World,"[139] Ishtar and Ea replace the earlier protagonists, Inanna and Enki. But there are other variations as well. In contrast to the earlier myth, Ishtar sends no message or threat to the gods. However, the central difference seems to be a more constricted view of what the death of Ishtar will jeopardize, namely human and animal reproduction. This view throws Ishtar back into the company of pre-third-millennium fertility goddesses rather than that of Inanna.

Whereas Enki understands that the level of civilized development is at stake should Inanna remain a perpetual prisoner in the realm of the dead, Ea decides to rescue Ishtar when he hears from Papsukkal, the vizier of the gods:

> Ishtar has gone down to the nether world,
>   she has not come up.
> Since Ishtar has gone down to the Land
>   of No Return,
> The bull springs not upon the cow, the
>   ass impregnates not the jenny,
> In the street the man impregnates not
>   the maiden.
> The man lies down in his (own) chamber,
> The maiden lies down on her side.[140]

The Wide-Ranging Power of Goddesses

If the beneficent aspect of Ishtar's power is here linked with reproduction, she was also described in other terms. In the "Hymn to Ishtar," written about 1600 B.C.E., she is portrayed as:

> The goddess—with her there is counsel.
> The fate of everything she holds in her hand.

Who—to her greatness who can be equal?
Strong, exalted, splendid are her decrees.
She is sought after among the gods; extraordinary is her station.
Respected is her word; it is *supreme* over them. . . .[141]

Ishtar's ferocity as the goddess of war in the "Prayer of Lamentation to Ishtar"[142] rivals that of Inanna in *The Exaltation of Inanna.* And in *The Epic of Gilgamesh,* when Ishtar woos that hero and is refused by him, she flies into a terrible rage. She asks her father, Anu, to create the Bull of Heaven for her to destroy Gilgamesh, and says:". . . but if you refuse to make me the Bull of Heaven I will break in the door of hell and smash the bolts. I will let the doors of hell stand wide open and bring up the dead to eat food with the living; and the hosts of dead will outnumber the living."[143] The power of Ishtar is here shown as enormous. Anu accedes to her demand once she assures him that she can provide enough grain for cattle and food for people in order to counteract the seven years of drought that were sure to follow the destruction unleashed by the Bull of Heaven.

By the first millennium, other major fertility goddesses also exercised great and wide-ranging powers. The Greek Demeter was not an earth-goddess but a "Grain-Mother," or the goddess of the cultivated field, of agriculture, and of the civilizations based on them. Even in the period of Olympian ascendance, after the forcible loss of her daughter, Demeter refused to do her job, causing such barrenness on earth that she unilaterally brought humanity to the edge of extinction. Zeus and Hades were compelled to bow to Demeter's power, return Korè, and negotiate peace with her mother. Hades managed to retain his queen for one third of the year not through the use of countervailing power but only through duplicity, when he tricked Persephone into eating a few addictive pomegranate seeds before she left Tartarus.

It is noteworthy that Demeter autonomously defied Zeus's decision, and in this instance established the primacy of the mother-daughter bond, or female affiliation, over the conjugal relationship. In addition, rather than suffering punishment for her act of defiance, the powerful Demeter is shown as benign, blessing the earth once her conditions are met. After Korè was restored to her mother, Demeter lifted her curse from the land and consented to send the Eleusinian Triptolemus around the world to teach people the arts of agriculture.

Isis was another towering, autonomous goddess. As already noted, early Egyptian myths relate how she taught her brother-husband, Osiris, the secrets of agriculture; how, through her knowledge of magic, she rescued and revived him after his murder; how, through her active sexuality, she bore a son fathered by the dead

Osiris, thereby avenging his death and ensuring the stability of royal succession; and how, in her wisdom, she administered Egypt as "the throne" and assured Osiris his place as lord and judge of the dead. By the first millennium, Isis was to incorporate in her syncretistic evolution many of the attributes of the greatest Egyptian and Mediterranean fertility goddesses, of Osiris himself as chthonic deity, and of other male divinities who were believed responsible for both weather and civilization. Isis became in her illimitable power the most universal of all goddesses, ruling in heaven, on earth, in the sea, and in the world below. She was seen as endowed with the power to decree life and death, decide the fate of people, dispense rewards and punishments to humanity, and to hold out the promise of life after death. Her cultic worship was both intensely personal and social, and by the second century B.C.E. in Rome was extended to all classes of women and men in society.[144]

The Relation of Gender to Power

From the third through the first millennium, the wide spectrum of activities attributed to goddesses was matched by the wide-ranging powers of gods, and both shared sovereignty over fertility, life and death, war, justice, wisdom, social order, and the arts of civilization. To our modern consciousness, perhaps the most remarkable aspect of these ancient conceptions of divine power and divine sex roles is how minimally they seem to be related to the sex of the deities, and how gender as a category, at least in the divine sphere, was not seen as a necessary or natural correlative of power or powerlessness. The crucial concerns of ancient polytheistic Near Eastern societies centered in understanding and propitiating the sources of fertility; the regularity or irregularity of the food supply with which they were blessed or cursed; their conceptions of the afterlife and the rituals required to achieve immortality, where these were pressing communal concerns; their need for social order; and their thoughts about the nature and maintenance of creation itself. Within this context, the basic aim of these societies in a religious sense seems to have been the fulfillment of these personal and social needs, without any irrevocable notions of what could most fittingly be performed by a goddess or a god.

In the dominant myths of this period, the figures of strong, autonomous goddesses emerge, in every way as important as gods in their roles and functions, and with no fixed or limited roles determined by their sex. In fact, conspicuously absent are any denigrations of divine attributes or powers applied to divinities as a group on the basis of gender. Goddesses were not seen as constricted in their activities by their maternity and were not considered ritually impure or sinful by virtue of their sexual functioning or role in childbirth. Frequently, major goddesses shared attributes or powers with major gods or exercised them along with male deities, as was the case with Isis and Anath. Frequently, deities of the same sex had close affiliations and acted together, as was the case with Osiris and Thoth, Isis and Nephthys, Demeter and Korè. And frequently, goddesses as well as gods were seen as responsible for the progress of civilization and the orderly functioning of society, as was the case with Inanna, Isis, Themis, and Athena.

The precise connection between conceptions of divine power as related to gender and conceptions of secular sex roles in this period can, of course, only be guessed at, but it is likely that some connection existed. Generally, since deities in the major myths and epics were conceived of in anthropomorphic terms, and some of the greatest like Gilgamesh, Osiris, and Isis were thought to have been actual rulers before they were deified, it is conceivable that assignments of sex roles to goddesses and gods may have corresponded to some segment of the real experiences or imagination of the possible in the societies that produced them. Moreover, whatever the enduring literature and art of any age can reveal about the attitudes and values of their cultures may likewise be found in that of the ancient Near East. And what is striking in much of the extant literature is the representation of divinities and mortals of both sexes in a wide variety of roles.

The Varieties of Sex Roles

One of the most widely disseminated literary works, *The Epic of Gilgamesh,* shows its protagonists as ranging across a broad span of behavior and feelings, irrespective of their sex. The hero Gilgamesh (mentioned in an excavated king-list as reigning fifth in line from the founding of the First Dynasty in Uruk after the flood)[145] is described as two-thirds god and one-third man. His father was a high priest, responsible for his mortal part, and his mother was the goddess Ninsun. She had a palace-temple at Uruk, and Gilgamesh often sought her advice because she was "one of the wise gods" and "gifted with great wisdom."[146] In counterpoint to the portrayal of the goddesses Ninsun and Aruru, a creation-deity who in her benevolence shapes Enkidu to tame Gilgamesh, is the portrayal of the goddess Ishtar as capricious, cruel, sexually predatory, and terrible in her anger.

On the human level, there is the temple harlot (possibly one of Ishtar's priestesses, for her "people" are referred to as "the dancing and singing girls, the prostitutes of the temple, the courtesans").[147]

She is sent out into the countryside in order to seduce Enkidu and alienate him from his animal companions. But through intercourse with her, Enkidu is humanized, made wise, and longs for a human comrade.[148] Enkidu "listened to her words with care. It was good advice that she gave." "Like a mother," she teaches him how to eat, drink, and behave like a civilized person.[149] In similar fashion, when Gilgamesh tries to discover the secret of immortality because he fears his own death, it is the wife of Utnapishtim, a deified former king, who has compassion for Gilgamesh because of the long and dangerous journey to the end of the world that he undertook in his quest. She prevails upon her husband to disclose the secret of everlasting life, which Gilgamesh first finds and then loses.

Likewise, the range of sex roles for divine and human males is very broad. Gods are portrayed as wise and merciful, e.g., Anu and Ea, and evil and uncaring, e.g., Enlil and Humbaba. Men like Gilgamesh and Enkidu are shown as loving, emotional, ambitious for fame, brave, and fearful. For instance, the arrogant, brave, and ambitious Gilgamesh speaks as an equal with the goddess Ishtar when he rejects her love and is fearless in his battle with Humbaba and his search for immortality. But he also openly expresses all the agony of separation and grief when his beloved friend/servant Enkidu sickens and dies, the divine punishment for killing the Bull of Heaven.

Art surely does not precisely mirror or tabulate social realities. Nevertheless, it would appear that polytheistic conceptions of divine sex roles and power as not especially linked to gender, found from the third through the first millennium in many myths, hymns, epics, and the like, were certainly not outside the comprehension of participants in popular worship in the religion-centered universe of the ancient Near East. *The Epic of Gilgamesh* is an example of a widely proliferated work that portrays divine as well as human beings with qualities that at most might be termed androgynous, and at least seem to have been understood as attributes shared by females and males alike in the divine and secular realms. And the likelihood that conceptions of sex roles and power were not most significantly based on gender is enhanced by what is known about the involvement of women and men as participants in ritual life and the roles of women and men who officiated in priestly capacities at sacred rites.

CHAPTER 4

The Relation of Gender to Participation in Cult:
Polytheistic Practice

I F myths were sometimes altered over time to accommodate changing historical circumstances, social needs, and visions, sacred rites tended to be more fixed, enduring forms of collective religious response to the inevitable incidence of change, repeated at prescribed intervals in order to assure continuity and stability in nature and society. Central to the meaning and function of religious rituals was their probable origin in beliefs and emotions widely shared by the community of believers, which then sustained and supported their performance based on an apparently consensual trust in their effectiveness.

Goddess-Worship and Sacred Rites

It may therefore be anticipated that those ancient cultures which worshiped both female and male divinities and appeared to have held religious views more androgynous than our own would have involved both women and men in some fashion in their sacred rites. What is more surprising is that even in some very early Near Eastern civilizations generally believed to have been overwhelmingly dominated by goddess-worship, there may have been no exclusion of men from participation in cult on account of their sex.

For example, in contrast to most other Neolithic sites, which yielded only "Mother Goddess" figurines, in Catal Hüyük, where the cult of the goddess was apparently firmly entrenched, excavated shrines dating from 6500 to 5700 B.C.E. yielded cult-statues of male as well as female deities. Although the latter far outnumber the former, many of the statuettes are clustered in groups that illustrate various aspects of divine activities. The deities are of many ages and are shown as performing what seems to be a Sacred Marriage, as pregnant, giving birth, and exerting authority over wild animals and the like. While these portrayals conform to the traditional concepts of goddess-dominant religions, and the goddess is shown ruling over all life and death, the young god was also present. Unquestionably, his position was absolutely subordinate to hers, but by then the male's role in reproduction may have been understood. For instance, one plaque shows a couple embracing on one side, and a mother with a child, possibly the offspring of the union, on the other.[1]

Perhaps more telling, while the cult of the goddess seems to have been presided over mainly by women, and the material in the shrines points to the probable burial of priestesses in them, ceremonial garments found only in male burials suggest that male priests might have been interred there as well. In short, though the early Neolithic society of Catal Hüyük was demonstrably one in which women were preeminent in both social life and religion, there is some acknowledgment of the importance of men for the perpetuation of life. And it is possible that male priests, though fewer in number than priestesses, were not barred from sacred rites devoted to the cult of the goddess.[2]

A few thousand years later, after the settlement of Crete in the third millennium by a people who came to be known as the Minoans, archaeological remains indicate that the cult of the goddess flourished there too. Though Minoan religion was dominated by a female divinity, the important vegetation cycle was represented by the annual death and resurrection of the young god, the son-consort of the Great Goddess. The same sacred story and its attendant rites were, of course, to be found elsewhere in the ancient Near East, revolving around the figures of Dumuzi, Tammuz, Baal, and Adonis. But a novel and suggestive feature of Minoan religion was that the young male god had a direct female counterpart, the young vegetation-goddess Ariadne, who also died and was reborn each year.[3]

Furthermore, despite the indisputable dominance of the Great Goddess, men were incorporated into many levels of Minoan ritual and worship. In some representations of the young god, he possesses a number of his mother's attributes, e.g., he is shown as a tamer of wild beasts, or armed with a shield, bow, or spear, or accompanied by a lion, wild goat, or griffin. Also, though priestesses are more frequently portrayed in service to the goddess, there was no apparent exclusion of men from the performance of cultic rites.[4]

Indeed, there was a High Priest of Knossos, and the worshipers of the goddess are shown as both female and male. Priestesses and men dressed in women's robes participated in some of the ceremonial processions, but so did male youths who probably belonged to the retinue of a priest. In some of the sacred rites, male members of the royal family or the priesthood are shown assuming the role of the young god. Other pictorial representations of rituals show the Prince with the Lily Crown, who very likely personified the incarnated god just as priestesses at times personified the goddess; female and male dancers in addition to priestesses and priests participating in ceremonial processions; and a male priest shaking a sistrum, a musical instrument known to have been used in Egypt by women in rites dedicated to Isis.[5] Hence, as was possibly the case in Catal Hüyük as well, the dominance of the Great Goddess in Minoan Crete did not seem to exclude men from involvement in cult solely because of their sex.

The Evidence from Egypt

In contrast with what is known about Minoan Crete, in Egypt the dominant divinities were both female and male, and from earliest times there is evidence of the inclusion of both women and men in many of the most important religious activities and sacred rites. During the predynastic period, long before the unification of Upper and Lower Egypt into one nation, each village, town, or settlement had a divinity whose worship waxed or waned according to fluctuations in the prosperity of the community in which it resided. In addition, the whole country was divided into more than forty *hesps* or *nomes,* and in the capital of each of them was a temple dedicated to a deity or a group of allied deities of either sex.

Attached to the service of each nome-deity in its temple was a group of priests who divided among themselves the several duties connected with the service of their goddess or god. Among their responsibilities were maintaining the buildings of the temple, making copies of religious works, and providing for the religious education of the community. In Upper Egypt, the care of the dead seems to have been the principal responsibility of the living, and the lower orders of the priesthood probably conducted a lucrative business from mummifying the dead, inscribing funeral papyri and amulets, and conducting funerals.

In what were probably the most primitive stages of the priesthood's development in these early times, the "wise woman" very likely assumed a leading role. She was referred to in the nomes of Upper and Lower Egypt as the "Nurse" where the priest was called the "Child" or as the "Appeaser of the Soul" where the priest was called the "Favorite Child." Elsewhere, she was variously called the "Protector,"

"The Robed," the "Dark Woman," the "Divine Mother," or the "Watcher." The relationship of priestesses to priests may be inferred from their respective titles in the same nomes. For instance, in nome #8 of Lower Egypt, priestesses were known as "The Great Ones," while priests were called the "Roaming brethren." At Gynaecopolis or "Women's town" in nome #6 of Lower Egypt, the priestess was titled the "Commander" and the priest the "Hidden One." In general, though they also performed religious functions, the nominal designations of the male priests would seem to suggest that their occupations were more frequently civil than religious.[6]

In the capital cities of the nomes, both high priestesses and high priests occupied positions of prestige and power, and there are records of their titles and names. The High Priest of Thebes was called the "first servant of the god Rā in Thebes"; in Heliopolis he was the "Great one of visions of Rā-Atum"; in Memphis he was the "Great chief of the hammer in the temple of him of the Southern Wall, and Setem of the god of the Beautiful Face (i.e., Ptah)"; and in Saïs he was called the "governor of the double temple." Their female counterparts, the high priestesses, were likewise accorded titles or referred to by name. The High Priestess of Thebes was named Nefer-tutu; in Saïs she was called Utu or the "great one"; in Sekhem she was the "Divine Mother"; and in Mendes she was named "Utcha-ba-f."[7]

The widespread worship of the goddess Net (or Neith) in many parts of Egypt, dating from the latter part of the predynastic period and lasting through the first four dynasties, is evidenced by the many sanctuaries built in her honor. In earliest dynastic times, Neith was the chief deity of Saïs in the Delta. She was titled "the great lady, the mother-goddess, the lady of heaven, and queen of the gods" as well as "mother of the gods," and "the great lady who gave birth to Rā, who brought forth in primeval time herself, never having been created."[8]

Very early records from the Old Kingdom relate that Neith was served at that time only by priestesses. But it is clear that in other early times both priestesses and priests were involved in her cultic rites, because several members of both sexes were buried in mastaba tombs in and near Sakkâra. Indeed, the service of deities in a priestly capacity was not always along same-sex lines, i.e., priestesses serving female deities and priests serving male deities. For example, when Hathor was the most popular goddess, it was recorded that she was served by sixty-one priestesses and eighteen priests. Three priestesses but no priests of the god Upuaut are recorded, and one priestess and one priest are recorded for the god Tehuti. In the latter period of the Old Kingdom, a high priestess generally held that rank along with the chief priest. Moreover, though the records indicate that the pharaohs in the first half of the third millennium were normally served by priests, at least one priestess was in service to Khufu, and one served Teta.[9]

It seems rather obvious from the foregoing that virtually from the inception of the Egyptian priesthood, both women and men were involved in priestly functions in the service of both female and male deities. In addition, from the time of the Old Kingdom there are visual artifacts portraying ladies of rank, priestesses and unidentified women holding sistra in their hands, all of whom probably assisted in the musical ceremonies of the temple.[10] And quite early, the active participation of both laywomen and men in cultic celebrations is well attested.

For example, an extensive mortuary literature was engraved upon the walls of Fifth and Sixth Dynasty pyramids, where they have been preserved in large numbers. Commonly referred to as Pyramid Texts because of their location, many of them originated in predynastic times. The goddess Bast—amalgamated with Sekhet and with many other goddesses, among them Mut or Isis at Thebes—is mentioned in the Pyramid Texts but not in the later Theban recension of the *Book of the Dead.* Representing the milder heat of the day, Bast was believed to encourage the growth of vegetation and the germination of seeds. Called the "Lady of the East," in early dynastic times she became the preeminent goddess of the eastern part of the Delta as a lunar deity, who was thought to exercise special influence over women in childbirth. Much later, she was considered the Egyptian counterpart of the Roman goddess Diana.

The chief festivals in her honor were held in April and May in the city of Bubastis. They were described by the classical authors Herodotus, Diodorus, Strabo, and Pliny, and the city is referred to in the Old Testament as Pibeseth (Ezek. 30:17). During these two months of celebration, as many as seven thousand women, men, and children joined in the jubilant sacred rites, the women playing drums and tabors, the men pipes, and there was singing and dancing in the streets as they followed the image of the goddess from sanctuary to sanctuary.[11]

Likewise, there is evidence for the inclusion of women in a number of ritual occasions of national significance. For instance, in a ritual dating from the earliest dynastic period, the pharaoh and his queen participated in a sacred rite on behalf of all Egyptians, the Festival of Min. With the exception of Horus, it is probable that very early the god Min was more closely affiliated with kingship than any other deity, since he personified the fertility of the land and animals, and Egyptian kingship was seen as guaranteeing the benefits of nature's abundance to society. The festival itself seemed to symbolize the harmony of nature and society, the annual renewal of fecundity, the virility of the king, and the prosperity of the whole land.[12] Millennia later, by the time of the New Kingdom, the king and queen might have engaged in ritual sexual intercourse as part of the ceremony.[13]

Another ritual dating from the First Dynasty, the Sed Festival, was a periodic renewal of the king's rule, sometimes held thirty years after his accession to the throne, sometimes at shorter intervals. It consisted of a most elaborate reinvestiture of the king in his role as mediator between heaven and earth, and it involved the participation of large numbers of royal relatives, the priesthood, and women and men selected from every social class and area of Egypt, who came to witness the homage paid to the goddesses and gods by the king. The focal point of the festival was the dedication of "the field" (i.e., all of Egypt) to its mistress, and in this ceremony the pharaoh performed a ritual dance in which he is described as facing the god Thoth sometimes, but the goddess Mert far more frequently.[14]

The "Mystery Play of the Succession" is based on the text of a play dating from around 2000 B.C.E. in its present form, or from about the beginning of the Middle Kingdom dynasties. But there seems to be no doubt that many of its elements antedate this time by many centuries, and it was probably a variant of a ritual performed at the accession of each new ruler. The performance itself was repeated over and over at many sites at the time of transition from the reign of one pharaoh to the next. Apparently it was considered a crucial ritual, in which the new king received the right to rule as the new Horus by establishing his religious ties with the whole country. The many stages of the ceremony are described in a surviving papyrus, and they involved a mingling of real happenings and mythological constructs. On the human plane, at the coronation of the new king, two priestesses, representing Isis and Nephthys, were chosen to serve as part of the cult of the dead pharaoh in his role as Osiris.[15]

For thousands of years, providing for the possible resurrection and immortality of the dead was to be the primary and abiding preoccupation of Egyptian religion. While it has been observed, and perhaps rightly so, that at least from the time of the Middle Kingdom there are increasing numbers of written references to the inadequacy of death as compared to life, and at times a clear aversion to the former, it nevertheless is also evident that simultaneously the religious view of death continued to play a central role in Egyptian life.[16] People of all classes desired a ritually correct burial, and toward that end bodies were mummified, tombs erected, papyri inscribed, and sacred rites performed. Indeed, a huge number of the remains of ancient Egypt are sepulchral in nature. Furthermore, despite some changes in attitudes toward death, which might be predicted for a period spanning several thousand years, what is remarkable is that so many of these attitudes remained fairly stable even after Egyptian religion ceased to develop along mostly autochthonous lines.

Very early, before the erection of sumptuous tombs and the development of a priesthood with specialized mortuary functions, women were included among those who might perform sacred rites for the dead. Simple offerings were placed at the burial site by a son, brother, or wife of the deceased. It is likely that in this period human sacrifice was practiced, and it is thought probable that slaves of both sexes were sacrificed at "tombs of Osiris" in order that they might somehow protect kings or nobles after death. Two human heads, one female, one male, are found on tombs of upper-class people, who, at their death, "became" Osiris. And throughout the history of Egypt, unidentified women are shown as participants in the ritually precise funeral processions as mourners and singers of dirges. For example, there is a reference from the Sixth Dynasty to a burial ceremony at which two women represented Isis and Nephthys.[17]

Moreover, it seems that women were not only participants in sacred rites for the dead but were themselves recipients of such ritual service. Before the thirty-fourth century B.C.E., the belief became prevalent that the deceased might return every day if they were appropriately buried. By the thirtieth century, the first architecture in stone, the royal tomb, was produced. These royal tombs are extremely impressive, and give a notion of the importance attached to fitting mortuary provisions. The largest of them all, the Great Pyramid of Gizeh, was begun in about 2885 B.C.E. and was to house the remains of the Pharaoh Khufu, so revered in his own time that he was not even mentioned by name. He was called only "Pharaoh," which in Egyptian means "Great House," or the palace where he lived, just as by that time Isis meant "The Throne."

The tomb of Khufu's mother, Queen Hetep-heres, had been ransacked, and therefore Khufu had her remains moved to a place adjacent to his own pyramid. Her tomb is so magnificent, containing gifts of such royal splendor conferred upon her in death by her surviving son and husband, that it has provided one of the pieces of evidence for the likelihood that women then, at least those of upper-class or royal rank, might have enjoyed equal status with men.

There are other indications that women as well as men were recipients of the all-important rituals for the dead, namely one or two passages in the Pyramid Texts that relate that there were women in the

Egyptian heaven just as there were goddesses. And even before the spread of the belief in equality of opportunity with regard to the divine by 2000 B.C.E. (referred to earlier), opening up the prospect of immortality to Egyptians of all classes, the possibility of everlasting life after death may not have been confined to upper-class women. For instance, from early dynastic times there is a record of a mortuary priest who contractually provided for the endowment of his daughter's tomb in order to insure its ritual service after her death.[18]

Among the most enduring texts that recount the sacred rites connected with the dead is *The Liturgy of Funerary Offerings,* found in funerary inscriptions on tombs and papyri in association with another work, the *Book of the Opening of the Mouth.* The former consists of a list of the precise offerings made to the dead in 114 ceremonies, and includes the consecrating formulas recited by the chief priest as he presented the offerings to a mummified body or, in later times, to a statue of the deceased. It probably described a ritual performed for kings and other royal personages and for people of high civil and ecclesiastical rank. The latter work was in existence by the Third or Fourth Dynasty (ca. 3800 B.C.E.). It seems to be the written service accompanying the daily offerings of meat and drink by qualified priests, and the object of its recital was to bring about a reconstitution and resurrection of the dead. The textual changes in *The Liturgy of Funerary Offerings* were few, and copies were found in many tombs dating from the period of the Old Kingdom through the Twenty-Sixth Dynasty (ca. 666–527 B.C.E.), and on papyri written in the first or second century C.E. In other words, these funerary rituals were in use age after age, in practically unaltered form, for approximately four thousand years.[19]

Egyptians believed in dual souls, only one of which was immortal. The other lived just as long as it was fed with daily offerings and provided with a residence, i.e., statue. As different from the *Khu,* the spirit-soul, the *Ka,* or double of the person, and the *Ba,* or heart-soul, fed on material offerings. If the supply of food and drink failed, the *Ka* and *Ba* literally died of starvation. Through the use of proper ceremonies and formulas, the intent of the rituals was to restore the *Ka* either to the dead person from whom it was temporarily separated, or to a statue representing the deceased. When this was accomplished, it was considered obligatory to continue providing meat and drink for its sustenance.

Just as the words spoken by the Kher-Heb, or chief officiating priest, from the *Book of the Opening of the Mouth* were believed to change meat, bread, and wine into divine substances, so the formula said over each element from *The Liturgy of Funerary Offerings* was supposed to change it into divine and spiritual food to be shared by the souls of deities and the dead. When the material elements of the offering were eaten by priests and relatives of the dead, it was believed that it brought them into communion with the blessed dead and the deities. This belief in the transmutation of offerings was current at least by the time of the Fifth Dynasty, and probably even earlier.

As far as we know, the priests who conducted these rituals were male. But women were involved in them in rather interesting ways. For example, the Papyrus of Nu from the Eighteenth Dynasty (ca.1500–1400 B.C.E.) says that the deceased expected a house to be provided, to which women and men were to bring oblations.[20] In light of the importance assigned to the ritual "feeding" of the dead, the participation of both women and men seems significant.

The twenty-third ceremony in *The Liturgy of Funerary Offerings* describes the offering of the breast of some animal by the Sem priest, which symbolized the act of embracing the deceased. It was a vital ritual because it was thought that life was given to a statue by embracing it. The account of the ceremony explains that when a living person, priest or relative, embraced a mummy, *his* or *her* object was to reunite the bones, knit the flesh together again, and give order to the members of the body—which, in early times, were thought to be to be dislocated at death, like those of Osiris when he was dismembered by Seth—before putting them together, piece by piece.[21] Again, since the intention of these mortuary rituals was the restoration and resurrection of the dead, the involvement of both women and men in this ritual process seems important.

As always, divinities were freely named as participants in sacred rites, and the incidence of female involvement in the divine sphere may have reflected to some extent the attitudes toward the involvement of women in the secular one. There is yet another ceremony that describes how the Sem priest offers two linen sashes or bandlets to the deceased while the chief officiating priest says the sacred formula. These sashes were presumably woven by the goddess Täat, who presided over the apparel of the dead. She was believed to have made the bandlets with her own hands and to have woven into them her magical protection, which not only covered the nakedness of the dead but also assured them of the respect of the deities and spirits who saw them. One of the sashes carried the protection of the Horus-god who resided in the city of Pe-Tepor Buto, while the other carried the protection of the Horus-god who dwelt in the city of Net (or Neith).[22]

Though it is by no means certain, it may be that priestesses as well as priests came to preside over these critical rites for the dead. A copy of the *Book of the Opening of the Mouth* was found written on a papyrus placed on the coffin of a priest, Butehai-Amen, of the Twentieth

Dynasty (ca.1200–1100 B.C.E.). When it was deciphered, it appeared that its liturgy was totally different from the ordinary funerary text. Further, it was most unusual because it mentioned the various priests of different orders who normally officiated at funeral ceremonies and described each individual's role.[23] The papyrus was prepared for the priestess Saïs, and one can only speculate about the reason for the explicit details. One possibility, of course, is that she was being instructed on how to officiate herself at these ceremonial offerings, particularly since there is also a Papyrus of the Priestess Anhai from about 1000 B.C.E., in which part of the ceremony of "the weighing of the heart of the dead" is recorded.[24]

The performance of some of the critical sacred rites for the dead by both women and men was not inconsistent with the view, by the second millennium, that the goddess Isis was intimately involved in the momentous judgment of the dead, even as Egyptian religion became Osirianized. Everywhere in *The Book of the Dead* her presence is attested —as the source of food and life to the deceased, and as one of the two Maat goddesses who stands behind Osiris as he judges the dead. Indeed, one Egyptian scholar believes she may by then also have been regarded as one of the judges of the dead.[25] In addition, before her worship spread throughout the Mediterranean world in the first millennium, she represented for Egyptians not only the union in herself of all the attributes of all the goddesses of Egypt known to us—water goddess, earth goddess, corn goddess, star goddess, queen of the underworld—but she appears to have been viewed by them as a *woman* as well.[26]

The Book of the Dead is the title usually given by Egyptologists to the editions of prayers and litanies in the Eighteenth Dynasty and later that dealt with the welfare of the deceased in the next world. It described the nature of existence in the latter and the dangers that had to be averted in order to achieve immortality. They were generally based on accepted religious dogmas and mythological beliefs. Though it is difficult to fix an exact date of origin, these written prayers existed side by side with established rituals recited and performed by priests and relatives on behalf of the dead, and together they apparently were in use by Egyptians, in revised forms, from about 4500 B.C.E. to the early centuries of the Common Era.

The largest, best preserved text from the Eighteenth Dynasty is the Papyrus of Ani. It consists of vignettes, hymns, and chapters with introductory and descriptive material. Although it contains less than half the chapters usually associated with *The Book of the Dead,* Ani's high official position as chancellor of ecclesiastical revenues and endowments for Abydos and Thebes suggests that the material found in his tomb was then considered sufficient for his spiritual welfare in the hereafter. Also, a number of revised versions of *The Book of the Dead* recovered from different periods sometimes include commentaries on the actual historical events of those times. Therefore, the Papyrus of Ani not only is regarded as typical of the funeral book in use by the Theban nobility of his era, but it may indicate as well the extent to which upper-class women and men of that time and place did or did not experience different treatment at their death as recipients of sacred rites, and the extent to which women and men participated in these rites by the middle of the second millennium.

The very first vignette of the papyrus introduces Ani's wife, Thuthu, who died before him. She is dressed exactly like Ani and is identified as Osiris, or as having successfully overcome all the obstacles to eternal life and therefore, in death, is at one with the god. She is described as having been in the service of one of the greatest gods of the time, Amen, and she holds objects used by priestesses at religious festivals. The translation of the relevant passage and note reads:

> The scribe Ani . . . wears a fringed white and saffron-coloured linen garment; and has a wig, necklace, and bracelets. Behind him stands his wife "Osiris, the lady of the choir of Amen, Thuthu," similarly robed and holding a sistrum . . . in her right hand, and a *menât* in her left.[2]

> [2]The *menât* . . . consists of a disk, with a handle attached, and a cord. It was an object which was usually offered to the gods, with the sistrum; it was presented to guests at a feast by their host; and it was held by priestesses at religious festivals.[27]

Apparently the *menât* was used in the worship of Hathor. In another vignette, Ani's wife is once more called "Osiris, the lady of the house, priestess of Amen, Thuthu."[28]

There is nothing in the Papyrus of Ani to suggest that his burial accommodations were different from those of his wife. Thuthu, like Ani, became "Osiris" at her death. Their mummies literally shared the same room in a tomb that had many rooms. And from the following description, one is led to believe that as much care was taken for Thuthu's suitable burial as for his own:

> Close by her is a table of alabaster covered with shapely vessels of the same substance, filled with wine, oil, and other unguents; each of these fragile objects is inscribed with her name. On the table are spoons made of ivory of the most beautiful workmanship. The body is stained a deep creamy colour, the colour of the skin of the Egyptian lady, who guarded herself from the rays of the sun; the hair is black, and we see that it is movable; when we lift it off we see that it is movable; when we lift it off

we see the name of "Tutu, the sistrum bearer," engraved beneath. On a second stand, made of wood, we find the articles for her toilet, mirror, kohl pot in obsidian, fan, etc., and close by is the sistrum which she carried with her, so that she might be able to praise that god with music in his mansions in the sky. Chairs and her couch are there too, and stands covered with dried flowers and various offerings. Removing the lid of the coffin we see her mummy lying as it was laid a few years before. On her breasts are strings of dried flowers with the bloom still on them, and by her side is a roll of papyrus containing a copy of the service which she used to sing in the temple of Amen in the Apts, when on earth. Her amethyst necklace and other ornaments are small, but very beautiful. Just over her feet is a blue glazed steatite ushabti figure . . . whose duty it was to perform for the deceased such labours as filling the furrows with water, ploughing the fields, and carrying the sand, if he were called upon to do them.[29]

When this equivalence of treatment after death for upper-class Theban women and men is joined with the democratization of mortuary beliefs by about 2000 B.C.E., and with what seems to have been the rough equivalence in the status of women and men within each class that apparently marked so much of Egypt's long history,[30] it would appear that the prospect of immortality was open equally to women and men of every class, or that access to the heart of Egyptian funerary ritual was not contingent on gender. Indeed, the accessibility of proper burial and therefore eternal life would seem to have depended far more on financial resources than on sex.

The female presence in the funeral procession transporting Ani to his tomb is conspicuous in several of the illuminations. One shows the mummy of the dead man lying in a chest or shrine mounted on a boat. At the head and feet of the mummy are two small models of Isis and Nephthys. At the side of the boat is Thuthu lamenting his death. At the center of another illumination of the procession, a group of wailing women are portrayed. They frequently are shown in attendance at funerals, since the occupation of professional mourner in sacred rites for the dead was one open to women, particularly those of the lower classes. Sometimes the female divinities Isis and Nephthys, as mothers and sisters, are depicted as beating their breasts in grief at Ani's death.[31]

One might well ask why there is a Papyrus of Ani rather than a Papyrus of Thuthu, or why there is not also a Papyrus of Thuthu just as there were Papyri of the Priestesses Saïs and Anhai at a later date. Naturally, the answer is uncertain. It may have been due to the fact that Ani was a scribe and prepared his own papyrus. Or it may have been a consequence of the high rank he held as chancellor of ecclesiastical revenues, while Thuthu was merely involved in the ritual of the temple. But we do have scattered bits of information from the Eighteenth Dynasty that suggest the possibility that around that time, and perhaps at other times as well, some highly placed men might have resented the prominence of women in civil and ecclesiastical life.

For example, the scribe played an indispensable role in the life of the temple, both as recorder of religious texts and liturgies and as preparer of inscriptions and papyri for the dead. By 2000 B.C.E. at the latest, there was a word in Egyptian for female scribes, and it seems curious that we have no sure records of their work even though they must have existed.[32] Also, during the Eighteenth Dynasty, when Thutmose III succeeded Hatshepsut as ruler of Egypt after her successful reign as pharaoh, he attempted to obliterate all references and physical monuments to her rule. It is impossible to know precisely what accounted for this violent reaction to his female predecessor's twenty-year rule. All that we know is that he attempted to erase all evidence of Hatshepsut's accomplishments, and that she was the only woman who ruled Egypt as pharaoh in her own name. (She "legitimized" her right to the throne by claiming to be the divine offspring of a Sacred Marriage between the god Amon-Rā and the queen mother, and this marked her, in a ritual sense, as different from the male pharaohs who claimed to be the living incarnations of the god Horus.)

It may be that the reaction of Thutmose was a measure of either the real or perceived power of royal women at that time, or an indication of widespread opposition to the rule of a woman, or an expression of personal hostility perhaps occasioned by his own frustrated aspirations to the throne as a possible heir. But whatever the reasons for his overt hostility, or how broad the support for it might have been, it seems likely that it was not expressive of a universally shared attitude toward women in positions of power. If such an attitude prevailed, there probably would not be so much evidence from that time for the participation of women as priestesses in sacred temple rites, nor would there have been a female pharaoh ruling Egypt for twenty years in the first place.

Thuthu is described as both a musician and a priestess of the god Amen. By the Eighteenth Dynasty, an important part of the services in the temple of Amen was the many choruses, hymns, and litanies sung by the *shemāt*, or women singers, who accompanied themselves by rattling sistra. These *shemāt* customarily included all the women of high rank in Thebes, who formed companies of priestesses, collectively titled the "harim of the god." At their head was the queen or crown princess, who normally participated in the cult through a substitute, and who held this position as "wife of the god" by virtue of her supposed sacred union with the deity.

From the Eighteenth Dynasty on, the High Priest of Thebes was one of Egypt's wealthiest and most influential officials. In addition to his control over the properties of Amen, he possessed great houses and estates and had a large retinue in his service. For the most part, it seems that few of the high priests were distinguished by their ecclesiastical backgrounds. Apparently, they most usually functioned as administrators on behalf of the pharaoh, served at royal pleasure, and sometimes also held high civil posts.[33] But despite the fact that for several hundred years the high priesthood of Thebes was occupied by men, in the later period the use of sex as the basis for determining who might participate in or be excluded from the performance of sacred rites, or who might assume high ecclesiastical office, continued to be notably absent from Egyptian religion.

In the records kept of royal tomb robberies, mention is made during the Twentieth Dynasty (ca.1200–1100 B.C.E.) of "The tombs of the singing women of the house of the Divine Votress,"[34] the sacerdotal princess of Thebes. Among the building inscriptions of the Twenty-first Dynasty (ca.1100–966 B.C.E.), there is a reference to "The— matron, singer of Amon-Re, King of gods, Fetonemut, triumphant, daughter of the High Priest of Amon, Payonekh, triumphant."[35] She was the daughter of one of the Priest-Kings who ruled Thebes in that era, and it was a time when a number of women in the "harim of the god" exercised great power and occupied many offices. For instance, Nesi-Khensu is referred to as the viceroy of Nubia, the wife of Amen-Rā, and the mother of the god Khensu, as well as the Priestess of Amen-Rā, Nekhebet, Osiris, Isis, Horus, and Hathor. Her daughter, Nesitanebtashru, was the official copyist and arranger of the hymns and music in the temple of Amen-Rā. She was also a singer, possibly a soloist, in the temple of Mut, the female counterpart of Amen-Rā. Her copy of *The Book of the Dead* might have been inscribed by her, and she may have been the author of some of its revisions.[36]

During the Twenty-second Dynasty (ca.966–760 B.C.E.), we read of much attention being paid to the ministering women of the Theban temple at a jubilee commemorating the king's assumption of responsibility for the whole land. The inscription reads:

> Year 22, fourth month of the first season (occurred) the appearance of the King in the temple of Amon, which is in the jubilee-hall, resting on the portable-throne; and the assumption of the protection of the Two Lands

by the King, the protection of the sacred women of the house of Amon, and the protection of all the women of his city, who have been maid-servants since the time of the fathers, even the maid-servants in every house (i.e., Temple), who are assessed for their service yearly.[37]

At approximately the same time, there is a record of a gift of land to a princess, a singer in the temple of Amon, but it is unclear whether the gift is for her support in the temple or for her tomb.[38]

Finally, by the Twenty-sixth Dynasty (ca.666–527 B.C.E.), through a series of adoptions of the pharaohs' daughters by the Divine Votresses, a woman became the High Priest of Thebes. Nitocris, the daughter of Psamtik I, was adopted by Shepnupet, daughter of Taharka, the Divine Votress, and had conferred upon her all the extensive properties and titles of her adoptive mother in a series of splendid ceremonies and celebrations.[39] Nitocris, in turn, adopted the daughter of Psamtik II, Enekhnesneferibre. At her adoption, the latter received the title of High Priest of Amon. After the death and burial of Nitocris, the following inscriptions describe the induction and reign of her successor:

> Now, when twelve days had elapsed after these events, (in) the fourth month of the third season, day 15, went the King's daughter, the High Priest, Enekhnesneferibre, to the House of Amon-Rē, King of gods; while the prophets, the divine fathers, the priests, ritual priests and lay priests of the temple of Amon were behind her, and the great companions were in front thereof. There were performed for her all the customary ceremonies of the induction of the Divine Votress of Amon into the temple, by the divine scribe and nine priests of this house. She fastened on all the amulets and ornaments of the Divine Consort, and the Divine Votress of Amon, crowned with the two plumes,[40] the diadem of her forehead, to be queen of every circuit of the sun. . . . There were done for her all the customary rites and all the ceremonies as was done for Tafnut in the beginning. The prophets, the divine fathers, and the lay priests of the temple came to her at all times when she went to the house of Amon, at his every festal procession.[41]

She served as High Priest of Thebes until she was almost eighty years old.

In sum, for just about the entire course of ancient Egypt's recorded history, the fairly continuous incorporation of women as well as men in cultic life was widely attested. From earliest to latest times, the extant documents reveal that both women and men not only participated in some of the most important sacred rituals but were themselves beneficiaries of such observances, including those which dealt with fulfilling the requirements for eternal life. Also, the doctrine of equality of opportunity before the divine, promulgated at the end of the third millennium, extended the chance for immortality to people of every class irrespective of sex.

Moreover, while some distinctions in ritual were made on the basis of sex, e.g., only women comprised the "harim of the god," and for hundreds of years only men served as the high priests of Thebes, for the most part the gender of the participant seems to have figured only minimally in Egyptian cult. Persons of both sexes had access to positions of religious prestige and power, even in some periods when civil and ecclesiastical functions touched at many points, and even when the performance of sacred rites in these high posts entailed great influence and wealth for the individual who officiated over them. More generally, during the several thousand years of ancient Egypt's existence, its religious tradition appeared to minimize the significance of gender as a basis for inclusion in most aspects of cult.

Relation of Gender to
Religious Practice and Social Structure

Now it may be argued that the lack of importance attached to gender in the ritual life of polytheistic cultures like Egypt or Minoan Crete was a corollary of the relatively high status of women within those cultures, and therefore was typical only of specific and localized patterns of congenial, perhaps even accidental, historical circumstances rather than indicative of attitudes characteristic of ancient Near Eastern polytheism itself. However, though religious beliefs and rituals apparently interacted in crucial ways with social life, it is difficult to establish a clear and linear relationship between polytheistic attitudes toward sex roles in the divine sphere, or the extensive participation of women as well as men in cultic rites, and the actual legal and social status of women as compared with men in ancient societies.

Again, religious views undoubtedly reflected in many ways the cultures of which they were a part, and in turn very likely exerted a shaping, or at least legitimizing, influence on the beliefs of their cultural milieus. But the relation of religious views to the social and political realities of secular life was extremely complex, often characterized by inconsistencies and disjunctions in time. For instance, the prominence of goddesses at any given time did not in itself signify the high status of women in the earthly societies of those same times. Sometimes the two seem to have gone together—as may have been the case in early Sumer with respect to upper-class women, or during some periods of Elamite and Egyptian history—but most often they probably did not. The worship of powerful goddesses during the Classical period of Athens seemed to bear little relation to the diminished status of upper-class Athenian women in real life, just as the later exaltation of the Virgin Mary by the early Church Fathers did not seem grounded in the actual status of most European women at that time, nor did the worship of Mary elevate that status.

Perhaps the most that can be said is that some polytheistic cultic practices apparently continued in their old forms long after secular views and customs changed, and that the relationship between the secular and the divine was further complicated by the persistence of folk religions and rituals long after official theology took other turns. Much more important, no matter which society is scrutinized—Elam, where the status of women as compared with men remained high and actually improved over a long period of time; Sumer, where the status of women as compared with men deteriorated over time; or Athens during the Classical period, when the status of upper-class women as compared with men of the same class was relatively low—where there was a polytheistic pantheon and cultic practices directed toward its propitiation, the presence of both sexes in the priesthood, in cult, and in popular religion was almost universal.

There were, of course, some notable exceptions. For example, the "women's festivals" of Greece—the Thesmophoria, Arrephoria, Skirophoria, Stenia, and Haloa—were of immemorial antiquity and involved only women. But in the course of time, the Haloa came to be dedicated to Dionysus as much as to Demeter and Korè, though it was still presided over by priestesses and celebrated only by women.[42] By the first millennium, with the increasing popularity of mystery cults, which held out to their adherents the prospect of union with the divine or the promise of immortality, women and men participated as priests, initiates, and celebrants in the central rites of purification and the viewing or handling of the *sacra,* or sacred objects. Indeed, the Eleusinian Mysteries and the cult of Isis, both of which gained a large following in the Mediterranean world, not only included women and men in their priesthood, but embraced as initiates and votaries persons of both sexes from every class in society.[43]

Even the customary Hellenic practice of priestesses in service to goddesses and priests in service to gods was not invariable. At Delphi, his presumed burial-place, Dionysus was served by the Thyia, his priestess. She and her assistants alone knew and performed the secret rites of the god.[44] As has been noted, in Egypt the traditional occupancy by men of the high priesthood of Thebes in the second millennium gave way to the appointment of a woman to this post by the first. And as we shall see, in many parts of Mesopotamia even the dedication of "holy women" to the service of Ishtar, which was contingent on their sex and sexuality, probably had more to do with the preeminence of that goddess in her sexual aspect in those times, and with the prevalent attitudes toward sexuality in those locales, than with the use of these women as sex objects, or with the exclusion of men from sacred rites on account of any kind of inferiority or ritual impurity associated with their maleness. Moreover, there were male counterparts to some classes of these "holy women" in service to a number of the temples. In short, from the third through the first millennium, the participation of women as well as men in Near Eastern polytheistic cult was extensive, and it seemed to hinge more on psychologically androgynous qualities inherent in the polytheistic outlook than on unique circumstances peculiar to specific cultures.

The Evidence from Elam

The civilization of Elam, which flourished from the third to the first millennium, provides an example of a culture that might be located at one end of the spectrum in terms of the high status of both female divinities and real women. Bordering on an expansionist Mesopotamia, it was for most of the second millennium first under Babylonian and then under Kassite rule, and therefore was subject to foreign cultural influences. Religion apparently played a very influential role in Elamite culture and in its legal system. All earthly things were seen as emanating from divine sources, and fulfilling the material requirements of the temples became a paramount concern of its population.

For the first thousand years of its existence, a goddess headed the divine pantheon. By the second millennium, when male deities were ascendant, the major holy triad included a great goddess as Great Wife, who seems to have been in a serial, polyandrous relationship with her two divine male siblings (mirroring the actual practice of incest and levirate marriage in the royal family, in which the queen's successive husbands were also her brothers), but the powers of the divine husbands increasingly expanded. While women always seemed to enjoy relatively high status socially and legally, it is noteworthy that during the time that the gods were elevated to equal rank with goddesses, the legal position of women actually improved over that of earlier times.

Throughout its long history, which saw many political changes and radical shifts in the rankings of goddesses and gods, the existence of numerous priests of both sexes, and their participation in civil life and sacred rites, are attested in Elamite art and written records. The high priest at the capital city of Susa was always male, and his affluence stemmed from his control of the vast temple estates and all the material offerings made to the goddesses and gods. But priestesses also were involved in administrative and business affairs. One group of priestesses who dedicated themselves to the great goddess owned real estate and managed it for a profit. And from the middle of the second millennium, there is a text that describes a temple guarded by fantastic figures personifying two goddesses. In its precincts, secret rites were engaged in nightly by four priestesses, assisted by a number of high-ranking civil and ecclesiastical officials who were male.[45]

The Evidence from Sumer

Sumer provides a somewhat different scenario, but one that reinforces the contention that a genuinely polytheistic religion would, as a matter of course, include both sexes in its cult regardless of the civil status of women, and even as the latter declined over time. There are some indications that in the third millennium women and men, at least of the ruling class, may have enjoyed social and economic equality. In about 2350 B.C.E., King Urukagina ruled the city-state of Lagash. During his reign he instituted some reform measures, one of which referred to what he considered the evil practices of earlier times and his remedy for them. It reads: "The women of former days used to take two husbands, but the women of today (when they attempted to do this) were stoned with stones inscribed with their evil intent."[46]

The evident prior practice of polyandry, coupled with the facts that Urukagina's wife, Shagshag, administered her own large estates, as did his predecessor's wife, Baranamtarra, and that the latter sent diplomatic missions to queens in other city-states without first consulting her husband, all testify to the very high status of at least upper-class women. But from about 2000 B.C.E. on, men came increasingly to dominate civil life, theology, and ritual, and the status of women suffered a proportionate decline. Nevertheless, though the deterioration of women's position in society had its counterpart in the divine sphere with the derogation of some of the earlier, most powerful goddesses "by the male theologians who manipulated the order of the divinities in accordance with what may well have been their chauvinistic predilections,"[47] goddesses as well as gods continued to be worshiped. In particular, the preeminence of the goddess Inanna, "Queen of Heaven," was never seriously threatened to the very last.[48]

Again, the genuinely polytheistic nature of this religion, encompassing divinities of both sexes, was reflected in the inclusion of both women and men in cult and rite. The Sumerian word *en* may be translated as high priestess or high priest, and the appointment of either to the main temple in each Sumerian city-state depended on the sex of its tutelary deity. If the deity worshiped there was male, then the *en* of the main temple was female, and if the deity was female, then the *en* was male.[49] Therefore, it would seem that in ancient Sumer the sex of the deity was of primary importance, and that gender alone was not considered a deterrent to the inclusion of either women or men in the highest echelons of religious life.

The first of the royal high priestesses we know of by name is Enheduanna, *en* of the moon-god Nanna at Ur, and later possibly *en* of the heaven-god An at Uruk as well. Her appointment to this post in about 2300 B.C.E. by her father, the Accadian ruler Sargon the Great, apparently was part of an attempt to consolidate his political control over all of Sumer and Accad. By designating his daughter as High Priestess and "bride" of Nanna in the Sumerian city of Ur, and at first possibly his sister as High Priestess and "bride" of An in the Sumerian city of Uruk, Sargon not only initiated a significantly novel cultic practice (which reflected his political ascendance in these two city-states) but also assigned to his daughter a pivotal role in his campaign. These high priesthoods helped unify the nations of Sumer and Accad by the cultic union of the major sacerdotal offices of Ur and Uruk in the person of Enheduanna, and by equating the Sumerian goddess Inanna, to whom Enheduanna was devoted for all of her public life, with the Accadian goddess Ishtar.

While Enheduanna's initial elevation to high priestess seems to have admirably served the political ends of her father, her final reputation rested on her own accomplishments as theologian, poet, and hymnographer. Her poems were widely popular in the Old Babylonian period, and a testament to her stature in the eyes of her people may be found in her virtual deification in later theological writings. Just as her literary influence on subsequent hymnography was likely great,[50] so her dual role as princess and priestess established a precedent. There was a long line of royal successors to her position, and we now know the names of many of those women who held that rank for the next five hundred years. However, the long, unbroken tradition of royal high priestesses existed simultaneously with the occupancy of high priesthoods by men in cities whose principal deities were female.

It was not only as *en* that women and men participated in early temple life and sacred rites. As in Egypt, in ancient Mesopotamia both women and men served the temple in many ways. Men were commercial agents, overseers of workmen, gardeners, superintendents of temple granaries, shepherds and doorkeepers, as well as scribes, judges, diviners, and members of the various classes of priests. Likewise, women's roles in early temple life were varied. They served as votaries, singers, enchanters, prophets, witnesses of legal documents along with men, judges, scribes, and members of the several classes of priest-esses.[51]

The Evidence from Mari

Recent studies of women connected with the royal family of the Middle Euphrates Kingdom of Mari in the Old Babylonian period (ca.1790–1740 B.C.E.) indicate the widespread involvement of women as well as men in most areas of official and private cult. Letters recovered from the royal archives of Mari, though mostly written by royal family members and therefore certainly representative only of the highest levels of society at that time, reveal that women, like men, served in the priesthood, offered prayers and sacrifices on behalf of the king, served as intercessors with the divine, and transmitted revelations received in dreams.[52]

The following letter to King Zimri-Lim from Addu-duri, a woman of uncertain relation to the royal family but obviously in possession of jurisdiction over important civil and ecclesiastical affairs in Mari,[53] provides a sample of the many cultic roles of women, and of the authority of their voices:

> To my lord
> Thus speaks Addu-duri, your servant.
> Since the establishment of your father's house
> Truly, I have never seen
> Such a dream. My former omens
> Were
> Of this kind.
> In my dream, I went to the temple of Belet-ekallim
> But Belet-ekallim
> Was not there. Besides, the statues
> Which stand before her were not there.
> When I saw this, I began to cry.
> I had this dream in the first part of the night.
> I had another one: Dada, the high priest
> Of Istar-pisra
> Stood at the door (of the temple) of Belet-ekallim
> And in a hostile voice
> Cried unceasingly
> These words: "Return Dagan,
> Return Dagan." It is thus
> That she cried unceasingly. Another matter.

An ecstatic stood erect
In the temple of Annunitum
And she said: "Zimri-Lim,
Do not go on a journey.
Stay in Mari, and
Thus, I myself, I will answer continually to you."
May my lord not neglect
To maintain his guard.
I sealed here the lock of hair
And the fringe of the coat
Of [the woman] and
I have had them sent
To my lord.[54]

Perhaps most significant, at a time when it was widely believed that the destinies of individuals and nations were governed by information yielded by omens and magical foresight, it appears that women prophesied as frequently as men, and the oracles from goddesses and gods were given equal credence whether delivered by female or male prophets. For example, in a letter from Nur-sin, Zimri-Lim's envoy in Aleppo, he writes: "Previously when I resided in Mari, I would relay to my lord whatever message a prophet or a prophetess would say to me."[55] Likewise, in a letter sent to Zimri-Lim by his principal wife, Queen Sibtu, in which she describes her efforts to ascertain the outcome of a battle to be fought between her husband and Išme-Dagan, she writes: "For a report of the campaign which my lord is on, I waited (?) on signs. I asked a man and a woman, and the word is very favorable to my lord. Similarly, with regard to Išme-Dagan I asked the man and the woman, and his prognosis is not favorable."[56]

If both women and men were prominent in the cultic life of Mari before the middle of the second millennium, elsewhere in this period, the growing temple organizations in Babylonia tended to augment the prestige and prosperity of their personnel. Priestesses and priests engaged in commerce with their surrounding communities, and in these business transactions, women and men enjoyed fairly equal status under the law.[57] In fact, some have conjectured that the relatively high status of women in early Babylonia derived from their high position as priestesses in cult. But whatever the case, the last may be partially inferred from the fact that some rulers of Mesopotamia, e.g., Sargon and Nabonidus, claimed priestesses as their mothers.

As the second millennium moved to a close, the roles of women in official cult, apart from their priestly functions, came to be severely curtailed. For example, from the thirteenth century on, even mentions of priestesses became less frequent in the texts of the increasingly male-dominant society of Assyria, as it consolidated its military and political sovereignty over Mesopotamia.[58] However, the growing tendency to exclude most women from participation in official religion did not mean that they played no part in extra-official religion, in some of the dominant popular cults, or in the service of the great generic Mesopotamian goddess Ishtar and her several counterparts. Indeed, what is somewhat remarkable is that long after the status of women declined in official theology as well as in the secular social structure, earlier attitudes seem to have persisted about the residence of special and magical powers in women as well as in men.

Gender, Divination, and Practical Magic

While the roots and practice of magic were incalculably ancient, from the third through the first millennium there was widespread faith among all classes of people in the efficacy of divination, omens, oracles, incantations, spells, and exorcism. Armies moved, rulers acted, and ordinary people made decisions about their lives on the basis of portents, omens, and prophecies. Though magic and religion coincided in many areas, the former was above all essentially practical in its aims, and most often involved the use of precisely ordered ritual words and acts that by their very nature guaranteed the achievement of specific results.

The belief in the potency of merely viewing the *sacra* in the mystery cults has already been mentioned, and, in fact, this practice constituted one of the central rites in the initiation ceremonies at Eleusis and elsewhere. The mortuary inscriptions of Egypt, especially those of the later period, beginning with the Coffin Texts, may be viewed as fundamentally magical. Ordinary people believed they could become "Osiris" at death, or could assume the sacrosanct character of the pharaoh in his relation to the deities of the afterlife, simply through verbal means, namely the recitation of appropriate liturgies. In Assyria, omens that related to the king were particularly important, because the well-being of the country was seen as based on the well-being of the king. Therefore, complex rituals and practices were developed in order to avert the consequences of evil omens for the ruler. In one instance, an omen predicted the death of an Assyrian king. A substitute was proclaimed king for one hundred days, and after this term of office he was killed and suitably buried. Thus the omen was fulfilled, and the true king could live.[59]

Among the Hittites, the use of precisely ordered ritual words and acts to achieve specific ends was engaged in by both women and men. In the "Ritual for the Purification of God and Man," the "Ritual to

Counteract Sorcery," the "Purification Ritual Engaging the Help of Protective Demons," the "Ritual Against Impotence," and the "Ritual Against Domestic Quarrel," the person performing the rite in each instance was referred to as "she," and is believed to have been a priestess titled the "Old Woman."[60] In other Hittite rituals, such as the "Ritual Against Pestilence," the "Evocatio," which summoned divinities back from other lands to Hatti, "The Soldiers' Oath," the "Ritual Before Battle," the "Removal of the Threat Implied in an Evil Omen," and the "Festival of the Warrior God," the person performing the rite in each instance was male.[61]

Another area of practical magic was the issuance of prophecies by oracles, and here there is clear evidence that women as well as men were relied upon to foretell the future. It has been seen how the omens and oracles obtained from the female and male diviners, ecstatics, and prophets of Mari were conveyed to King Zimri-Lim in order to assure his safety and victory. An Egyptian text dating from the second millennium, "The Prophecy of Neferti," recounts how that sage was called in by a pharaoh of the Fourth Dynasty for whom he foretold the collapse of the Old Kingdom, and the reestablishment of civil order and peace by a king of the Twelfth Dynasty.[62] About a thousand years later, during the reign of the Assyrian king Esarhaddon (ca.680–669 B.C.E.), prophecies of his protection by the divinities Ishtar and Bel were delivered, in this case by women, among them Ishtar-latashiat of Arbela, Sinqisha-amur of Arbela, Rimute-allate of Darahuya, Baia of Arbela, Ishtar-bel-daini, "oracle-priestess of the King," and Belit-abisha of Arbela.[63]

In the first millennium, the Oracle at Delphi was probably the best known and most influential in political and personal life throughout the Mediterranean world. While the Pythia was always female, the priests or "prophetes" who translated and transmitted the words of Apollo yielded through her divination were male. Yet in other parts of Greece, the words of Apollo were received directly by male oracles. Furthermore, though women were permitted to consult the Pythia herself only through an intermediary, they were not by any means totally excluded from other sacred rites associated with Delphi. For example, it was believed that Apollo left the sanctuary for several months in the autumn. Every other year at this time, fourteen girls and women from the best families in Athens were selected by the chief priest to act as Thyiads. They walked and danced along the mountainous, long road from Athens to Delphi, the supposed burial site of Dionysus, and with their sister-Thyiads from Delphi participated in the solemn rites and orgiastic revels characteristic of his worship, in which a young male impersonated the god.[64]

Gender, Omen and Exorcism Rites

Moving in even more closely on the everyday concerns of people in those times, we find there is a large body of omen and exorcism literature from Babylonia and Assyria, apparently copied, recopied, and stored in many temples over a very long period of time. It consists of a voluminous number of spells and magical formulas prepared for every contingency of life and was available to all people. When the specialized interpreters of omens in the temple came to be the male *Shailu* priests, outside of the temple and official religion there was a group of female interpreters of omens, the *Shailtu* diviners. They were employed especially by women in order to determine the will of the goddesses and gods, and apparently their powers were believed to be much broader than those of the *Shailu* priests.[65] Indeed, woven into the very fabric of Babylonian and Assyrian worship were the numerous strands of a strong belief in the power of magic, sorcery, and witchcraft, and many of the prayers recited during the sacred rites were akin to spells, charms, and incantations.

The incantation texts dealing specifically with devils and evil spirits, which were conceived of as attacking people and causing natural catastrophes for individuals and communities, are believed to be of great antiquity. Written in Sumerian, they are thought to have undergone little substantial modification from the time of their early use in Sumer to their use by Babylonians and Assyrians until the very end of the first millennium. Thus they provide some clues about those Mesopotamian beliefs, shared by many people for thousands of years, which had to do with phenomena threatening everyone, namely, sickness, death, and all the other calamitous events of daily life. Concern about the sources of these calamities and attempts to devise ways to avoid them led, in turn, to speculations about the existence of supernatural forces in the unseen world that might explain afflictions in this one.

Babylonian religion rested on the duty of laypeople and priests to please divinities in every possible way, to offer sacrifices and perform rituals in return for divine favor. For most of the second millennium, before the exclusion of women other than priestesses from participation in official cultic rites, both women and men were seen as responsible for the propitiation of divinities. The occurrence of misfortunes of all kinds was seen as the result of divine anger, originally understood as provoked by human transgression of ritual laws or the commission of sin. It was believed that the usual method used by goddesses and gods to vent their anger on transgressors was to inflict sickness on them, women and men alike, and thus mark them as sinful. Even more, since illness represented a state of impurity or sinfulness, it rendered people of both sexes unfit to participate in sacred rites, which was, of course, an additional sin.

At first, evil spirits were looked upon as messengers of divine anger that materially entered a person's body and did their work. Early Babylonian religious literature treats sin, uncleanliness, possession by evil spirits, and sickness as synonymous. For example, one exorcism ritual reads in part: "Mayest thou be freed from ... transgression, wickedness, curse, sickness, sighing, witchcraft, spell, charm, evil machinations of men."[66]

Since sickness and sinfulness were equated, the sick woman or man became a pariah, and the process of exorcism assumed some importance, as it became the means of at once magically curing illness, materially expelling evil spirits, and expiating sin. Priestesses as well as priests served as exorcisers, and the language in some of the incantations indicates that their knowledge was applied for the relief of women as well as men.[67]

Eventually it became apparent that evil sometimes struck at unexpected times those who deserved it least. From this perception came the notion that evil originated not with the great deities themselves but with the messengers of divine wrath, who thus became endowed with power of their own to inflict evil. Divinities then began to be conceptualized as "good" and as hostile to the evil spirits, who were, in turn, distinguished from one another, systematized, and named. Some of them were seen as personifications of specific illnesses or of disease itself, others as demonifications of storms and floods, but, in any event, they were viewed as responsible for every calamity suffered by people.

The power of exorcism was believed to derive partly from the greater power of the good deities, at the very mention of whose names the evil spirits trembled and vanished. Arrayed in the arsenal of the sick and victimized, to protect them from assault by evil spirits, were their personal goddess or god, thought to be present with them from birth, their household deity, and the god or goddess of the city. The existence of all these deities indicates the important role popular religion played beside official religion. And where these deities were male, their female counterparts were also invoked. For instance, as part of one elaborate ceremony to purify the palace and the king after his illness, exorciser-priests offered sacrifices and prayers. The last, spoken in the name of the king, and in an attempt to render them more effective, were addressed to pairs of female and male deities: Anu and Anatu, Bel and Belit, Ea and Damkina, Ninib and Gula, Sin and Ishtar, Nabu and Tasmet.[68]

Evil spirits fell into several classes. Official theology portrayed them as offspring of the deities Anu, Ea, and Damkina, and finally Bel and Ereshkigal, rulers of the underworld. But popular religious views tended to minimize the significance of their divine parentage and considered them as fairly autonomous and always dangerous. And the means of dealing with evil, focusing in the incantation-texts on how to expel malignant spirits from people's bodies, constituted an ever-present and continuing problem for Babylonian religion.

The interesting thing about these evil spirits is that, for the most part, their sexual designations indicated an absence of any particular association of either sex with evil or sin. For example, some of the most feared in a cosmic sense were The Seven, mentioned in many poems and incantations, who were thought to be the source of storms, tempests, unrest, disorder, and confusion in the world. Seen as so powerful that they even attacked divinities, who did not easily repulse them, in time they became the carriers of sickness and plague. And they had nothing in common with humanity. They were, in fact, sexless. The following is part of an incantation used against them:

> Seven are they, seven are they,
> In the Ocean Deep seven are they,
> Battening in Heaven seven are they,
> In the Ocean Deep as their home they were reared,
> Nor male or female are they,
> They are as the roaming windblast,
> No wife have they, no son do they beget;
> Knowing neither mercy or pity,
> They hearken not unto prayer or supplication.[69]

These seven spirits frequently reappeared in many shapes and forms in the legends of other Semitic nations, and the old Palestinian tradition of the Unclean Spirit may be partially based on their activities. In an old Syriac charm they were portrayed as male:

> "Seven accursed brothers, accursed sons! Destructive ones, sons of men of destruction! Why do you creep along on your knees and move upon your hands?" And they replied, "We go on our hands, so that we may eat flesh, and we crawl along upon our hands, so that we may drink blood."[70]

There were other kinds of evil spirits that could afflict people, such as the ghosts of women or men who died violent or unnatural deaths, or did not complete certain obligations before death, or reached a marriageable age but did not marry, or were not buried with the proper rituals so that their spirits could not rest. The last could come back and fasten onto anyone who had been in even a chance way connected with them in this world. And just as these evil spirits could be of either sex, so their victims could be women or men.

There were still other classes of demons that were of both sexes. There was the male Lilû, his female counterpart, Lilîtu, believed to have been the prototype of the Hebrew Lilith, and the female Ardat Lilî. The Semitic derivations seemed to associate the Ardat Lilî (apparently more intimately connected with humans than Lilîtu) with "abundance, luxuriousness, lasciviousness, wantonness,"[71] and she was sometimes described as she who had no husband, a restless ghost forced by her sexual desire to roam abroad until she was satisfied. In one text a sick man had been "married" to her, and it is likely that she was seen as the mother of the Alû or devil, half-human, half-spectre. In one explanatory text she was described as "The Night-wraith that hath no husband," but this is followed directly by the line, "The Night-fiend that hath no wife."[72]

A whole series of incantations was directed against the female demon, the *Labartu,* whose particular victims were children. But references to the evil man were not uncommon. He was seen as "an evil being, whose face is evil, whose mouth is evil, whose tongue is evil."[73] Through his evil mouth and tongue he was believed to bewitch people, and anyone who approached him might fall under his spell.

Gender and Witchcraft

There was yet another source of evil, which did not consist of spirits but of workers of evil. They were the female witches and male sorcerers, and the prevalent certainty of their existence probably sprang from the Babylonian belief in omens. Almost everything, and certainly everything unusual, portended good or evil. In time, any women or men who looked unusual came to be associated with evil, and later were believed to cause evil as witches and sorcerers. Seen as possessing powers greater than those of ordinary people, which they used for destructive purposes, their evil machinations were thought to affect individuals, families, and whole communities. So great was their presumed power that even evil spirits obeyed their commands, and therefore the goal of the exorciser was to reverse the process of bewitchment and send the same evil spirits back against the witches or wizards.

It seems significant that although witches were believed to outnumber wizards, suggesting that more women than men were isolated as looking unusual or as possessing extraordinary, destructive powers, many of the exorcism rituals against witchcraft were directed against both witches and wizards. For instance, in *Maqū,* an incantation series used against the effects of witchcraft, there were instructions that images of witches and sorcerers were to be fashioned and then burned, since it was held that these malignant ones practiced their craft through the torture of images of intended victims. Thus the process of torture might be reversed back upon the bewitcher. The routine inclusion of the image of a male sorcerer in the incantations would seem to indicate that witchcraft at that time was not exclusively associated with women.

Gender and Purification

The other chief means of combating witchcraft was through the use of pure, sweet water. And again the exorcism rituals involved images of both the witch and the sorcerer. In the incantation "Catcher of Catchers," for example, the exorciser instructed the sick person as follows:

> An image of a wizard and a witch,
> Shalt thou form out of meal in the copper wash-bowl;
> A clay image of a wizard and a witch,
> Shalt thou put to the image of meal;
> He shall wash his hands above (them);
> with sap of cedarwood he shall sprinkle
> (his hands) three times;
> Because of (or above?) thy witchcraft,
> thy sorcery he washes his hands; . . .[74]

When the water from the invalid's hands fell upon the images of the witch and wizard, it would transfer to the images, and therefore to those they represented, the uncleanliness and sin of the afflicted, who would thus, it was hoped, be restored to health. In effect, the exorcism achieved the washing away of evil spirits—the cleansing and purification of the sick. In time, spoken prayers accompanied the sprinkling of "holy" water over the sick, and the prayers came to assume greater prominence than the rite of sprinkling. But the act of expelling evil spirits, the *Kuppuru,* originally meant "to wash away," and a synonym for it was *"qudussu,"* or "to make pure." Used as a verb, it meant the purification of the exorciser-priest preparatory to the performance of her/his holy duties. A secondary meaning, rare in Assyrian but common in Hebrew, was "to dedicate something for holy purposes."[75]

The practice of purification as a sacred act and the use of very special water for this purpose were widespread and very important in ancient Near Eastern cultic rites. Babylonian bathhouses used for purification initially were for persons of both sexes, and the focal point of every Mesopotamian religious service was purification. References to members of the Egyptian priesthood making or keeping themselves ritually pure before performing sacred rites are scattered throughout the literature. At Delphi, before consulting with Apollo the Pythia went through a purification ceremony, the most important part of which was her ritual bathing in a sacred spring. The latter was also used by visitors of both sexes to Delphi for purification purposes. Indeed, many of the Greek festivals included among their sacred rites the purification of initiates in sacred water—e.g., the ritual immersion of participants before they attended the celebration of the Eleusinian Mysteries.[76]

Since access to membership and participation in the sacred rites of these later cults were open to women and men alike, it was apparently taken for granted that people of both sexes required purification in order to divest themselves of sin or mortal imperfections. More generally, neither sex seems to have been regarded as especially in need of purification, or especially sinful by virtue of their sex. And this absence of any association of ritual impurity or uncleanness with gender, and in particular with the female sex and female sexuality, was conspicuous in some of the most enduring and widely observed polytheistic rites.

The Sacred Marriage and Female Sexuality

One of the most well-attested rituals performed throughout Mesopotamia for two thousand years was the Sacred Marriage, the sacred drama of an ancient fertility cult dating back to the early part of the third millennium. Most of the priestly and poetic texts are in Sumerian, and they focus on how to assure the fertility of the land and the people. The rite itself involved the sexual union of the king, as representative of the community, with an avatar of the great goddess Inanna, probably her chief priestess. Judging by the jubilance and bliss marking its celebration it may well be, as maintained by Thorkild Jacobsen, that the Sacred Marriage was associated with the harvest, and with the community's feelings of well-being and security engendered by an abundant food supply.[77]

The first of the Sacred Marriage rites recorded by poets involved the ruler Dumuzi. Here, as in all other instances, it was the goddess Inanna who selected him for "the godship of the land." She bathed and dressed herself in her "special garments of power" and summoned Dumuzi to her shrine at Erech, filled with prayers and songs, to cohabit with her. Typical of the literature describing the rite is the account of Inanna's sexual initiative and activity, and the explicitness of the language. Enamored with Dumuzi, the Queen of Heaven says:

> "As for me, my vulva,
> For me the piled high hillock,
> Me—the maid, who will plow it for me?
> My vulva, the watered ground—for me,
> Me, the Queen, who will station the ox there?"[78]

The response is:

> "Oh Lordly Lady, the King will plow it for you,
> Dumuzi, the King, will plow it for you."[79]

And Inanna, overjoyed, says:

> "Plow my vulva, man of my heart!"[80]

After her "holy lap" is bathed and they have intercourse, the result is a luxuriance of vegetation that springs up around the king, and it is therefore a blessing for the whole community:

> At the King's lap stood the rising cedar,
> Plants rose high by his side,
> Grains rose high by his side,
> . . . (and) gardens flourished luxuriantly by his side.[81]

The issue of their union is not the offspring of Inanna but the fertility of the land. Once happily "married" to Dumuzi, she asks her shepherd husband for cream, milk, and cheese and in return promises the following to him (and to the people of Sumer):

> "My husband, the goodly storehouse, the holy stall,
> I, Inanna, will preserve for you,
> I will watch over your 'house of life.'
> The radiant wonder-place of the land,
> The house where the fate of all the lands is decreed,
> Where people and (all) living things are guided,
> I, Inanna will preserve for you,
> I will watch over your 'house of life,'
> The 'house of life,' the storehouse of long life,
> I, Inanna, will preserve it for you."[82]

Although it is uncertain just how often this *hieros gamos* occurred during a king's reign, what is fairly sure is that the ruler of Sumer, as a sort of incarnated Dumuzi, had to become the "husband" of Inanna in order to guarantee the fertility and prosperity of his country, and therefore the stability of his throne. For example, the "Blessing of Shulgi" relates how one of the rulers of the Third Dynasty of Ur (ca.2500 B.C.E.), as a reincarnation of Dumuzi, journeyed by boat to Inanna's shrine at Erech, sacrificed to the goddess, and dressed himself in ritual garments. Inanna was so impressed with his beauty that she broke into a passionate love song:

"When for the wild bull, for the lord, I shall have bathed,
When for the shepherd Dumuzi, I shall have bathed,
When with . . . my sides I shall have adorned,
When with amber my mouth I shall have coated,
When with kohl my eyes I shall have painted,
When in his fair hands my loins shall have been shaped,
When the lord, lying by holy Inanna, the shepherd Dumuzi,
With milk and cream the lap shall have smoothed (?) . . .,
When on my vulva his hands he shall have laid,
When like his narrow boat, he shall have brought life to it,
When like his black boat, he shall have . . . it,
When on the bed he shall have caressed me,
Then shall I caress my lord, a sweet fate I shall decree for him,
I shall caress Shulgi, the faithful shepherd, a sweet fate I shall decree for
   him,
I shall caress his loins, the shepherdship of all the lands,
I shall decree as his fate."[83]

The importance of the Sacred Marriage rite to the king and, through his person, to the people he ruled over may be gauged from the fate she decrees for her lover/husband Shulgi:

"In battle I am your leader, in combat I am your helpmate (?),
In the assembly I am your champion (?)
On the road I am your life.
You, the chosen shepherd of the holy (?) house (?),
You, the sustainer (?) of An's great shrine,
In all ways you are fit:
To hold high your head on the lofty dais, you are fit,
To sit on the lapis lazuli throne, you are fit,
To fix the crown on your head, you are fit,
To wear long garments on your body, you are fit,
To gird yourself in the garment of Kingship, you are fit,
To carry the mace and the weapon, you are fit . . .,
To guide straight the long bow and the arrow, you are fit,
To fasten the throw-stick and the sling at the side, you are fit,
For the holy scepter in your hand, you are fit,

For the holy sandals on your feet, you are fit . . .,
To prance on my bosom like a 'lapis lazuli' calf, you are fit.
May your beloved heart be long of days.
Thus has An determined the fate for you, may it not be altered,
Enlil the decreer of fate—may it not be changed,
Inanna holds you dear, you are the beloved of Ningal."[84]

In later Semitic renditions, the protagonists Inanna and Dumuzi were supplanted by Ishtar and Tammuz. But, despite variations in the accounts of the various rituals attendant on the marriage or at the feast celebrating it the next day, there were some constant features in all accounts of the Sacred Marriage. One was the jubilant quality of its celebration. Another was the dominance of the goddess in the Sacred Marriage. In some Sumerian and Old Babylonian royal inscriptions, the passages that describe the king's relationship to Ishtar refer to that goddess as "the carrier, the fountainhead, of his power and prestige,"[85] often in terms of her personal intervention on his behalf. In fact, it appears that those Mesopotamian kings with divine determinatives before their names could lay claim to deification only after they had been chosen by Inanna or Ishtar as "bridegrooms." Thus in the Sacred Marriage, the king not only represented the community but also came to play the part of Dumuzi or Tammuz, former kings who had themselves been deified through unions with the goddesses. But in all the texts, it is the goddess who plays the commanding role.

Still another feature common to all the Sacred Marriage rites was that the active sexuality of the goddess was portrayed only as good, and it was seen as a precursor to the blessing of the whole community. At least in the divine sphere, as expressed in this rite, female sexuality had no connotations of evil or danger for men. And the goddess's sexuality was displayed as totally extrafamilial, i.e., it was nowhere linked to her own reproductive abilities nor was there any implication of monogamy on her part. The heart of the Sacred Marriage rite was Inanna/Ishtar's great power over life, fertility, and destiny, the energizing character of her sexuality in her aspect as goddess of love and fertility, and her role in actively seeking out and sexually enjoying the king.

Women and the Cult of the Dying Young God

Related to the Sacred Marriage rite, but quite different in emotional content, were the cultic observances of the tragic, untimely death of the young Mesopotamian vegetation god. Worshiped under different names in different places as Dumuzi, Tammuz, Baal, or Adonis, his annual death and resurrection paralleled the annual cycle of the seasons and the alternate barrenness of the earth and rebirth of vegetation.

In the Sumerian tradition, an explicit reason was given for Dumuzi's annual death and resurrection. As described earlier, after Inanna's release from the Netherworld by Enki she had to find a substitute to take her place in death. When her son/lover/husband Dumuzi showed no signs of grief at her approach, surrounded as she was by the awful ghouls of the Netherworld, it so angered the goddess that:

> She fastened her eye upon him, the eye of death,
> Spoke the word against him, the word of wrath,
> Uttered the cry against him, the cry of guilt, . . .[86]

Inanna handed Dumuzi over to the demons, who were impatient for their surrogate-victim, and they pursued, tortured, bound, and beat him before transporting the king to the realm of the dead.

Dumuzi was consigned to the underworld for just half of each year only because of the intervention of his sister Geshtinanna, "the divine interpreter of dreams" and "an expert scribe."[87] First she demonstrated her love for him by refusing to reveal his whereabouts to the harpies of the Netherworld even after they tortured her mercilessly. Then she offered to take his place in the world of the dead. Inanna could not refuse altogether to honor Geshtinanna's generosity, but since she did not want Dumuzi to escape punishment for his faithlessness, she decided that each of them should alternately spend half the year in the Netherworld.

Thus in the Sumerian version, the young dying god of vegetation suffered death as a punishment for his lack of deference to the dominant partner in the Sacred Marriage. At the same time, he was rescued from death for half the year through the absolute devotion of his sister, whose name indicates some link with the goddess. The critical influences on Dumuzi's fate were female—primarily, the will and desires of Inanna and secondarily, the love and self-sacrifice of his sister.

But it was the death of the young Semitic god Tammuz, the counterpart of Dumuzi, that was commemorated and bitterly lamented all over Mesopotamia and Palestine, even by the women of Israel at one of the gates of the temple in Jerusalem (Ezek. 8:14). It is possible that when Mesopotamian laywomen were increasingly barred from participation in official religion toward the end of the second millennium, the cult of Tammuz was initiated and maintained by women outside of the temple, in Babylonia as well as in Israel. For it was principally, if not exclusively, a cult of women, and the many poetic references to the circumstances surrounding his death imply that he was mourned with the feelings of a bride, widow, mother, and sister.

As already noted, Jacobsen theorizes that the general feeling of bliss associated with the Sacred Marriage was induced by a bountiful harvest, and he sees the characteristics of Tammuz in terms of the particular qualities of the food harvested. What is especially striking is his description of the god as ethically neutral, like the food, and void of any separate individuality. He was adored by his worshipers because of the necessity of his presence to those who loved him, whether they were brides, widows, mothers, or sisters, who variously represented the community of believers. In this view, the essential quality of Tammuz is that he was the beloved, the object of women's love, all brides, all mothers, all sisters, and was in effect a projection of the emotional needs of those who loved him. In the lamentation for his death, in a near-reversal of roles between deity and worshiper, it is the god who was loved for his very helplessness and powerlessness. He was in his death young, hardly mature, passive, fearful, dependent, beloved, and possessed by his female worshipers.[88]

What seems so anomalous here is that all these qualities should have been ascribed by Semitic women to Dumuzi/Tammuz at a time when Mesopotamia was undergoing great changes—military invasions, expansion of trade, shifts in political power, and an increasing masculinization in social structure—and when Mesopotamian men frequently lived active lives as purposeful kings, warriors, priests, traders, agriculturists, craftsmen, and the like. Through the filtered vision of the women who dominated his cult, Tammuz emerged in death as a strangely immature and unmasculine figure for those times, perhaps almost androgynous for those cultures. In one of his aspects he was a desirable lover who aroused the sexual passion of the Queen of Heaven in their Sacred Marriage, providing in his person, and in the persons of the kings who became his avatars, for the fertility and prosperity of the whole community. That was the image of Tammuz in his sexual vigor and mature responsibility. In his other aspect, as the young dying god, his image was transformed by the women who mourned him with a sorrow that seemed to ignore his annual resurrection, into a gentle, tragic, doomed, passive object of love. Insofar as his cult was extraofficial, composed of Semitic women who were suffering a decline in their own status both within and without the temple before the second millennium was to end, the intensity of their grief for his death might have represented a projection of the sorrow they felt over their own lot in life.

Sexuality in the Service of the Divine

Finally, the active and beneficent sexuality of Inanna/Ishtar denoted an attitude among polytheistic Mesopotamians toward sexuality in general, and female sexuality in particular, that was very different from what is found in biblical literature. In many parts of the ancient Near East from the third to the first millennium, priestesses and female devotees of Ishtar, or her counterparts Kybele, Asherah, Aphrodite, or Astarte, lived in and around temples devoted to these divinities. Although they have sometimes since been described as "harlots" or "ritual prostitutes," they were known in their own times and places, especially in the earlier years of this period, as *quadishtu,* "holy women," or *ishtaritu,* "women of Ishtar."

They engaged in sacred rites that often included a free and active sexual life, in celebration of the active sexual aspect of the goddess they served, who was seen by people of those times as the source of fertility and abundance for the community. They were the hierodules of the temple just as Inanna was the hierodule of Heaven. And as representatives of the goddesses, the chief priestesses of Inanna/Ishtar participated in the Sacred Marriage rites, commemorated in rapturous poetry qua theology for two thousand years.

In Egypt for a long time there were women attached to the temple who served in a sexual capacity. Most of them probably were dedicated to the ithyphallic god Min and very likely were drawn from the lower classes in society. But the belief in the sacrosanct character of female sexuality extended to all social classes. If the second millennium produced the "harim of the god," the first saw the High Priestess of Thebes, who may have performed part of her ritual obligations in a sexual manner. Necessarily a member of one of the highest-ranking families and a virgin of great beauty, she was required to take any man she chose for a month, after which the community mourned her as if she had died. Subsequently she married and left the priesthood. This practice seems to have been a carry-over of the older concept of the chief priestess being the wife of the god, and therefore bound to accept any man who impersonated the god, just as the pharaohs formerly were believed to represent the god Amen during the Eighteenth Dynasty.[89]

In Mesopotamia there were several classes of priestesses, but there is only limited information about a number of their functions. It appears that some of these sexually active priestesses could marry, but few were permitted to bear children to their own husbands, so they sometimes provided the latter with substitutes for this purpose. When priestesses did bear children they evidently retained them. That the early status of these *quadishtu* was high, and that the sacred sexual rites, which involved having intercourse with men outside of marriage, were indeed considered sacred, are attested by the references to these priestesses as "the sacred ones," "the pure ones," "the holy ones." In Babylonia and Assyria, the active sexuality of the priestesses attached to Ishtar's temples in many cities was recognized as part of the goddess's religious rites.[90]

From about 1910 to 1840, and then from about 1813 to 1781 B.C.E., Assyrian merchants penetrated Asia Minor. The region was then divided into small city-states, each of them ruled by a princess or prince whose subjects were Hittites, Luwians, Hurrians, and Semitic Amorites. In many aristocratic families from this area, at least one daughter would be dedicated to the service of the god Ashur, or to one or another of the female or male protective deities, as *gubbātim* or *quadishtum,* the holy women of Ishtar.[91] The Babylonian Code of Hammurabi (ca.1700 B.C.E.) mentioned various classes of women connected with the temples, of whom the most exalted in rank was the *ēntum,* or high priestess and "bride" of the male deity. Some of them were the daughters and sisters of kings. Another numerous class of priestesses from upper-class families, the *naditum,* were simultaneously regarded as the wives of the reigning male deities and the hierodules of the temple, and they also were prominent in local civil and economic life.

In addition to these upper-class women who were votaries of the tutelar goddess and practitioners of her sacred sexual rites, there were still other groups of temple women mentioned in the Code, such as the *sikirtum* or *kulmasitum.* Though their specific duties are obscure, it seems fairly clear that they were also part of the general class of hierodules. And the sanctity of the sexual rites practiced by both the priestesses and the lay votaries of the goddess was widely acknowledged. Hierodules frequented the Phoenician temples of Astarte, the Ashtoreth of the Old Testament. Ritual sexual practices played an important part in Semitic religious ceremonies, and it was not uncommon for them to occur in places like threshing-floors, associated with the earth's fertility. But gradually, by the first millennium, the holiness of sexual acts performed in and near the temples gave way to profane prostitution.[92]

What may be less frequently realized is that there were male counterparts to these "holy women" who also practiced the sacred sexual rites of the great goddesses. For example, men as well as women were hierodules of some of the same temples of Ishtar in Babylonia. The fertility-cult of Canaan had its full complement of "ritual prostitutes" of both sexes, *quedesim* and *quedesoth.* By the mid-Assyrian period, and under Greco-Roman rule, Near Eastern temples employed thousands of hierodules of both sexes.[93] And while Josiah ruled over the Hebrews (ca.639–609 B.C.E.), he destroyed the quarters of the *qedeshim,* the "male cult prostitutes" who were housed in the Temple of Jerusalem, in fact in the very part of the temple where women wove clothing for Asherah, the mother-goddess (2 Kings 23:7).

What seems to have been the case in the ancient Near East, then, for most of the period from the third to the first millennium, is that both women and men performed sacred sexual rites in the service of female and male deities and, once again, the sex of the priest or participant was not a determining ground for inclusion or exclusion from these rites. While the purpose of these sexual rites apparently moved from the sacred to the profane with the passage of time, and perhaps especially so by sometime in the first millennium, attitudes toward sexuality in the earlier millennia appear to have been far more open, less judgmental, and different from our own. In most instances, female sexuality was not regarded with fear or ambivalence but was seen as an integral part of sacred rituals and therefore important to community life. Hierodules either represented goddesses in their sexual aspect or were "brides" of gods, and apparently monogamy and motherhood were not particularly linked with the roles of women in cult. There was no denigration of either sex involved in sacred rites on the basis of their biological functions, and the consequences of sexuality were often viewed as divinely inspired and beneficial to the community.

Sexuality, Ritual Uncleanness, and Female Biology

Even after economic, political, social, and philosophical developments transformed some of these cultures into more androcentric and male-dominant societies, older attitudes toward sex roles in religious life seemed to persist. For instance, Assyrian law codes from the thirteenth century or earlier imposed penalties on women for miscarriages and abortions. By the mid-Assyrian period (ca.1380–1080 B.C.E.), there were strict rules about purity for royal harems, and "unclean" wives and concubines were forbidden to come near the king.[94] But the ramifications of this basically new and unpromising concentration on the "purity" and "cleanness" of women, which related to their normal biological functions and sexuality, were far from simple or linear in their influence on views about the proper place of women in religion. Furthermore, if the Assyrian King Ashurbanipal (reigned ca.668–626 B.C.E.) begged forgiveness from a deity for having employed a female scribe when he asked for an oracle,[95] it is important to note that this incident corroborates the use of female scribes by the king even at that late date.

As already remarked, popular religious alternatives became available, perhaps even preferable, to those who came to be excluded because of their sex from official cult, and that alone says something about the relative lack of importance attached to gender in the polytheistic universe of belief and ritual. Where ordinary women were largely denied access to participation in official sacred rites, as in later Babylonia and Assyria, they maintained and presided over popular, extra-official cults of their own, as in the worship of Tammuz. And simultaneous with the increasing denigration of the "nature" of women and their deprivation of legal rights during some periods in ancient Athens, and the exclusion of women from most rights of citizenship because of the alleged imbecility of their sex in ancient Rome, in those same places the first millennium cults of Demeter and Isis incorporated women and men into every level and facet of their worship.

To be sure, the beginnings of the association of female sexuality with ritual uncleanness was ominous. For example, among the Hittites temple officials were not permitted to perform any of the sacred rites after having had intercourse with women until they bathed and restored themselves to cultic purity. Failure to observe this rule was thought especially offensive to deities and deserving of death.[96]

But it would appear that it was not female sexuality alone that was considered a source of ritual contamination. Some groups of Babylonian priestesses lived cloistered lives as well. At Eleusis, both priestesses and priests played enormously important roles in the cult, and some of them held office for life. Like some of the priestesses, the Hierophant, or chief priest, was allowed to marry. But if he was required to remain chaste during the period of initiation into the Greater Mysteries, there was likewise a group of "panageis priestesses," or "all-holy ones," who lived in special dwellings at Eleusis only with other priestesses, apart from men.[97] Also, during some periods of ancient Rome, the chastity of the powerful Vestal Virgins was supposed to insure the well-being of the state. Therefore it would seem that it was primarily sexuality itself that was coming to be seen by some religious communities as threatening to ritual purity, whether it originated with women or men.

Related to the notion of ritual uncleanness was the practice of ritual isolation of individuals from the community at times when experiences in their lives posed what was perceived as a threat to the safety of the group. For example, Canaanite social customs dating back to the early part of the second millennium indicate that though the birth of a child was an occasion of rejoicing, it was also considered a time of transition, when the whole community was believed to be particularly vulnerable to supernatural influence, and therefore possible harm. Thus, after childbirth there were "rites of separation," or the ritual isolation of the mother from the rest of the community. And "wise women" were employed to chant incantations at the birth to guard the social group from possible harm during these "periods of passage."

Likewise, death was thought to present the same kinds of dangers for society as birth. Its occurrence was viewed as another "season of passage," when the next of kin, on behalf of the community, observed a period of ritual isolation during which the bereaved meticulously performed all the necessary rituals required for burial and mourning. And again, the rituals were properly observed for the safety of the social group.[98]

The same type of reaction to birth and death might, of course, have meant many things, among them fear of changes in the community, and therefore fear of the introduction of unknown elements and possible danger; or the association of birth (or sex?) with death; or the solemn marking of the beginning and end of the existence of the individual and, by extension, the social group. However, while both birth and death required ritual isolation, in the case of childbirth, even after the paternal contribution to birth was familiar, it was *only the mother* who had to endure separation from the group and therefore became the symbol of potential danger. One can only speculate about the possible reasons for this practice, which, in turn, raises a host of questions about Canaanite attitudes toward the biological nature of women and their status as a sex. Was this ritual isolation imposed only on the mother for her own protection from sexual intercourse as a means of population control? Was she considered ritually "unclean" because of childbirth, or was the latter regarded as rendering her particularly potent? Was she considered the more important parent, or was she more dispensable to the community's ongoing functions than the father? Did she in childbirth become the scapegoat for the community's ritual transgressions or sins? But whatever the underlying rationale, ritual isolation after childbirth was mandatory only for the mother, and it does not seem extreme to conclude that the community in some way may have felt itself endangered by her natural bodily processes at that time.

Participation of Women and Men in Cult

In discussing religious attitudes, it is difficult, if not impossible, to remove them from their social context. Obviously there is always interaction between the two. And there is no question that in Canaan, the social conventions that connected women in childbirth with danger for the community were very important and potentially threatening for women. Nevertheless, with this one large exception, it seems that in general where there were deeply held polytheistic beliefs in the ancient Near East, the earthly corollary was the participation of both women and men in fairly equivalent roles in its sacred rites.

Along with the presence of persons of both sexes in the priest-hood and in a variety of positions in the temple, women as well as men were involved in significant ways in popular cults. Participants in sacred rites were not necessarily of the same sex as the deity worshiped, nor is there much evidence that either women or men stood in a particularly close relationship to the divine simply because of their sex. Ritual exclusion of persons of either sex on the basis of ascriptions of "natural" biological inferiority or stereotypic sex roles was alien to the religious temper of those times. Neither sex was exclusively stigmatized as dangerous or evil, by virtue of its sex alone, in the demonology of extraofficial religion. And at a time when religion seems to have played a far more central role in social life than it does today, in societies that were in many ways highly advanced and productive, if different from our own, some of the most crucial rites and cultic practices exhibited degrees of psychological androgyny in their conception, imagery, symbolism, and performance that has since been unparalleled in Judaism and Christianity.

PART III

BIBLICAL ATTITUDES TOWARD GENDER

CHAPTER 5

Gender and
the Nature of the Divine:
The Biblical View

I N estimating the importance attached to gender in biblical literature, it is, of course, necessary to distinguish between the Old Testament and the New and to examine them as discrete documents, bound as they are by their focus on a single deity, whose presence and activity is central to the vision of both, and by the many references in the New Testament back to the Old. Just as the mythic portrayals of goddesses and gods shifted somewhat over time, so biblical conceptions of the nature of the divine and their relation to the issue of gender naturally evolved and changed over the millennium and more during which the canon was finally formulated and set in place. Nevertheless, despite the many differences between the two testaments, there are some large similarities as well.

The Biblical and Polytheistic Outlooks: Some Similarities

It is by now a commonplace of much biblical scholarship that the early roots of monotheism may be located not only in the life experiences and social needs of its proponents, and in the influence of prevailing customs and ideologies, but also deep in the outlook and practices of the polytheistic religions in its environment, even as they were appropriated, altered, or rejected by biblical authors. To cite but a few random instances by way of illustration, some have maintained that Yahweh was likely a Canaanite fertility deity before he was taken over and transformed by the early Hebrews, or that Aaron was conforming to customary practice when he fashioned a graven image of the divine while Moses was on Mount Sinai receiving the Ten Commandments.

135

Others have pointed to the impact of surrounding cultures, as when the reformer-king Josiah expelled vestiges of idolatrous worship from the temple, or when Yahweh is represented as demanding a real human sacrifice from Abraham as a test of his faith. And still others have observed that there was a monotheistic pharaoh, Ikhnaton, who ruled Egypt within the early period of biblical evolution, and that the Greek philosophical orientation, which came to perceive reality in terms of a matter-spirit dualism, was to have a profound effect on the thought of early Christians.

Beyond these specific influences and parallelisms—and there are many—is a more general congruence. As was evident in most Near Eastern polytheistic cultures, the monotheistic world view encompassed a belief in the interpenetration of the divine and the secular in everyday life, in which divinity was seen as immanent and interventionist in both nature and human history, and in which some individuals had access to the divine.

Like polytheistic texts, biblical literature is infused with trust in the efficacy of omens, prophecies, magic. Like Egyptian ideas about the afterlife or those of first-millennium mystery cults, biblical writings raise the possibility of personal salvation based on individual righteousness or communal observances of appropriate rituals. Like some of the deities of polytheism, the intentions of Yahweh are not always comprehensible to his worshipers. Above all, despite the more graphically anthropomorphic depictions of goddesses and gods in polytheism, both the latter and monotheism conceived of divinity as overwhelmingly powerful, and of humans as correspondingly vulnerable to divine edicts and dispensations. In short, as recounted in the Bible, the universe of both the early Hebrews and Christians, like that of polytheistic societies, was essentially religious in nature.

The Biblical View of the Divine

However, unlike the polytheistic beliefs in the indwelling of divinity in nature, the assignment of sexual identity to the various elements of the natural world, and the consequent view of the proper functioning of nature as closely affiliated with the survival and prosperity of society, the biblical view of the divine is that God is more than only immanent in nature; he creates nature just as he creates people, and he is immortal, while nature itself may change or die (Ps. 102:25–27). After his creation of nature and humans, he is seen as both immanent and transcendent. God rather than nature is divine, and while he might address his selected prophets in specific physical places, no one part of nature is rendered uniquely divine by his presence. Indeed, until the time of the monarchy, altars and sanctuaries were erected in his honor in many places, consonant with the existence of a nomadic people, and there were no geographically fixed sites of cultic worship that excluded others.

This modification in the view of divine immanence and transcendence was one important link in a chain of differences that was to set monotheism apart from the religions in its environment and ultimately was to yield a set of radically different attitudes toward the importance of gender. Since the god of monotheism was not geographically localized, immanent, or interventionist only in particular parts of nature or in specific aspects of human existence, his power came to be seen by his followers as virtually universal.

Thus, unlike goddesses and gods whose scope of power was limited by their particular attributes, Yahweh came to be worshiped as the sole creator and sustainer of life, the source of fertility, social order, wisdom, and justice, the champion of his adherents in battle, and the supreme judge in this life and the next. This different conception of the residence and breadth of divine power in a single deity had the effect of enormously enhancing the significance of his every action and judgment, including those which pertained to sexuality and appropriate sex roles in the secular community, all of which were then made applicable to believers and nonbelievers alike.

Yahweh was above all conceived of as ineffable. Possessing many names and therefore no name, he is nominally nonsexual, nonfamilial, and thus neither the parent nor the offspring of other deities. Moreover, though competing religious beliefs and divinities are mentioned in both testaments (usually in association with idolatry), God is not usually shown as interacting directly with them but, instead, interacts with his special prophets and the human community. If humans follow the teachings of other gods, they are threatened with divine punishment. Hence, while in polytheistic religions the characteristics of the divine become apparent through the many relationships of goddesses and gods with one another as well as with people, the attributes of Yahweh emerge solely from the nature of divine-human encounters. Consequently, the nature of the human community and its kind of involvement with the divine assume far greater prominence in monotheism than in polytheism.

Female Metaphors for God

Biblical descriptions of the content of divine-human interactions (and sometimes the signal importance of the patriarchs and male prophets in the Old Testament and Jesus and his male apostles in the New) all have led many theologians and laypersons alike to personify and think of God, though he is by definition ineffable, as nevertheless also male. He is portrayed as issuing commands, warnings, and instructions to the human community on matters of central ethical or ritual concern, and he does so far more frequently through specially chosen men than through women. These more numerous, more significant interactions with men are mirrored in the numerous designations of God as masculine in the Bible (and in later commentaries, prayers, and hymns as well)—e.g., in the recurrent use of words like "He," "His," "Him," "Lord," "King," and the like.

Countering this view of God's "sex" established by the use of typically masculine God-language, Phyllis Trible has uncovered the presence of "gynomorphic" imagery in Old Testament descriptions of the ways in which the divine interacts with the human community, or female metaphors for God. While acknowledging the more common usage of "andromorphic" language, she concentrates on the use of womb and breast imagery as metaphoric symbols of divine compassion, mercy, nurturance, and grace. Citing such imagery in a number of passages, Trible claims that the allusion by uterine analogy to God as mother, nurse, and midwife in some accounts of Yahweh's relations with Israel tends to subvert the more usual perception of God as a male deity.

In addition, she contends that the use of female as well as male imagery in reference to God's transactions with people was distorted in early and subsequent translations from the Hebrew. The translators assigned more sexually restrictive, or only masculine, traits to Yahweh, e.g., in Deut. 32:18, whereas the original Hebrew was more sexually inclusive in its meaning. The last suggests an initial monotheistic view of divinity as God the Mother along with God the Father, both of which, according to Trible, were finally abandoned in favor of a more transcendent and less limiting, or asexual, conception of the divine.[1]

Certainly the use in some of the early monotheistic texts of more sexually inclusive language, which refers to either the female or male attributes of Yahweh, is very significant as rediscovered history. However, contrary to Trible's implied conclusion, namely that there were no negative connotations in the shift to the later view, which ascribed asexuality and transcendence to Yahweh or saw divinity as transcending the limitations of sexual attributes, the latter might very well have contributed to the development of an essential ambivalence toward femaleness, threaded through the content and imagery of many of the narratives in both testaments.

God As Transcendent and Asexual

The depiction of God in his more transcendent and asexual character lies at the center of some of the most cultically crucial biblical passages, and it was this aspect of the divine which was to become dominant in the Western tradition. But even as God came to be seen as overarchingly ineffable, the portrayal of how this deity sometimes interacted with the secular community in specifically sex-related ways established monotheistic attitudes toward the importance of gender as novel and quite different from those of polytheism.

For example, while a more complete discussion of the Old Testament story of creation as it relates to sexual identity, moral capacities, and power must be reserved for later, a comparison of the general polytheistic and monotheistic attitudes toward that event may indicate a few of the implications of the view of God as asexual and transcendent. As remarked earlier, polytheistic religions often envisioned the creation and organization of the universe as a process and product of sexual unions between goddesses and gods, even when the primary divine source of life was presented as female, as in the instance of the Sumerian Nammu, or male, as in the case of the Egyptian Ptah. As noted, some creator-deities were apparently thought of as bisexual. All of this reflected the slight emphasis placed on the importance of divine gender, as well as the polytheistic view that there was no natural division or conflict between body and spirit. The divine was celebrated as actively sexual, and the fruits of sexuality in either the divine or the secular sphere frequently were seen as good for the whole of society.

By way of contrast, in the Old Testament (Gen. 11–3) the importance of the act and agent of creation is considerably magnified. As a universal deity seen as the source and arbiter of everything in life and death, Yahweh does not perform the act of creation by identifying himself with any physical elements in nature, e.g., the earth or sea, but rather almost at once creates all inanimate and animate matter. Thus existence itself dates from the time of his first creative acts.

The god of monotheism creates by his words rather than his body, and there is no subsequent involvement in that process of any other divinities of either sex. Further, the supreme power of the divine will and words in the creation of the universe sets up an implicit and, considering its source, perhaps eternal dichotomy between the physical and the spiritual.

Both sexuality and bodily reproduction (the latter in this world visibly restricted to women) are rendered as correspondingly less important than the type of activity engaged in by God, indeed almost counter to the divine. Both are placed forever in a more limited, earthly sphere, producing none of the grand results of material abundance or stability for the secular community provided, for instance, by the Sacred Marriage, the issue of which rested on a view of the beneficence of female sexuality. Interestingly, and even ironically, God blesses his human creations and enjoins the man and woman to "be fruitful and multiply," but it is within the larger context of his creation and provision of the means for re-creation of every kind of life, in order to fulfill his divine purpose (Gen. 1:27–31).

In God's asexual creation of every living thing, in the face of all human experience to the contrary, the female involvement is conspicuously absent. From the perspective of human understanding, that which remains as the source of life can, by analogy, only be called male. And from God's vantage, the successive stages of creation demonstrate his power and transcendence and are seen as good. Moreover, he endows the man with the power to name every living creature, including his wife (Gen. 2:19–20, 23; 3:20). This act was extremely significant because of the prevailing Near Eastern belief in the almost magical potency of names associated with the divine, and because of the enhanced importance attached to words as the means of divine creation. Reinforcing the masculine imagery, then, the primary act of the creation of every living thing by the word of God is replicated in the secondary act of their verbal identification by the first man.

The Moral Universe of Yahweh

It is, perhaps, in the representation of Yahweh as the origin of universal moral laws, and in biblical reactions to the relation between "official" and "popular" religion, that examples of the most cogent evidence for the new significance accorded to gender may be found. Some of the biblical narratives dealing with both of these areas picture God as responding and judging differently on the basis of sex alone, and in this respect the monotheistic mentality is most sharply marked as radically different from that of Near Eastern polytheistic religions.

In contrast with polytheistic representations of the divine, the conception of Yahweh as immanent in a less localized way, as more universal in his power, and as at once immanent and transcendent, had as its corollary the requirement that his worshipers offer more than merely ritualistic propitiation, sacrifices, and liturgical services. For example, as late as the middle of the first millennium, the reformers and prophets of the exilic and post-exilic periods, for all their passion, were not religious innovators but, for the most part, were exhorting the Hebrews to return to their ancient traditions. And central to this "return" was an insistence that mere participation in traditional forms of worship, unaccompanied by a wholehearted commitment in daily life to divine moral commands, was not only reprehensible in the sight of God but would elicit divine retribution (Jer. 7:1–15).

In lieu of the specific powers possessed by goddesses and gods in polytheistic pantheons, the one deity of the Bible was seen as possessing more general attributes, which, of course, were unshared. While Yahweh does not always conform to these attributes and also acts out of seemingly "human" motives—e.g., anger, jealousy, caprice—he is most frequently portrayed as a god of righteousness, compassion, justice, and, to a lesser extent, omnipotence and omniscience.[2] Even evil becomes an instrument of divine will and retribution. But all these divine qualities operate within the bounds of what was then perceived as God's overriding concern with moral issues, a preoccupation vastly expanded from the expression of polytheistic concerns for righteous behavior. While it was not always the case, it appears that those polytheistic concerns could sometimes be satisfied by merely verbal or ritualistic professions of virtue, as in the Egyptian Negative Confession of sins.

Gender and the Divine Covenant

As different from divine-human relationships in official polytheistic religions, in which the king or ruler was either considered divine or was seen as embodying the prosperity or misfortune of the human community in his own person, through his own personal standing with goddesses and gods, Yahweh is described as making a covenant with the *people* of Israel, independent of its existence as a political state or its particular geographic location. While women are undoubtedly included among the people of Israel, this covenant was periodically initiated and renewed by God with men like Abraham, Isaac, and Jacob, who then most often, though not always, relayed its terms to the community. Thus it was the male leaders, prophets, and reformers who most frequently transmitted the divine laws and commandments that people had to morally choose to obey in order to benefit from the fulfillment of the divine promise or to escape divine wrath. Indeed, the concept of a divine-human convenant was so central to the worship of the one god of Israel that Old Testament authors saw human history as the working out of this pact over time. More than anything else, what the covenant required was a commitment from people as moral beings.

The roles of women and men are different in God's covenant. Therefore, while there are divine expectations of individual as well as collective responsibility for behavior, in compliance with or rejection of the specific provisions of the covenant, the expectations of moral responsibility on the part of women and men are sometimes different. And as recorded in the Old Testament, the unfolding of God's covenant, or the human historical experience, has sometimes been quite different for each sex.

Abraham, Sarah, and Hagar As Moral Beings

What all of this meant for women is perhaps most explicitly conveyed by the nature of God's compact with Abraham, and it is therefore worth looking at this relationship in some detail. During the long period in which Yahweh promises title to the land of Canaan to him and his posterity in return for Abraham's fidelity and obedience, there is a good indication of what was understood as God's view of the appropriate roles for women in this divine covenant and an implicit value judgment about the moral capacities of women.

The transactions between God and Abraham—God's promises, Abraham's misgivings and his difficult moral decisions—all exclude Sarah. At God's instigation, Abraham leaves his family, takes his wife along with his other possessions, and travels to Canaan without any prior consultation with Sarah, beyond telling her that, wherever they go, she is to pose as his sister. (And of course she is his half-sister, the daughter of his father, as well as his wife.) While Sarah does not participate in the divine covenant, her beauty and Abraham's half-truth, the latter evidently endorsed by God, lay the basis for the patriarch's material prosperity (Gen. 12, 13:1–2) and for his final peaceful settlement in the land promised to him and his descendants by God.

First a famine drives them to Egypt. Because of her great beauty, Sarah is taken into the pharaoh's palace, "And for her sake, he dealt well with Abram: and he had sheep, oxen, he-asses, menservants, maidservants, she-asses, and camels" (Gen. 12:16). God afflicts the pharaoh and his household with plagues, presumably because Sarah has been included in the royal harem. The pharaoh rebukes Abraham for not having disclosed that Sarah was his wife, returns her to him, and orders him out of Egypt with all of his possessions. Abraham was by then vastly enriched by Sarah's sojourn in the pharaoh's harem: "Now Abram was very rich in cattle, in silver, and in gold" (Gen. 13:1–2).

When they reach Canaan, Abimelech, the king of Gerar, sends for the beautiful Sarah to make her one of his women. God appears to Abimelech in a dream, informs him that Abraham is a prophet and that Sarah is his wife, and threatens him and all his people with death if he does not return her to her husband. Abimelech confronts Abraham with the danger he had exposed him to, through no fault of his own, and Abraham replies: "Because I thought: Surely the fear of God is not in this place; and they will slay me for my wife's sake" (Gen. 20:11), and he explains that she is also his half-sister. Whereupon Abimelech restores Sarah to Abraham, provides him with restitution for her in the form of sheep, oxen, slaves, and silver, and gives him leave to live wherever he wants to in his land. In return, Abraham intercedes with God to restore the fertility of all the women of Gerar (Gen. 20).

Recent evidence from the Nuzi archives has uncovered the existence of a Hurrian practice of that time that enabled a man to buy, and legally adopt as his sister, an unrelated woman at the same time that he married her. Apparently wife-sisters then enjoyed extra privileges and protection not normally accorded to wives. Some scholars, in what may be an attempt to mitigate what seems to be the use of Sarah's beauty and sexuality as a means of enriching Abraham, saving his life, and fulfilling God's promise to him, have pointed out that the designation of Sarah as his sister, in line with that Hurrian institution, might have represented Abraham's attempt to elevate Sarah's status.

However, according to the biblical account, Sarah is not adopted by Abraham but is really his half-sister. This seems to provide her with no protection whatsoever from either the pharaoh or Abimelech. Indeed, she is released by those rulers not because they know she is Abraham's sister (which is why they took her into their harems in the first place), but because God tells them she is Abraham's wife.

Furthermore, when questioned by Abimelech about his reasons for concealing their marriage, Abraham himself says that he did it not in order to raise Sarah's status but in order to save his own life (Gen. 20:11). In other words, Sarah, who is not an active partner in the divine covenant, is used as a virtual pawn in the negotiations between God, Abraham, the pharaoh, and Abimelech. And it is her physical beauty and sexuality alone, not her relationship to God or her moral decision to enter into such a relationship, that results in the prosperity of Abraham and his peaceful settlement in Canaan, in fulfillment of the covenant.

In addition, circumcision of males became the divinely ordained sign of the covenant, the outward mark of conversion to monotheism. When first introduced by God, it was apparently considered so momentous that not only was it accompanied by the divine promise to Abraham that he would father "a multitude of nations," but also it occasioned the name-change of Abram to Abraham and Sarai to Sarah, further heightening the significance of the conversion (Gen. 17:9–15, 23–27). But though Sarah obviously shares in the divine promise, just as she does in the name-change, as the future mother of multitudes, she and all other women were forever barred from this sacred, commemorative ritual of circumcision solely on account of their sex, with no parallel rite permitted to them.[3]

The expulsion of Hagar and Ishmael after the birth of Isaac portrays Sarah in a most unsavory light (Gen. 16, 21:1–21). Because of her prior sterility, and in conformity with prevailing Near Eastern customs —and not to fulfill any part of the covenant with God—Sarah provides Abraham with a concubine, her Egyptian slave woman Hagar. She does this in order to guarantee *his* posterity, or she uses Hagar as she herself was used, in order to satisfy Abraham's needs and fulfill his destiny. While Abraham treats Ishmael like a loving father and has him circumcised, it is Sarah who treats both Hagar and Ishmael abominably.

Sarah is shown as motivated not by any moral concerns but rather only by material considerations when she refuses to let Ishmael share the inheritance with her own son Isaac. It is important to note that God tells only Abraham, not Sarah, that Ishmael will father a whole nation, "because he is your offspring," and "through Isaac shall your descendants be named" (Gen. 21:12–13). And throughout, the fine hand of a patriarchal god may be detected.

Sarah's sterility was, of course, her greatest shame, since the role of women as childbearers, especially son-bearers, was overwhelmingly important. The impregnation of Sarah when she was ninety serves the divine purpose admirably, since it demonstrates the tremendous power of God. The siding of God with Sarah in her dispute with Hagar, which terminates with the casting out of Hagar and Ishmael into the desert (or granting them their "freedom"), does not confront Sarah with any moral dilemma or compel her to accept the consequences of her moral or immoral behavior, but instead merely pits woman against woman as reproducer.

Furthermore, despite the divine pledge that Ishmael would father another great nation, God's attitude toward Hagar is rather curious in the context of his continuing concern for the just and humane treatment of slaves, the poor, the widowed, the orphaned, and the alien. While Ishmael's future is assured, even with God's intervention it could not have been easy for Hagar alone in the desert with an infant. But what happened to her apparently was considered so inconsequential, all that is recorded is that Ishmael grows up in the wilderness under God's protection, and that Hagar selects a wife for him (Gen. 14–21).

Indeed, in this section of the covenant narrative, it is as though the most significant thing about free and slave women alike in their relationship with God was their ability or inability to bear children, or as though their most important role in observing the provisions of the covenant was reproductive. But even in this role they were not honored as coprogenitors with Abraham but were seen as only instrumental, since it is the offspring of *Abraham* who were destined to fulfill the divine promise.

This subsidiary function of women in the covenant is underscored in the most dramatic test of Abraham's faith in God, namely the latter's command that the patriarch sacrifice his only son, Isaac (actually his second son, after the machinations of Sarah and God had effectively disposed of the first). There seems to be no doubt whatsoever that it was a human sacrifice that was required. By the second millennium, while animal sacrifice was usually regarded as a satisfactory substitute, human sacrifice was still resorted to in extraordinary circumstances in Canaan and elsewhere. Moreover, the prophetic preachings against human sacrifice would seem to indicate that in Israel this practice was not wholly eliminated from popular attitudes toward the range of acceptable behavior until the time of the Babylonian exile (Lev. 18:21, 27; Deut. 12:31, 18:9; Jer. 7:31; Mic. 6:7).

What is so striking here is the biblical treatment of Sarah as the other parent of Isaac, and its possible larger significance as symbolic of the role of women in God's covenant with Israel. Sarah waited ninety years to become a mother. And God clearly recognized the importance of that role, since he made it possible for her at such a late age, used it as a vehicle for the display of his power, and supported Sarah in the expulsion of the other mother and child in furtherance of his own aims for Israel through her son.

Yet, though the test of Abraham's faith in God hinges on his resolution of the conflict between the divine order that he sacrifice Isaac and his paternal love, Sarah is not likewise required to make such a moral choice as a sign of her faith in God, nor is she even made aware of the necessity for such a choice. At no point are Sarah's maternal feelings or her opinion about the impending sacrifice of her son taken into consideration. By not being consulted and not participating in the decision to sacrifice Isaac she becomes, in effect, only marginal to the covenant between God and Abraham, except that her body bore Isaac.

While women, like men, are bound to obey God's commands and therefore must have been judged as capable of making moral choices, nowhere in this crucial divine-human covenant are there provisions that indicate the capacities of women as moral beings. The supreme act of faith in God, enacted in the near-sacrifice of Isaac, cements the covenant between God and Israel in a scenario in which all the main actors are male, and women, whether slave or free, occupy a peripheral place. Except as beautiful sex-object, wife, concubine, or mother—all roles established by their relationship to men, not God—women *have* no part in the covenant (Gen. 12, 13, 15, 18:1–15, 21:1–21, 22:1– 19).

Women and Men As Morally Accountable to God

It should go without saying that there are many images of women, sometimes conflicting ones, in different parts of the Old Testament, depending on the time of the final redaction, the type of literature, and the prevalent social and political conditions. But in this God-centered document, which has at its heart the transmission of Yahweh's moral laws to the human community, including women, and the conveyance of the divine promise, or covenant, contingent on the faithful obser- vance of these laws by individuals and the social group, again certainly including women, seminal distinctions of a moral nature are made on the basis of sex.

In a religion that stresses moral accountability to God above all, women, even as they are surely included in the community of believers, are not infrequently portrayed as either less morally responsible than men in their relationship to God, or are shown as moral agents only by virtue of their primary relationship to men. In short, women as moral persons are regarded with profound ambivalence.

For example, if a man makes a vow to God, he is bound by it. If a woman makes a vow to God, it is binding on her only if her father or husband hears it and says nothing, or tacitly approves. But if a woman makes a vow to God, and her father or husband says he disap- proves, she is not bound by that vow, and the Lord will forgive her (Num. 30:2–8). Since fathers and husbands do not need *any* woman's concurrence in their vows to God, the moral double standard in this instance is glaring, and, indeed, the prophets and patriarchs relate to God as individuals, outside of any family affiliations. Their primary moral affiliations are quite properly to God, not to mothers, wives, sisters, or daughters.

The vows to God of a widow or a divorced woman would stand as though made by a morally responsible person, but only if these vows were made outside of her husband's house, or only if he concurred with silence and did not immediately void them before his death or their divorce (Num. 30:9–14). Even if the husband negated his wife's vows after some time had elapsed, and therefore they remained intact, it is not the woman who would suffer, but her husband would "bear her iniquity" (Num. 30:15), as though she were far less morally accountable to God than was her husband.

In addition, it must be remembered that both widows and divorced women had a precarious existence in the family-based social structure of ancient Israel. If the divorced woman remained perpetually unattached, she was likely to be regarded as something of a pariah and was certainly deprived of the legal status that had accrued to her through her husband. The widow was part of the group repeatedly selected by God as especially deserving of compassion.

While these conditions probably faithfully reflect the attitudes toward women of ancient Israel in those times, namely that they were the property of their fathers and husbands, or that the father or husband "epitomized" or represented all the members of the family in many of its dealings with the outside community,[4] there is still another dimension to these divine commands.

God was seen not only as the deity of Israel but also as a universal deity. In this latter aspect, vows made to him involved a commitment to the laws of this single god rather than to the many divinities in Israel's environment, under threat of divine punishment, and obedience to God's universal laws was required of all people, Hebrews and non-Hebrews alike. Therefore, though written from the viewpoint of ancient Hebrew society and its attitudes toward women and men, these divine commandments regarding the moral propensities of the former mark women off as a sex, standing in a different and more peripheral moral relationship to God than men in all societies, at least in those times.

Illustrative of the other face of this deep ambivalence toward women as fully moral persons, both men and women were offered the option of dedicating their lives to God as Nazirites, or consecrating themselves to an austere mode of life for a period of anywhere from thirty days to two years. This special vow to God, often taken by persons of either sex for purely personal reasons, such as gratitude for the birth of a child or recovery from illness,[5] was one of the few which, for women, did not necessitate any endorsement by fathers or husbands (Num. 6:1–21).

However, the most well-known Nazirites are, of course, Samuel and Samson, and it would be difficult to find female counterparts of equal stature. Furthermore, Samuel is dedicated to God not because of the special purity of either of his parents, but because of God's response to the tragedy and shame of his mother's inability to bear children until his birth (1 Sam. 1:1–22). And when Samson's hitherto barren mother is told by an angel of the Lord that she will bear a son who will be a Nazirite, she is warned by him not to drink wine or eat anything unclean (Judg. 13:2–7, 13–14)—two of the outward signs of those who consecrated themselves to God—not for her own sake, for she makes no vow, but to protect the purity of her future off-spring.

The differentiation between women and men in terms of the ca-pacity of each sex for making moral decisions is reinforced in another part of the Pentateuch that lists all of the sexual relationships prohib-ited by God. With the exception of forbidding women to have inter-course with animals (recalling the Cretan Queen Pasiphaë and the Sacred Bull of Poseidon), these prohibitions are directed almost exclu-sively toward men. They are not to lie with their mothers, sisters, daughters, aunts, daughters-in-law, etc. Even the prohibition of homo-sexuality is addressed only to men, as though it would not be a possible choice for women (Lev. 18:6–23).

But underlying all these sexual bans, again applicable almost solely to men, is the assumption that only the latter have a developed enough sense of right and wrong to choose to obey them, particularly since disobedience is described in no uncertain terms as "abomina-tion" and "defilement." Indeed, the phrase "defilement of the land," which God warns will follow disobedience, refers to moral offenses rather than ceremonial transgressions.[6] The language of the whole passage, in which Israelite and non-Israelite alike are warned away from the sexual practices of Egypt and Canaan, is couched in terms of universal moral laws (Lev. 18:1–5). And the punishment for what was seen as immoral sexual behavior is clear and awful since such be-havior is described as a transgression against God's laws (Lev. 18: 24–30).

However, while the injunctions against sexual misbehavior or, more properly, disobedience, are directed mainly to men, as those more capable of making a moral judgment, the punishments for violat-ing these sexual taboos are to be suffered by both women and men. This is yet another expression of the ambivalence toward women as moral beings. Yahweh simultaneously warns mostly men against com-mitting these transgressions but includes women equally with men as part of the moral community, or as recipients of divine punishment for moral sins. Death, burning, childlessness, iniquity, and being cut off from the rest of the tribe, all penalties for different types of sexual transgressions, are to be shared by persons of both sexes. And this is so even though the decision to transgress in these cases is apparently made primarily by men, since they are the ones warned against trans-gression in the first place (Lev. 20:10–21).

The Woman and Man As Moral Beings in the Creation Myth

Again, while a fuller analysis of the implications of the creation story must be reserved, some of the narrative bears directly on the question of whether women were seen to be as fully accountable as men for their moral behavior. It is noteworthy that after the fruit is eaten, God is portrayed as dealing differently with the serpent and the man than with the woman. He directly links his punishment of the serpent and Adam with their disobedience to his command, or to their moral transgression. His first words to the serpent are: "Because you have done this" (Gen. 3:14). His first words to Adam are:

> "Because you have listened to the voice of your wife,
> and have eaten of the tree
> of which I commanded you,
> 'You shall not eat of it.' " (Gen. 3:17)

When he speaks to the woman, he does not directly link her punishment to her moral transgression. He says only:

> "I will greatly multiply your pain in childbearing;
> in pain you shall bring forth children,
> yet your desire shall be for your husband,
> and he shall rule over you." (Gen. 3:16)

Once more, it is as though both the serpent and the man are thought of by God as more capable of making moral choices, or more morally responsible, than the woman.

The expulsion of people from paradise for their sin introduces the general notion of human responsibility for their behavior. Though the woman is the first to eat the forbidden fruit, there is an interesting difference between the divine punishment of the woman and the man. It is apparently assumed that the only roles possible for the woman are those of mother and wife, because nothing else is mentioned, and she is cursed in those roles. But the man's curse is not restricted to his roles as husband and father. God's punishment of Adam is longer, and involves a much more complex relationship between him, his work, the land, and his death (Gen. 3:17–19).

Also, when God summarizes the moral offense of the man and woman and expels them from Eden, the wording is curious:

> "Behold, the man has become like one of us, knowing good and evil; and
> now, lest he put forth his hand and take also of the tree of life, and eat,

and live for ever"—therefore the Lord God sent him forth from the garden of Eden, to till the ground from which he was taken. He drove out the man. (Gen. 3:22–24)

God's references here are singular and addressed only to "the man." Eve's sin and punishment are simply not part of the picture. It is as if they are considered so much less important than Adam's that they are not even worthy of mention—as if the moral identity of Eve is already incorporated into that of her husband.

Divine Ambivalence toward Women As Moral Beings: the Exodus

The different responses of God to the same moral offense, depending on the sex of the offenders, are to be found in other parts of the Old Testament. But in at least one instance, God's sex-related behavior is strikingly illustrative of the ambivalence with which women as a sex came to be regarded. Its significance is further heightened by its occurrence in one of the narratives central to the establishment of Israel as a people, confirmed in a special relationship to the divine.

The Hebrews' exodus from Egypt and their long journey to the land of promise constitute some of the more spectacular episodes in the long history of their interaction with Yahweh. Indeed, their deliverance from slavery by God was climaxed by their fusion into a people under a holy compact. As has been pointed out elsewhere,[7] a variety of women were involved as active and autonomous agents of that process of liberation, from the Hebrew midwives who refused to obey the pharaoh's orders to kill all the Hebrew male children because they "feared God" (Exod. 1:17, 21), to the women, both Hebrew and Egyptian, who disobeyed the pharaoh when they saved Moses and nurtured him to adulthood (Exod. 2:1--10), to Miriam, who is mentioned in the prophetic literature, along with Moses and Aaron, as one of the leaders of the exodus (Mic. 6:4).

Against this backdrop of strong and effective involvement by women in the struggle to free the Hebrews, there is a straightforward account of the dispensation of divine justice and compassion on the basis of sex alone, or the negative face of the ambivalence toward women. During the wanderings of the Hebrews, both Miriam and Aaron, on an equal footing, challenge the exclusive status of Moses as the only prophet of God and claim prophetic status for themselves as well (Num. 13:1–2). God is furious with both of them for questioning his decision to speak with Moses alone "mouth to mouth," but afflicts only Miriam with leprosy (Num. 13:6–10). After Moses intercedes on her behalf, God consents to exile her "in shame" for a week, like a rebellious daughter, and then permits her to rejoin the tribe and continue with them on their journey (Num. 13:14–16).

What can be made of this episode in which the apparent coleaders, Miriam and Aaron, both provoke God's anger, but the woman is punished and the man goes unpunished for the same act? Later rabbinical commentators theorized that Miriam sexually enticed Aaron to defy God, but there is nothing in the context of the chapter to suggest this, nor is there any difference indicated in their relationship with Moses beyond the fact that Miriam was female and Aaron was male.

Indeed, if one were to assume that God knew that Aaron and his sons were to become the priests of Israel, Aaron's transgression might have been the greater. In the early chapters of Leviticus, which list the several kinds of mandatory sin-offerings required of different groups in the population, God declares that if an anointed priest committed a sin he would bring guilt not only on himself but on all the people (Lev. 4:3).

Gender, the Advent of Monotheism, and Ethical Progress

Many have claimed that the development of monotheism denoted great ethical progress over earlier polytheistic religions because it introduced a belief in the existence of universal moral laws, and because it set a standard of righteousness for human behavior, since it was the outstanding quality of God. For example, the great biblical scholar William F. Albright maintained:

> In essentials, however, orthodox Yahwism remained the same from Moses to Ezra. From first to last ethical monotheism remained the heart of Israelite religion, though there were many crises through which it had to pass during the slow change from the primitive simplicity of the Judges to the high cultural level of the fifth century B.C.[8]

On this same theme, Sabatino Moscati wrote:

> In any case, apart from the question of the time at which it was fully manifested, ethical monotheism is the dominant feature of the religion of Israel. . . . it is a distinctive quality of Israel that it insisted on righteousness as the deity's supreme and constant characteristic.[9]

And some years later, Albright wrote:

One of the most remarkable features of Mosaic legislation—always using the term in its widest sense, of laws approved or introduced by Moses and developed in later Israel—is its humanity to man. It is the most humanitarian of all known bodies of laws before recent times.[10]

The use of terms like "ethical monotheism," "righteousness," and "humanitarian" by Albright, Moscati, and others suggests a moral universality at the center of Israelite monotheism that bears looking at as it applied to women and men.

Lot and his Daughters

For instance, as a universal deity, God destroys the pagan cities of Sodom and Gomorrah because of their wickedness, but it is interesting to note that he does not fault them for practicing idolatry or neglecting to worship him. Not much is said in Genesis about the nature of their sin except that God has heard the "outcry" of the suffering in those cities. Ezekiel describes the sins of Sodom and Gomorrah in some greater detail: "Behold, this was the iniquity of thy sister Sodom: Pride, abundance of food, and prosperous security were hers and her daughters'; but the hand of the poor and the needy did she not strengthen" (Ezek. 16:49). There is the assumption here that Sodom violated some universal moral laws laid down by God, just as people of Noah's time did, and that God's retribution may be dealt to *any* people who defile themselves or commit abominations in a *moral,* rather than purely ritual, way.

In light of this universal God's concern with morality, it must be noted that when Lot extends his hospitality to the two angels of the Lord who come to Sodom (an ancient and honored custom among nomadic peoples), and all the men of Sodom surround Lot's house and press him to bring his guests out so they might "know" them carnally, Lot offers the mob his two virgin daughters instead. He says: "I pray you, my brethren, do not so wickedly. Behold now, I have two daughters that have not known man; let me, I pray you, bring them out unto you, and do ye to them as is good in your eyes; only unto these men do nothing; forasmuch as they are come under the shadow of my roof" (Gen. 19:7–8).

The two visitors are identified as angels at the beginning of the chapter, *but not to Lot.* He addresses them as "My lords" (Gen. 19:2), and refers to them only as "these men . . . (who) are come under the shadow of my roof." Evidently, in the hierarchy of moral values in those days, even universal moral values decreed by God, protecting male strangers in one's tent ranked above protecting one's own daughters. Lot does not even refer to the possible gang-rape of his daughters as "wicked." (The later rabbinical contention that Sodom was full of male homosexuals, that it was their *real* wickedness, and that Lot therefore knew his daughters would be safe, seems to be at the least interpretive and at the worst an apologia; otherwise, the intervention of the angels to save Lot's daughters seems inexplicable.) While the compassion of God is extended to "the poor and the needy," it is not extended to the same degree to Lot's daughters. Their father is not punished for violating any divine moral law by offering them to the mob of men, nor was that act apparently sufficient to cause an "outcry." On the contrary, along with his family he is saved from the general destruction of Sodom, "the Lord being merciful to him" (Gen. 19:16). And it is only his wife who is punished and turned into a pillar of salt for disobeying the angels' command not to look back.

What is even more curious is that biblical scholars today can write about the destruction of these wicked cities as illustrative of God's compassion and concern that all people obey universal moral laws without even noticing that (a) these moral laws *cannot* be universal, even in patriarchal times, if half the human race is somehow removed from their protection, or (b) if no "outcry" reached God about Lot's offer to have his daughters raped instead of his male guests, it may well have expressed social attitudes toward women and men at the time of the final redaction of Genesis but can hardly be recognized as a universal *moral* law.

In an otherwise fine book, for example, Nahum Sarna writes about this episode: "The 'outcry' of Sodom, then, implies, above all, heinous moral and social corruption, an arrogant disregard of elementary human rights, a cynical insensitivity to the sufferings of others."[11] Does the offering up of daughters for gang-rape in order to protect male strangers under one's roof not constitute "heinous moral and social corruption, an arrogant disregard of elementary human rights, a cynical insensitivity to the sufferings of others"? More plainly, do women not have "elementary human rights" or the capacity to suffer? Does the rape of a woman represent less "heinous moral corruption" or violation of "elementary human rights" than the rape of a man?

That Sarna is not confining himself to the social mores of that early period is fairly clear when he continues, further down:

> The sins are entirely on the moral plane, . . . the Sodom and Gomorrah narrative is predicated upon the existence of a moral law of universal application for the infraction of which God holds all men answerable. *The idea that there is an intimate, in fact, inextricable, connection between the socio-moral condition of a people and its ultimate fate is one of the main pillars upon which stands the entire biblical interpretation of history.* (Sarna's italics.)[12]

And a bit further along, Sarna elaborates on what this passage reveals about the monotheistic conception of God:

> The universality of God is presumed throughout the story. . . . He is "the Judge of all the earth" (18:25). . . . God is assumed to be the architect of a societal pattern which is universal in scope. . . .
>
> *Above all, the Bible is concerned with the problem of divine justice.* Just because God is universal and omnipotent mankind needs assurance that His mighty power is not indiscriminately employed and that His ways are not capricious. *God must act according to a principle* that man can try to understand, and that principle is *the passion for righteousness.* (Italics mine.)[13]

One can only conclude either that God does behave capriciously in respect to women, or that his passion for righteousness does not extend to women as fully as to men, or that he dispenses divine justice using a double standard based on sex, in which women receive far less justice than men. And what all of this has to do with "a moral law of universal application" (except that it includes pagans as well as nonpagans under its jurisdiction) is very elusive when one thinks of women and men. That this last is sometimes simply not a concern of scholarship—and, until recently, most scholars have not considered women as important a subject for study as men—may be seen in Sarna's discussion of the covenant between God and Abraham, which in its exclusion of any consideration of the roles of Sarah and Hagar might lead to the conclusion that Isaac was the product of a virgin birth by his father.[14]

The Levite and his Concubine

The same double standard of divine justice and compassion based on sex may be found in the last few chapters of the book of Judges. At the outset, it should be noted that later rabbinical commentators have pointed out that it was written early and represented a period in Israel's development when there was much confusion and reversion to pagan practices, and when great charismatic leaders or judges were required to bring some semblance of order to the people. But if the tribes of Israel were confused, presumably God was not. And though the action is described through the eyes of those earlier times, its inclusion in the final canon says something about its meaning to men of a later period. Since the aid of God is solicited and obtained in this passage, it becomes one of a number of sex-linked moral components in the divine-human relationship.

The story has to do with a Levite whose concubine leaves him and returns to her father's house. When he comes to reclaim her, the woman's father greets him joyfully and entertains him royally. After several days, the Levite and his concubine (silent, with neither of the men consulting her feelings) leave for his home, and they spend the night in Gibeah, among the Benjaminites.

The latter refuse to extend the hospitality of their homes to the travellers, which immediately indicates that something is amiss. But an old man from the Levite's part of the country, who just happens to be in Gibeah at that time, takes them in for the night. And just as the men of Sodom wanted to "know" Lot's guests, so the men of Gibeah come to the old man's house and demand that he yield up the Levite (Judg. 19:22). (Incidentally, for its bearing on what happens next, later commentary does not identify the Benjaminites as homosexual.) The old man replies:

> No, my brethren, I pray you, act not wickedly; since this man is once come into my house, do not this scandalous thing.
>
> Behold, here is my daughter a virgin, and his concubine; let me bring them out now, and humble ye them, and do to them what seemeth good in your eyes; but unto this man do not this scandalous thing.
>
> But the men would not hearken to him; so the man took hold of his concubine, and brought her forth unto them into the street; and they knew her, and ill-used her all the night until the morning; and they let her go when the day began to dawn. (Judg. 19:23–25)

The concubine lies on the doorstep, gang-raped to death. The Levite returns home with her body, cuts it into twelve pieces, and sends them to the tribes of Israel. Outraged, they decide to punish the guilty men, but when the city refuses to produce them and chooses instead to fight the other tribes, the latter, with divine approval, battle the Benjaminites. And as they are to be defeated, these men who committed and then condoned rape and murder are described as "men of valor" (Judg. 20:44–46).

The victors swear an oath not to give their daughters in marriage to the Benjaminites but lament the loss of one of the tribes of Israel (Judg. 21:3) and express compassion for the *men* of that tribe since so many of their wives died in the carnage (Judg. 21:6–7). So the men of the other tribes attack Jabeshgilead and kill every woman, man, and child in it, except for four hundred virgins, whom they turn over to the "valorous" rapists and murderers for wives. But even that number does not suffice, and in their concern that the tribe of Benjamin not die out, in their *compassion* for the Benjaminites, the tribes of Israel propose a plan whereby the men of Gibeah can abduct the daughters of Shiloh and take them as wives when they go out dancing in the fields (Judg. 21:15–24).

On one level, this narrates the social attitudes and practices of the Hebrews at the time when the book of Judges was written and finally redacted, and it may be understood as expressing the views toward women of male authors living in a male-dominant age that clearly considered women as lesser human beings than men. However, this male complicity in the use of women is rather difficult to fit under the shelter of God's righteousness, compassion, justice, and ethical concern, which seem, in this episode, to extend almost exclusively to the male Benjaminites, in fulfillment of the divine plan for Israel. The protection of male guests and the perpetuation of Israel certainly take precedence over the protection or even lives of women. The fathers and brothers of the virgins of Shiloh are absolved from guilt for permitting their capture by the Benjaminites. And though the book concludes with: "In those days there was no king in Israel: every man did what was right in his own eyes" (Judg. 21:25), it is clear that God's advice was sought and followed, and that he was implicated in the bloody confrontation: "And the Lord defeated Benjamin before Israel" (Judg. 20:35).

Furthermore, the battles and the scarcity of wives for the Benjaminites were precipitated by what was represented as an outrageous and immoral act, which in itself presumes that some standard of moral behavior was consensually held by most of the tribes. But it would seem that the moral outrage was not the gang-rape and murder of the concubine, or the offer of her to the Benjaminites, but the destruction of the female property of the Levite. Compassion is extended by Israel, acting under God's surveillance, to the male Benjaminites and not to the raped and dead concubine, the virgins of Jabeshgilead, or the daughters of Shiloh (Judg. 21:2–3, 14–16, 20–21).

While it is meaningless to transpose our current sense of morality back to those times, it is likewise meaningless for people in our own times to use general terms like "ethical monotheism," "justice," "righteousness," or "compassion" when discussing the concept of divinity in biblical literature. One must ask, "just, righteous, compassionate and ethical toward *whom*?"

As compared with polytheism, then, one aspect of the monotheistic conception of divinity was the elevation of gender to a more important role in establishing the nature of God's relationship with the human community in a manner quite alien to the polytheistic mentality. It seems as if the working out of the covenant in human history might have represented a moral advance or had ethical significance for the men of biblical times, but this progress was apparently less applicable to women. God sometimes was portrayed by biblical authors, themselves products of their own cultures, as dispensing a double standard of justice, righteousness, and compassion for women and men, with the former receiving a lesser share than the latter. If divine justice and compassion at times operated differently for women than for men, it might have been the result of the exclusion of women from full participation in the covenant with God, except in their sexual and reproductive capacities. Therefore, they were subsequently excluded from his full protection of every aspect of their personhood, or men were seen as standing in a closer moral relation to God than women.

But it cannot be emphasized enough that while all the above might be true, perhaps the most accurate description of monotheistic attitudes toward women is that they were profoundly ambivalent. For even as women were shown as somehow less capable of moral judgment than men, they were at the same time included as part of the community of believers, sometimes as coleaders with men, as in the case of Miriam. Likewise, though women's relation to God was sometimes shown as more indirect or peripheral than that enjoyed by men, they simultaneously suffered divine punishment for moral transgressions, or were subject to the same universal divine laws as men. Hence, while viewed to some extent as more marginal in an ethical sense, women, like men, were also seen as sharing a sense of right and wrong, or morality. And this fundamental ambivalence toward women also distinguished monotheism from polytheism.

If the Bible is compared with polytheistic writings, it may be that the former placed a greater emphasis on individuals bearing responsibility before God for their actions in a more substantive sense than required, say, by the Egyptian liturgical Negative Confession of sins; or that people in the Bible were assured that there were alternative courses of action open to them, some of which were more favorable in God's eyes because they represented moral behavior rather than mere propitiation of the divine; or that God compelled people to take into account and deal justly and mercifully with the special needs of disadvantaged groups like the poor, the orphaned and the enslaved. Thus the claims for the universal and ethical quality of biblical monotheism seem to be substantiated. If God is seen as just, righteous, and compassionate, then adherence to his commandments might produce a belief in the value of justice, righteousness, and compassion, or what we call a moral sense, among his worshipers.

But it must also be seen that women were not then considered disadvantaged because of their status or treatment. The justice and mercy that God commanded the community to show in meeting the special needs of the disadvantaged were not likewise extended to women, unless they were also poor, orphaned, or slaves. Correspondingly, adherence to divine commandments would not necessarily produce a belief in the value of justice, righteousness, and compassion, or "a moral sense," with respect to women. Thus the universal, ethical quality of monotheism is somewhat diminished.

However, the meanings of words change over time, naturally reflecting the attitudes and realities of the cultures that use them. Justice, righteousness, compassion, sin, transgression, even morality itself, may be understood today as encompassing social aspirations, ideologies, or realities that were, of course, inconceivable in, say, 500 B.C.E. And it may well be that if monotheism indeed represented a moral advance over polytheism, that advance had far less to do with the ethical qualities of the former, or with its view of women and men as moral equals, than with the fact that in place of the specific attributes with which goddesses and gods were endowed, the single deity was endowed with attributes broad enough to sustain the assignment of different meanings to them as social standards of morality changed over time, so that those general attributes might have meaning for people of all times.

The Positive Face of Ambivalence: Wisdom As Feminine

The positive side of this basic ambivalence toward femaleness may be found in the description of a strong feminine involvement and even collaboration with God, which enabled worshipers to understand and obey divine laws and thus fulfill their obligations under the covenant. In the book of Proverbs Solomon, king of Israel, offers moral instruction, much of it dealing with the importance of following wise teachings and avoiding the snares of sin and evil behavior. Wisdom, as both a personification and as a matter of grammatical form, is always feminine.

While the knowledge of divine commands was seen as the first step in the sure path to righteousness, it is wisdom that leads to knowledge (Prov. 1:2–7). She establishes herself as the source of all the secular authority of kings and those who rule with justice (Prov. 8:15–16). Further, she describes herself as having existed from the very beginning of creation (Prov. 8:22–31):

> "The Lord created me at the beginning of his work,
>   the first of his acts of old.
> Ages ago I was set up,
>   at the first, before the beginning of the earth." (Prov. 8:22–23)

And she pronounces the most extreme rewards and penalties for those who do and do not follow her teachings:

> "For he who finds me finds life
>   and obtains favor from the Lord;
> but he who misses me injures himself;
>   all who hate me love death." (Prov. 8:35–36)

In the Apocrypha/Deuterocanonical Books, The Wisdom of Solomon describes how that king, renowned for his own wisdom, prayed to God for the acquisition of her treasures. Addressing himself to other secular rulers about the importance of gaining Wisdom, he describes her as "radiant and unfading" (Apocrypha, Wisd. of Sol. 6:12), accessible to all who desire her (6:13–22), and the means of attaining immortality, closeness to God, and earthly power (6:26–30).

Solomon then proceeds to enumerate in greater detail both the attributes of Wisdom and her very special relationship to God. He describes her as possessing superlative qualities (Wisd. of Sol. 7:23–24, 29), and as "the fashioner of all things" (7:22); "a breath of the power of God, and a pure emanation of the glory of the Almighty" (7:25); "a reflection of eternal light, a spotless mirror of the working of God, and an image of his goodness" (7:26); and she is shown as tremendously powerful: "but against wisdom evil does not prevail. She reaches mightily from one end of the earth to the other, and she orders all things well" (7:30, 8:1).

Speaking directly to God, he amplifies on the relation of Wisdom to the divine and her advantage to humanity (9:9–12). Finally, Solomon places Wisdom at the very center of human history, right at the side of Adam, Cain, Noah, Abraham, Lot, Jacob, and Joseph. She is depicted in the forefront of Israel's deliverance from bondage, and participates in the exodus from Egypt to the Promised Land, when she enters the soul of Moses (10).

It may be argued with considerable justification that Wisdom as an abstraction and female personification has little to do with women, and of course that is so, except that goddesses too were personifications. To the extent that their presence along with male divinities seems to have been reflected in the widespread involvement of persons of both sexes in cult and rite, it may be no accident that Wisdom is not portrayed in the Pentateuch, and that her attributes and power are described most extensively in the Apocrypha. Further, it may be contended that she lacks autonomy, that, like everything else, her source and creator is God, and that she is, after all, shown only as his first enterprise even while she is his constant and glorious ally.

Actually, there is some ambiguity in the characterization of Wisdom. For example, at one point in the Apocrypha, she is described as having been present when "thou didst make the world" (Wisd. of Sol. 9:9). However, in most of her portrayals and self-portrayals, she is described as his first creation, derivative or reflective of God, and his supreme agent. She is not independently active in the story of creation (Gen. 1:1–3). Indeed, the divine commands transmitted by Moses or the prophets come from God, not Wisdom.

Nevertheless, she also displays an omnipresence that recalls the characterization of the Egyptian goddess Maat. Wisdom is not only presented as providing the knowledge necessary for righteousness but also becomes in these passages the very underpinning of earthly power, justice, and order, a prime shaper of the history of Israel, and she exists with God virtually from the beginning of time.

The Negative Face of Ambivalence:
Isaiah and Ezekiel

By way of contrast with the positive attitudes toward femaleness in the Old Testament picture of Wisdom as feminine, equally strong negative attitudes may be found in parts of the prophetic literature. These instances of the denigration of femaleness, not of individually "good" or "bad" women, are deepened by the genuine importance accorded to Wisdom in her close alliance with God, and by the association by some of the prophets of negative attitudes toward femininity with the worst of all sins, idolatry.

The degree to which biblical conceptions of the divine were different from the beliefs in many goddesses and gods prevalent in surrounding cultures, and the difficulty of impressing some of these radically new conceptions of divinity on the popular consciousness within their own culture and elsewhere, may be inferred from the many passages in the prophetic literature that plead and reason with, warn and threaten, those who adhered to the older polytheistic beliefs and cultic practices. The process of religious conversion apparently was of long duration, and evidently was marked by much inertia and resistance in popular beliefs and customs.

Indeed, one way of looking at the writings of the prophets is that the intensity of their messages, their claims to direct communication with God, and their self-proclaimed function as conduits of divine commands, warnings, and threats all might have derived from their assumption of the role of representatives of the official religion of Yahweh as it tried to stem the tide of popular religious inclinations and practices. Much of the Old Testament attests to the magnitude of the struggle in which, time and again, and seemingly for the longest part of their history, the ancient Israelites questioned, defied, and disobeyed divine laws and were repeatedly admonished and threatened by the prophets with divine punishment as Yahweh tried to win the exclusive allegiance of his people.

The straying of the community from the injunctions of God may be seen, therefore, as the effects of the persistent attractiveness of polytheistic practices in their surroundings to the people of Israel, or as part of their popular religion. While the schism between popular and official religion was by no means always clear-cut and broad, it was a sign of the real conflict between the beliefs and teachings of the prophets and the outlook and customs of the people. And this conflict, too, set monotheism apart from polytheism, for in the latter there most frequently seems to have been a fairly easy, more tolerant, even pluralistic coexistence of official and popular religion.

However, though the whole community sins against Yahweh, the language and imagery used by some of the Old Testament writers in identifying the abominations of polytheism and the sins of Israel when *she* breaks her covenant with God are often simultaneously feminine and pejorative. Moreover, there are passages in the prophetic books that exhibit such a close corollation of sin with the outward symbols of femininity or female sexuality that they can only be described as misogynistic.

Idolatry and Female Sexuality: The Prophetic Metaphor

For instance, the prophet Isaiah describes a time when Judah and Jerusalem are as sinful as Sodom, when confusion reigns and everything is topsy-turvy, when the elders and princes of Israel oppress the poor, and when "children are their oppressors, and women rule over them" (Isa. 3:2). And then, in an outburst of hatred for women, who become at once the symbols and scapegoats of Israel's sins, Isaiah relays the words of God, in which the idolatry of the Hebrews is represented by the "proud daughters of Zion," whose sexuality and nonspiritual concerns are displayed in their clothing, rings, bracelets, earrings, and mincing gait. Conversely, the return of Israel to righteousness is symbolized by the daughters of Zion being stripped of their finery and ornaments, or a time "when the Lord shall have washed away the filth of the daughters of Zion" (Isa. 3:16–26, 4:1–4).

If Isaiah links the straying of Israel from God and its general moral decay with the alluring dress of women, and the purification of Israel from sin with the washing away of the moral "filth" of the proud daughters of Zion, the prophet Ezekiel portrays the persistent attachment of the people of Israel to other religions in imagery that turns on female sexuality, female lewdness, and female prostitution. First, he writes in very sensual terms about the love of God for Israel, described as feminine, and the transaction of the covenant (Ezek. 16:1–14). Then God accuses Israel of playing the whore with every casual passer-by at his sanctuaries ("high places"), relying on her beauty, and indulging in harlotry with male images fashioned of the gold and silver ornaments God lavished on her in his love.

God threatens her with terrible violence from her former lovers, and while Israel is grammatically designated as feminine, Ezekiel shows God addressing her as if she were human. For example, Ezekiel has God say:

> "therefore, behold, I will gather all your lovers, with whom you took pleasure and I will judge you as women who break wedlock and shed blood are judged, and bring upon you the blood of wrath and jealousy. . . . they shall strip you of your clothes and take your fair jewels, and leave you naked and bare. They shall bring up a host against you, and they shall stone you and cut you to pieces with their swords." (Ezek. 16:37–40)

Interestingly, this violent retribution is to be witnessed by real women: "they shall burn your houses and execute judgments upon you in the sight of many women" (Ezek. 16:41). And all of Israel's sins are pictured in totally feminine imagery. God says of her, using human relationships and especially female relationships to describe her abominations:

> "Have you not committed lewdness in addition to all your abominations? Behold, every one who uses proverbs will use this proverb about you, 'Like mother, like daughter.' You are the daughter of your mother, who loathed her husband and her children; and you are the sister of your sisters, who loathed their husbands and their children. Your mother was a Hittite and your father an Amorite. And your elder sister is Samar'ia, who lived with her daughters to the north of you; and your younger sister, who lived to the south of you, is Sodom with her daughters. Yet you were not content to walk in their ways, or do according to their abominations; within a very little time you were more corrupt than they in all your ways. As I live, says the Lord God, your sister Sodom and her daughters have not done as you and your daughters have done." (Ezek. 16:43–49)

In a later passage, Ezekiel again laments the departure of Israel from God's laws and again employs feminine imagery, in which the sinning people are symbolized as both sexual women and prostitutes, perhaps in this case not an accidental association. The level of physical aggression that he foresees as inevitable divine retribution against women who flaunt their sexuality and consort with men of other religions and other cultures—and here female sexuality seems almost equated with harlotry—and, by extension, against the people who sin and indulge in idolatry, reveals a great deal about the intensity of Ezekiel's attitudes toward both sinning Israel and sexual females.

In a succession of images that fuse blasphemy, idolatry, female sexuality, and female wantonness, and that detail the consequences of these moral transgressions in God's awful punishment of sinning Israel as sinning female, Ezekiel closes this long passage with a warning to *real women*, and exhibits the stunning depth of his fear and hatred of femininity and female sexuality (Ezek. 23). Now it may be that the association of idolatry with femaleness stems partly from the fact that cities are always called "she." However, cities are not always designated as sexual, and it is the use of feminine metaphors that link idolatrous cities, cities portrayed as females, and cities described as sexually active (and if active, promiscuous and whoring) that is so illuminating.

What seems most remarkable in these passages from Isaiah and Ezekiel is that there are no corresponding symbols or imagery used to describe sinning Israel in terms of male sexuality, lewdness, lustfulness, or promiscuity with foreign women. Indeed, when King Solomon succumbs to the lure of other deities, it is blamed on the "foreign women." In cautioning men against marrying "outsiders," Nehemiah writes: "Did not Solomon king of Israel sin on account of such women? Among the many nations there was no king like him, and he was beloved by his God, and God made him king over all Israel; nevertheless foreign women made even him to sin" (Neh. 13:26).

In other words, the use of imagery describing female sexuality qua harlotry as equivalent to sin and moral transgression, deserving of the most violent divine reprisals, was widely enough accepted in popular belief by exilic times that it could be used as the basis for exhortations to radical religious reforms. And apparently the opposite side of the coin was blank. There seems to have been no corresponding association, in either the prophetic or popular mentality, of the sins of Israel with male sexuality or lust.

Just as female sexuality came to personify the transgressions of Israel, so, of course, the great polytheistic goddesses themselves were personifications of aspects of nature or human endeavors. And these prophetic attitudes toward female sexuality were dramatically and diametrically opposite to the polytheistic celebration of female sexuality in the Sacred Marriage, in which Inanna and Ishtar were seen as actively sexual and enjoying many lovers, and in which the consequences of their sexuality were viewed as advantageous to the whole community.

Evidence from the New Testament

If some Old Testament accounts of cultically crucial divine-human encounters express profound ambivalence toward femaleness in a moral sense, so too some equally important New Testament accounts of those encounters manifest the same depth of ambivalence toward femaleness in a spiritual sense. However, while God is, of course, at the center of both testaments, the variety of people who transmit his moral laws and record his long historical engagement with Israel in the Old Testament—the prophets, psalmists, chroniclers, judges, kings— are all supplanted by the single, towering figure of Jesus in the New. Therefore, in order to evaluate the importance attached to gender in conceptions of the divine in the New Testament, it is necessary to focus on aspects of the life and teachings of Jesus.

Given the importance to the earliest Christians of his birth or "coming," one might expect that the role of his mother Mary would be viewed as pivotal in the Gospels in order to establish the humanity of Jesus. But even in the very first instance of his presence, the woman chosen to physically enable his redemptive mission on earth is pictured, in relation to that divine event, with almost complete ambivalence.

The Negative Face of
Ambivalence toward Women: Mary

The New Testament opens with a recording of the circumstances surrounding the birth of Jesus, presented in this version from a masculine point of view. It traces the ancestry of Joseph back through the greatest leaders of Israel and their fathers to Abraham (Matt. 1:1–17) —a most curious opening because, except for the fact that he was later to marry the mother of Jesus, Joseph was not involved with the Virgin Birth. If, for example, Mary's ancestry had been traced back to Abraham, the significance of this genealogical line of descent might be explicable. While still a virgin, Mary "was found to be with child of the Holy Spirit" (Matt. 1:18), and in order to prevent Joseph from divorcing her (then his unilateral right under Hebraic law), an angel of the Lord appears to Joseph in a dream.

Reminiscent of the exclusion of Sarah and Hagar from any substantive moral role in God's covenant with Abraham, and of their use as reproducers of offspring in order to fulfill the divine promise, Joseph, not Mary, is informed of the special conditions related to her pregnancy; Joseph, not Mary, is told to name him Jesus; and it is to Joseph, not Mary, that the special destiny of her child is revealed, in fulfillment of the Lord's wishes spoken by a prophet (Matt. 1:19–23). Their subsequent wanderings to Egypt and then to Nazareth (again recalling the wanderings of Abraham and his household as a result of divine communication with the patriarch), are undertaken on the advice of an angel who appears to Joseph (Matt. 2:13–15, 19–23). In all these negotiations about the issue of her body, Mary is not only silent; she is almost absent.

Jesus has customarily been viewed as the son of God (e.g., Mark 1:1; Luke 1:32, 3:22; John 1:14; Gal. 4:4) or as divinity incarnate, and though the matter of his sex may or may not be significant, he is incontrovertibly male. While his was without question presented as a unique birth with enormous symbolic and real implications, the fact that a mortal woman *gave* birth poses the question of her stature as the earthly parent. And here she is scarcely outlined as a person but is nearly a paradigm of the Aristotelian conception of woman's role in reproduction as the incubator of the unborn child. In other words, Mary provides the "material" form rather than the spiritual aspect of Jesus.

A View of the Positive Face of Ambivalence: Mary

Describing the other side of this ambivalence, Rosemary Radford Ruether argues that the prebirth passages in Luke, in which Mary is informed of the coming delivery, make of her "much more than just a passive instrument of God. She becomes an active agent, cooperating with God through her personal will and consent to bring about the Messianic advent. She becomes a symbol of Israel, or the New Israel, the church, the redeemed people of god."[15]

Expanding on Luke's interpretation of Mary's role in the Virgin Birth, Ruether maintains:

> Luke makes Mary an active participant in the drama of Jesus' birth, accepting it through an act of free consent, and meditating upon the meaning of his future mission. Thus Luke begins that tradition which transforms Mary from being merely the historical mother of Jesus into an independent agent cooperating with God in the redemption of humanity. In other words, she begins to be a theological agent in her own right. This is espressed especially in her obedient consent to the divine command: "And Mary said, 'Behold, I am the handmaid of the Lord; let it be to me according to your word" (*Luke*, 1:38).[16]

To be sure, in the Lucan gospel Mary is addressed directly by the angel of the Lord: "Hail, O favored one, the Lord is with you!" (Luke 1:28), and she alone converses face-to-face with him (Luke 1:26–38).

But this apparently more active involvement by Mary must be quali-fied. It may be that Ruether's view of Mary as "an active agent, cooper-ating with God through her personal will and consent," "an independent agent cooperating with God in the redemption of human-ity," "a theological agent in her own right," all somewhat overstate the case.

Perhaps the role of Mary in the divine birth, "expressed especially in her obedient consent to the divine command," comes nearer to the mark, for in the culture of ancient Israel, as a young and pious Hebrew woman, what else could Mary's response have been? It was, after all, not too dissimilar from the response of Samson's mother to the angel when informed that the son she was to bear would be a Nazirite.

Moreover, it is tempting to project our current notions of power and autonomy backwards in time. In the biblical environment, power-ful men imposed constraints on women's behavior, and there is not much of a scriptural tradition of strong, independent, defiant women, except, for the most part, those who were aliens, idolatrous, or both. For example, it was unthinkable that Bathsheba should have refused to appear when summoned before King David, just as Esther, remem-bering the fate of Queen Vashti, risked her life by appearing unbidden before King Ahasuerus.

More generally, with rare exceptions like Deborah and Jael from an earlier period, if Hebrew women deviated from the commandments of God as translated by the prescriptions of men, they faced possibly heavy punishment (e.g., the confrontation between Tamar and Judah, Gen. 38:24). By approximately the middle of the first millennium, the discouragement of autonomy in women may be inferred from the metaphors of Isaiah, when he equates the sins of Israel with the pride of the daughters of Zion. Indeed, as already seen, it is only when these daughters are humbled and stripped of all the outward, public symbols of their pride and arrogance—possibly, in our own language, of their independence—that Israel can be cleansed and redeemed (Isa. 3:16–26,4).

Hence, despite her subsequent almost unsurpassed importance in the thought and writing of the early Church Fathers, in the Gospels Mary might have had no alternative but to obey. That she rather than Joseph is informed about the nature of the impending birth in Luke, as different from the version in Matthew, might have had less to do with her "active consent" than with the obvious reality that, in provid-ing for the humanity of Jesus, Joseph simply plays no part. Also, unlike male leaders who covenant and even question and remonstrate with God, e.g., Abraham and Moses, Mary deals with an intermediary, ques-tions nothing, and simply acquiesces. Once her son is born and embarks on his mission, Mary recedes into near-obscurity in the rest of the New Testament—as person, woman, or mother—so that Paul, for instance, never even mentions her by name.

Women, Men, and the Mission of Jesus

The life of Jesus is peopled with both women and men at many of its critical stages, and women as well as men are, of course, involved in the spread of his message after his death and resurrection. While a fuller discussion of women's role in cult must be reserved, it should be noted here that when Mary appears with her infant at the temple for the rituals of circumcision and purification, his identity as the redeemer is recognized by the devout man Simeon and the prophetess Anna (Luke 2:21–38).

Jesus convinces people of his divine origin by signs and healing, and he heals both women and men. People of both sexes are baptized (Acts, 8:12), and before Paul's own conversion, "if he found any belonging to the Way, men or women" in Damascus, he brought them back, or "bound them," as prisoners to Jerusalem (Acts 9:1–2). Women believers are mentioned by name—Damaris (Acts 17:34), Lydia (Acts 16:14–15)—and the apostles speak to the women of Philippi (Acts 16:13). Both Priscilla and her husband, Aquila, teach the converted Jew Apollos about Christianity and "the way of God more accurately" (Acts 18:24–26), and women pray with the apostles after the death and resurrection of Jesus (Acts 1:1–14).

Furthermore, men are sent to the Gentiles in Syria, Antioch, and Cilicia to tell them that they do not require circumcision in order to be saved (Acts 15:29), and the removal of circumcision as a sign of special dedication to God, it would appear, implicitly removed the automatic cultic barriers to women. (That the last was not necessarily the case shall be seen later.) And in a series of letters to converts in different places, Paul urges them to welcome women as well as men who work for Christ—the deaconess Phoebe (Rom. 16:1–2), Prisca (Rom. 16:3–5), Ap'phia (Philem. 2), Mary (Rom. 16:6), the mother of Rufus (Rom. 16:13), Julia (Rom. 16:15), Claudia (2 Tim. 4:21), and the like.

This dedication of both women and men to Christ's work is evident in the words of Peter, quoting the prophet Jo'el, about what will happen at the end of time:

> "And in the last days it shall be, God declares,
> that I will pour out my Spirit upon all flesh,
> and your sons and daughters shall prophesy,
> . . . .

yea, and on my menservants and my maidservants in those days
I will pour out my Spirit; and they shall prophesy.
. . . .
And it shall be that whoever calls on the name of the Lord shall be
saved."

(Acts 2:17–21)

Elsewhere, Paul extends the appeal to oppressed people, implicitly including women living under Mosaic law, when he writes that ". . . God chose what is weak in the world to shame the strong, God chose what is low and despised in the world" (1 Cor. 1:27–28). Jesus himself declares that "everyone who exalts himself will be humbled, but he who humbles himself will be exalted" (Luke 18:14). And since Christianity evolved out of a small Jewish sect, the appeal to Israelite women must have been powerful, for, in many places, faith in Jesus and his teachings rather than submission to Mosaic law is stressed as the route to salvation.

The View of Jesus As a Feminist

This kind of evidence, along with the oft-quoted passage Gal. 3:28, has prompted many to interpret the meaning of Jesus' message as sexually egalitarian, or as spiritually inclusive of all persons regardless of sex. For example, in an essay heralded by a number of feminist theologians as extremely perceptive when it was first published,[17] Leonard Swidler argues that in early Christianity (as well as in some of the other great religions) "the initial burst of human liberation extended to women as well as men in a very high degree."[18] This represents one important modern perspective on Christianity, namely that Jesus himself was somehow exempt from the misogyny or ambivalent attitudes toward women found in the views of later Christian commentators—Swidler himself sees Jesus as a feminist—and therefore should be looked at with care.

One of the examples he cites is Jesus' attitude toward Martha and Mary when he visits with them in their home. The biblical passage reads:

Now as they went on their way, he entered a village; and a woman named Martha received him into her house. And she had a sister called Mary, who sat at the Lord's feet and listened to his teaching. But Martha was distracted with much serving; and she went to him and said, "Lord, do you not care that my sister has left me to serve alone? Tell her then to help me." But the Lord answered her, "Martha, Martha, you are anxious and troubled about many things; one thing is needful. Mary has chosen the good portion, which shall not be taken away from her." (Luke 10:38–41)

From this, Swidler concludes that Jesus opposed the notion of woman's function as merely domestic and supported Mary's "intellectual" interest when she sat at his feet. It should be noted first that Mary was hardly being intellectual in any creative way, or initiating any original ideas of her own, by sitting at his feet and listening. In addition, and far more important, Jesus never said *for how long* it was appropriate for Mary to choose "the good portion, which shall not be taken away from her." For two hours? Two weeks? Two years? And this consideration was crucial for women. In the absence of the magical power to feed thousands with a few loaves and fishes, which only the son of God had, *someone* had to prepare the food until the end-times came. And those someones (except for Jesus) were usually women.

Given the radical nature of his teachings in other areas, namely that faith in him would alone guarantee redemption, if he was really concerned about women sharing in the intellectual and spiritual life with men, he might have taught something else equally radical. In short, he could have said that men, perhaps his apostles, had to get into the kitchen for part of the time so that the Marthas of the world could also sit at the Lord's feet along with the Marys. In other words, the notion of "service" exemplified in the life of Jesus is nowhere extended by him in admonitions to his male followers to share more fully in the material labor of cooking, spinning, and child care so that women might share more fully in the life of the spirit.

In like fashion, Swidler attaches importance to the fact that Jesus' first appearance after his death was to a woman, whom he then told to carry the news of his resurrection back to the Eleven. But when Mary Magdalene and the other women relayed the good news, the apostles did not believe them (Mark 16:11; Luke 24:8–12). Indeed, in one telling, it is only after Christ appears to Simon that the apostles believe in his resurrection (Luke 24:34).

The risen Christ is, of course, one of the central tenets of Christian faith, and therefore much has been made lately of whom Jesus appeared to first. However, while cultural influences and biases have been freely acknowledged as coloring the content of early translations and theological discourse, or even the thought of some of his early disciples—e.g., Constance Parvey locates the source of some of the attitudes expressed in 1 Corinthians in Paul's identification with the customs and social values he absorbed as a first-century Jewish teacher[19]—it seems strange that the widespread Near Eastern custom of women participating in funerals and rituals for the dead has been largely overlooked.

For thousands of years, in many societies in this area, there is a long history of women of all classes whose role as mourners and attendants on the dead is widely attested. Thus, in its cultural context, the presence of women at the cross or at the tomb of Jesus was not exceptional, and in itself might not have signified exceptional courage or devotion. Furthermore, just as the sex of Jesus might have been merely incidental to his purpose on earth, as some have claimed,[20] so his appearance after death to women first might have been also incidental. Moreover, if Jesus had demonstrated in his own life that equal treatment of the sexes was an integral part of his mission, possibly the apostles would have credited the testimony of the women.

Likewise, Swidler believes that Jesus went out of his way to reject publicly the ancient blood taboo suffered by women by calling the attention of a large crowd to the fact that a bleeding woman touched him. He was not repelled by her supposed "uncleanness," and he publicly cured her. But the ritual "impurity" or "uncleanness" of women under Hebraic law was specifically connected to their menstruation ("impure" in Hebrew means, among other things, "menstruant woman"), and the woman who touched Jesus was afflicted with a twelve-year issue of blood (Mark 5:25–34). That is a disease, and menstruation is not. Jesus himself refers to her condition as a disease: "Daughter, your faith has made you well; go in peace, and be healed of your disease" (Mark 5:34), and he nowhere confronts the whole issue of menstruation and childbirth, which marked women as either ritually unclean or sinful.

Swidler concludes that Jesus was a feminist in the sense that he "treats women primarily as human persons and willingly contravenes social customs in so acting."[21] But was he and does he? That he treats women as persons is certainly true. He speaks to them, instructs them in Torah, and holds out the hope of salvation to them, as he does to every other group of pariahs. But he does not in any radical sense oppose either social conventions or the law as they affect women. In other words, Jesus himself relates to women in a manner that was radical for his time, especially in the framework of Hebrew society. But except by setting a personal example, which was no small thing, he does not insist that everyone else must act in a like manner in order to follow him.

Women and the Life of the Spirit

It is not that Jesus was not a feminist. It is that he had other concerns, which were in some respects, whether intentional or not, most alienating for women. For example, throughout the New Testament one of the major emphases is on the paramount importance of the spiritual world, next to which all the preoccupations of the material world seem trivial and transitory, except for acts of faith and loving one's neighbor. Jesus says over and over, in many ways: "It is the spirit that gives life, the flesh is of no avail; the words that I have spoken to you are spirit and life" (John 6:63). He teaches about the unimportance and impermanence of the physical world: "Take heed, and beware of all covetousness; for a man's life does not consist in the abundance of his possessions" (Luke 12:15). "Therefore I tell you, do not be anxious about your life, what you shall eat, nor about your body, what you shall put on. For life is more than food, and the body more than clothing" (Luke 12:22–24). He tells people to: "Sell your possessions, and give alms; provide yourselves with purses that do not grow old, with a treasure in the heavens that does not fail, where no thief approaches and no moth destroys. For where your treasure is, there will your heart be also" (Luke 12:32–34).

He urges people to abandon their families, land and possessions, and follow him (Matt. 19:29, Mark 10:29–30), but only the fathers, husbands, or sons of Hebrew women owned land and possessions, and therefore, in reality, those women could not make that moral choice. When a man says to him, "I will follow you, Lord: but let me first say farewell to those at my home," Jesus replies: "No one who puts his hand to the plow and looks back is fit for the kingdom of God" (Luke 9:61–62). Jesus also says: "If any one comes to me and does not hate his own father and mother and wife and even his own life, he cannot be my disciple" (Luke 14:26). "God is spirit, and those who worship him must worship in spirit and truth" (John 4:24). "I am the bread of life; he who comes to me shall not hunger, and he who believes in me shall never thirst" (John 6:41).

And this emphasis on the *spiritual* affects women as a group more than men, because they are the ones who literally baked the bread and bore the children; very young children require material as well as spiritual nourishment and care; and nursing an infant and disposing of its bodily wastes are very *material* work. It has nothing to do with whether all mothers are naturally maternal or better parents than fathers, or with whether women do or do not want their babies, or with all the other things they do in addition to bearing children.

For despite the likelihood of high maternal and infant mortality in those times, in the absence of widespread contraception, or an absolute prohibition of sex and marriage, or a strong endorsement of homosexuality, with Christians (as well as Jews) set against infanticide, which was widely practiced in their environment, it was finally the woman who bore the consequences of human sexuality. Historically, in most instances either the mother or other women cared for the children. And with whom was the mother to leave her infant when she abandoned her family and everything material to follow Jesus? For every mother of infants who did, there must have been a Martha tied to the physical requirements of this world, and to children who needed material care.

There are certainly women among Jesus' followers in his lifetime, and there are women associated with the apostles and disciples who spread Christ's message throughout the Mediterranean world after his death. *But there is a conspicuous absence of children.* And that may be one meaning of Jesus' public rejection of his own mother and family. When told that his family is asking for him, he says: "Who are my mother and my brothers? . . . Here are my mother and my brothers! Whoever does the will of God is my brother, and sister, and mother" (Mark 3:33–35).

When a woman in a crowd listening to him cries out: "Blessed is the womb that bore you, and the breasts that you sucked," Jesus responds: "Blessed rather are those who hear the word of God and keep it" (Luke 11:27–28). What Jesus is repudiating here is not his mother as a person, because there is nothing in the narratives to indicate that she was anything but supportive or concerned about him. He is rejecting the *ties* of motherhood, the material responsibilities toward anything but his spiritual mission. It may also be why Paul on his own advocates chastity, if possible, so that all people might devote themselves entirely to spiritual matters. Hard-headed pragmatist that he was, Paul seems to have understood that as long as women and men have a sexual life together—and Jesus did not explicitly oppose heterosexuality but only the primacy of material and family affiliations—in the absence of a radical redistribution of labor between the sexes, the spiritual succession would probably have to be mostly male. Ironically, almost immediately after he speaks of the equality of *all* persons in Christ (Gal. 3:28), Paul describes this succession in all-male imagery:

> But when the time had fully come, God sent forth his Son, born of woman, born under the law, so that we might receive adoption as sons. And because you are sons, God has sent the Spirit of his Son into our hearts, crying, "Abba! Father!" So through God you are no longer a slave but a son, and if a son then an heir. (Gal. 4:4–7)

Unlike men, there appears to have been little a devout Christian woman could do if she wanted to devote herself totally to the spiritual life, except remain chaste or pray for sterility. However, there were many injunctions to preserve the status quo—to love one's oppressors, to refrain from judgment and condemnation (Luke 6:27–38), to be "subject to the governing authorities. . . . and those that exist have been instituted by God" (Rom. 13:1). Jesus said: "for I did not come to judge the world but to save the world" (John 12:47). Lacking a divine mandate, then, to restructure fundamentally the social relations between the sexes, because of their biology women more than men were placed in a somewhat more peripheral relation to the life of the spirit.

Without a divine definition of spirituality as necessarily based on the full personhood of both sexes, or a divine acknowledgment of the inherent contradiction between a dedication of all people to the life of the spirit at the same time that the status quo of sexual inequality was preserved in society, there was not much likelihood that men, who held most of the secular power, would share in the time-consuming requirements of the material world—the domestic and child-care chores—so that women might have increased access to the spiritual. Furthermore, it was *only* to men that Jesus imparted some of his magic. He made it possible for his male apostles to heal so that they might wander from city to city and preach his gospel. He did not make it possible for the Marthas of this world to feed people with a few loaves and fishes so that they too could proselytize.

It seems evident that redemption was not based on sex. What counted above all was faith in the divine, and Sarah's conception in her old age as well as the safety of Rahab the harlot are both attributed to their faith in God (Heb. 11:11, 31). But Jesus was neither a feminist nor a misogynist. His central message simply lay elsewhere. And in the context of his message, women more than men, because of their reproductive functions and customary kinds of labor, probably continued to be more torn between the real obligations placed on them by the material world and their own inclinations toward the promises of the spiritual one. In spite of what must have been the powerful appeal of spiritual egalitarianism to those women who were subordinated under the law and in cult, in a very deep way early Christian attitudes seem to have been more consonant with the lives (and biology) of men and women past the age of childbearing than with those of younger women.

It seems likely that in ways we can never measure, the preachings about the superiority of the life of the spirit may have been profoundly discouraging and alienating to mothers of very young children, who knew about the realities of their own lives and realized that these preachings were profoundly insensitive to those realities. For the women were not asked to choose between earthly power and riches and following Jesus, but instead were told to love their neighbors while they abandoned their living children (probably to other women) in pursuit of their own salvation. Indeed, it is not that Jesus viewed women with ambivalence, but his emphasis on the superior value of the spiritual may have placed women more than men in an ambivalent relationship to the divine.

Equality between the Sexes: Gal. 3:28

Paul's statement "There is neither Jew nor Greek, there is neither slave nor free, there is neither male nor female; for you are all one in Christ Jesus" (Gal. 3:28) has provided an emotionally appealing argument for the nonhierarchical inclusiveness of women and men in equality by early Christianity. But as pointed out elsewhere, this passage cannot be understood apart from Paul's ethics governing the age before the imminent new order, or end-times.

Indeed, this passage seems to have little to do with the ethics of ordinary relationships between people of unequal status in normal times. From the perspective of slaves or of most women living in Paul's time, there were naturally inescapable material differences between their conditions in life and those of free persons or men. And though Jesus came to save the world not judge it, and though one does not live by bread alone, in this life it is impossible to survive without it.

What Paul's formulation in Galatians does suggest, beyond his belief that the kingdom of God was at hand, is an equality of souls before God, perhaps at the time of judgment, and a more general theme recurrent in both testaments, namely, the transitory nature of secular wealth and status when measured against the permanent blessings of righteousness, a result of obedience to divine commandments. In other words, Paul seems to refer here to an extraordinary period, or to the afterlife, or even to the experience of having faith in Christ, but hardly to what might be applicable to all people as a Christian precept under ordinary circumstances in this life.

Just as Gal. 3:28 does not speak to the issue of the equal and ongoing participation of both sexes in religious ritual in this world, nor to the more general issue of social equality, so the immediate context of the verse is couched in male imagery. Thus, both immediately before and after his strong expression of equality for all persons in Christ, Paul represents the divine promise as moving through the male line of descent: "for in Christ Jesus you are all sons of God, through faith" (Gal. 3:26), and "if you are Christ's, then you are Abraham's offspring, heirs according to promise" (Gal. 3:29).

Idolatry and Female Sexuality: The Metaphor in Revelation

While the attitude of Jesus toward women is undoubtedly different and more positive in many respects than those expressed in many parts of the Old Testament, the negative side of the ambivalence toward femaleness in general, and the linkage of female sexuality with sin in early Christianity, are both strikingly evident in the concluding book of the New Testament. The last consists of an extended analogy on a projected conflict between the forces of cosmic good and evil, or the teachings of Jesus versus apostasy of every sort, in which the former finally triumphs. It is replete with images of portents, visions, angels, beasts, plagues, and the future of nations and multitudes of people.

The climactic scene is the confrontation of the true faith with idolatrous worship. The latter, symbolized by Babylon in all its earthly wealth and splendor, is described, like sinning Israel, as female, explicitly sexual and a fornicator, and she is finally laid waste with violence. The following are samples of the way in which competing polytheistic religions were clothed in feminine imagery, and of the level of aggression directed against these other religions perceived as universally female.

An angel introduces Babylon as a great whore. She is called "Babylon the great, mother of harlots and of earth's abominations" (Rev. 17:5), and she is promised divine punishment:

"Fallen, fallen is Babylon the great!
It has become a dwelling place of demons,
a haunt of every foul spirit,
a haunt of every foul and hateful bird;
for all nations have drunk the wine of her impure passion,
and the kings of the earth have committed fornication with her,
and the merchants of the earth have grown rich with the wealth of her
  wantonness."
Then I heard another voice from heaven saying,
"Come out of her, my people,
lest you take part in her sins,
lest you share in her plagues;
for her sins are heaped high as heaven,
and God has remembered her iniquities.
Render to her as she herself has rendered,
and repay her double for her deeds;
mix a double draught for her in the cup she mixed.
As she glorified herself and played the wanton,
so give her a like measure of torment and mourning."
. . . .
so shall her plagues come in a single day,
pestilence and mourning and famine,
and she shall be burned with fire;
. . . .
"So shall Babylon the great city be thrown down with violence, and shall
  be found no more;
. . . .
The smoke from her goes up for ever and ever."

(Rev. 18:2–8, 21; 19:3)

And the fate of the kings of the earth who were also fornicators?

> And the kings of the earth, who committed fornication and were wanton
> with her, will weep and wail over her when they see the smoke of her
> burning; they will stand far off, in fear of her torment, and say,
>   "Alas! alas! thou great city,
>   thou mighty city, Babylon!
>   In one hour has thy judgment come."
>   (Rev. 18:9–10)

While the level of violence directed against the feminine personification of sin against God is perhaps more restrained here than in the Old Testament, there is the same association of idolatry with femaleness, female sexuality, and harlotry. God judges Babylon and orchestrates the violent reprisals against her (Rev. 18:8, 19:2), but though the kings of the earth fornicate with her, there is no comparable imagery linking male sexuality with sin, idolatry, or abomination. Neither the fornicating kings nor their lands are violently destroyed. In short, there is no male counterpart, in image or fact, to the great whore of Babylon.

Gender and the Messianic Tradition

It is not only in the imagery used to describe idolatry and its consequences that differences based on gender may be found. In many of the areas in which God interacts with the human community, in both testaments, distinctions are made on the basis of sex. For example, the monotheistic conception of divinity encompassed different attitudes toward death than those held by polytheistic religions, and some of these differences had important implications with regard to the significance represented as attached to gender by the divine.

In contrast with the idea in Genesis that human sin caused death, in Mesopotamia just the *fact* of death was dealt with, and it was believed that the just and the unjust alike, of both sexes, suffered desolation. In Egypt, death was seen as possibly leading to immortality in a pleasant setting for both sexes if the Negative Confession of sins was performed properly in a ritual sense and was accepted by deities of both sexes who sat in judgment of the dead. The first-millennium Mediterranean mystery-cults held out the possibility of attaining immortality if persons of either sex first went through the proper rituals of purification, initiation into the sacred mysteries, and celebration of the sacred rites of a female or male deity.

The Old Testament prophets taught that divine retribution should be expected as the result of people's sins. But there is no great emphasis on this retribution immediately after death. *Sheol* is mentioned as the residence of the deceased, but there is no clear image of divine reward or punishment in that place. The closest approach to this notion may be God's warning in Deuteronomy that not only will those who disobey his commandments be cursed in every conceivable and practical way in this life, but also the curse will be inflicted on all their descendants as well (Deut. 23:15–68). The new idea introduced by some of the prophets is messianism, according to which concept a kind of catharsis and judgment would occur after people throughout human history, projected backward to the beginning of time, had been punished for their sins and undergone moral purification. But this event was to take place at the close of history, and a new and golden age would then emerge (Isa. 11:1–9).

In the New Testament version of messianism, Jesus is described as the Messiah, whose birth, suffering, and death in the body were seen as the means of expiating the sins of humanity. The prophetic vision of moral judgment taking place at the end of human history was transformed into the view that the end of time was imminent. And when that event failed to materialize, what was retained was the belief in the actual resurrection and immortality of the dead based on faith in the reality of Christ as the son of God, or divinity incarnate, and on the faithful observance of his teachings.

While the messianic beliefs of Judaism and Christianity obviously include persons of both sexes, the extent to which women of those times might have been seen as capable of participating in the process of moral purification, or seen as deserving of equal treatment with men at the final judgment, might well have depended on how fully or unambiguously they were incorporated as participants in the divine covenant with the human community. In the biblical view, to the extent that women as a group were set apart from men on account of their sex and regarded with ambivalence, they suffered under the constraints of a more marginal relationship to God in a moral or spiritual sense. In like fashion, to the extent that the worst of all sins, idolatry, came to be symbolized by rampant, unbridled female sexuality, the final judgment of women on moral or spiritual grounds alone might have been somehow diminished.

The Inflation of the Significance of Gender

Divine judgment is not by any means shown as always dispensed on the basis of sex. It is not so much that women as well as men were not punished for their disobedience to God's ordinances, as of course they were, or that women were punished more than men, which they sometimes were and sometimes weren't. It is in the finer sense that, in the androcentric view of some of the biblical writers, women seem to have had a smaller moral and spiritual stage than men on which to live out their lives, and this established a difference in the nature of women's relationship to God and men's relationship to God. In comparison to men, women are shown as more susceptible to definition by their sexual, biological, or reproductive functions. Insofar as these in any way limited their moral or spiritual capacities, it is as though women, at the same time that they are without doubt an integral part of the community of believers, are somehow considered less worthy of divine engagement.

There is no counterpart to the book of Job that features the torments and moral struggles of a woman, just as there is no daughter of God in any way comparable with Jesus. The queens of Israel are not like David or Solomon. Except for a few women like Deborah, Jael, and Chuldah, the judges, soldiers, and prophets of Israel are male, and while there are women among the followers and close associates of Jesus, they neither became his apostles nor wrote the New Testament.

There is no woman like Moses, who speaks "mouth to mouth" with Yahweh. There is no female counterpart to Abraham, who bargains with God to spare Sodom and Gomorrah if a few good men can be found there. And the resurrection of Lazarus may represent more an act of divine grace and a demonstration of the power of faith than an acknowledgment of any power that the sister of Lazarus has in her relationship with Jesus.

Thus, it would seem that the monotheistic conception of divinity elevated the importance of gender in a manner quite foreign to the outlook of polytheistic religions, whether it was used to describe the basis for divine judgment or action, or the interactions of people with the divine through their participation in cult. In a literature that stresses as central the existence of universal moral laws of divine origin, which all people are required to observe, those sections of biblical narratives that view women as suffering a more peripheral relationship to God in a moral sense, or see them as less developed moral beings than men, or portray them as having lesser access to spirituality than men not only are exclusionary of half the human race by their nature, but also make these distinctions only on the basis of sex.

At times female sexuality, or the very existential being of women, was viewed as a dangerous threat to the pursuit of righteousness by men, as shall be seen in the discussion of sex roles in the next chapter. At the very least, especially from the period of the exile on, women in their sexual aspect were easily associated with idolatry and rival religions in the prophetic and apparently the popular mind as well.

Even in cultically crucial narratives, such as those which describe God's covenant with Israel or those which establish the mortality of Jesus, some biblical authors present women as less significant than men in these transactions, or as more defined than men by their sexual or reproductive functions, especially in areas which involve moral choices or an ongoing, active commitment to the aims of the divine.

Sometimes, divine priorities with regard to the importance of women are made fairly clear, as, for example, in those passages which suggest that the safety or respect for the full personhood of women are not as much a matter of God's concern as a number of other issues that closely involve men, such as guaranteeing the survival of the offspring of Abraham or the male Benjaminites, in fulfillment of the divine promise. Proceeding from this representation of the divine, God therefore is at times shown as dispensing less justice and compassion toward women than men. And all these distinctions based on sex are considerably enhanced by the biblical conception of the divine as singular, transcendent, and universal in authority.

The Biblical Ambivalence Toward Women

Nevertheless, both women and men constitute the human community, and both are included within the moral and spiritual domain of the divine. In the Old Testament, there is the image of the powerful role played by Wisdom along with God in assuring the right and righteous ordering of the universe almost from the beginning of time, even though "she" is not mentioned in the Pentateuch. In the New Testament, the significance of Jesus' birth is revealed by the angel Gabriel to Mary alone in Luke, even if Mary diminishes in importance after his birth.

Also, in a body of religious writings that place a high value on moral redemption and resurrection, there is the passage in Galatians which assumes the full equality, probably after death, of all persons who have faith in Christ. In terms of the attitudes toward women of the Hebrews of that time, the inclusion of male and female is every bit as startling as that of slave and free, and it considerably reinforces the notion found in the Old Testament of equal accountability of pagan and Hebrew alike to universal moral laws. However, it introduces nothing substantially new, since it must be remembered that the foreign Jezebel was subject to divine retribution, just like her husband Ahab. And its sexually egalitarian sound must be qualified somewhat by the absence of any specifics, i.e., when, where, and how that sexual equality was to be achieved.

In short, what all the foregoing strongly suggests is that the monotheistic conception of divinity, recounted in biblical literature through the unfolding of God's relationship with humanity, placed a far greater emphasis on the gender of people and the sexual preferences of God than seems to have been characteristic of the polytheistic literature of those same times. In the Old and New Testaments, men tended to play a more powerful, autonomous, and morally responsible role than women, even as the nature of men's lives enabled them, more than women, to make moral choices about following divine commands.

Essentially though, given the inclusion of women in the community of believers, the attitude toward women as compared with men seems to have been characterized by much ambivalence. Women, like men, were held morally accountable and were punished for transgressions of divine laws, even if they were sometimes punished for the same offenses in different ways than men. Women, like men, were recipients of Jesus' healing and compassion. On the other hand, we find strongly pejorative attitudes toward women, the most fearful of which seem to have centered on female sexuality. But perhaps the most punitive of these negative attitudes—equal in importance to the positive side of biblical ambivalence toward women—were those expressed in simultaneous descriptions of God's moral laws as universal and of distinctions made by the divine that, in effect, treated women as lesser moral beings than men, or as less capable than men of making moral choices, or as more marginal than men in the divine covenant. Moreover, to the extent that God was shown as treating women and men differently, his laws were not only universal, but the reasons for this differential treatment of women and men by the divine, and the evidence for a moral double standard—within the religious universe established by Yahweh, in which ethical concerns were represented as paramount—had nothing to do with morality, righteousness, or compassion, but with sex alone.

CHAPTER 6

Sex Roles and the Relation of Power to Gender:
Biblical Narratives

I
T has been argued that parts of both testaments are radically different in outlook from much of ancient Near Eastern polytheistic literature in their emphasis on the importance of gender in divine-human encounters. Moreover, both testaments are characterized by profound ambivalence toward women as moral or spiritual persons, and both portray female sexuality as sometimes dangerous, sometimes sinful, but, in any event, as an easily recognizable symbol of depravity and idolatry in the human community.

Just as biblical conceptions of the divine as they relate to the significance of gender may be ascertained only from the nature of divine-human interactions, so early monotheistic attitudes toward sex roles and the relation of power to sex may be gauged only by the secular roles designated as appropriate for women and men as their societies interacted with the one, ineffable, nominally asexual God. In conformity with the ambivalence with which women are viewed in their relation to the divine, some of the narratives exhibit a correspondingly deep ambivalence toward the proper roles for women in the community of believers.

Obviously, these views do not appear with unvarying consistency in the Bible, nor are they central to all the books of the Old and New Testaments and the Apocrypha. But there is enough to suggest that biblical writers correlated gender with prescribed roles to a greater extent than did polytheistic literature. And in contrast with the latter, biblical texts are marked by the emergence of a sharper linkage of sex with power and powerlessness, with women suffering more of the last

181

partly as a result of their sexuality and normal biological functioning, even as they are simultaneously shown as essential to the fulfillment of the divine covenant and are portrayed in a variety of roles.

The Old Testament: Women in Leadership Roles

In the Old Testament there are references to women in a number of leadership roles. For example, Athaliah ruled Israel for six years (2 Kings 11:1–3). In the time of the prophet Jeremiah, the prophetess Chuldah was appealed to for advice by the reformer-king Josiah after "a book of the Law," Deuteronomy, was discovered in the temple. Josiah instructs his priest and some of his retinue to approach Chuldah, or "inquire of the Lord for me, and for the people, and for all Judah, concerning the words of this book that has been found" (2 Kings 22:13). Chuldah transmits the words of the Lord in genuine prophetic fashion and lays the groundwork for Josiah's reforms (2 Kings 13:1–30; 2 Chron. 34:23–33, 35:1–34). She says:

> "Thus says the Lord, Behold, I will bring evil upon this place and upon its inhabitants, all the words of the book which the king of Judah has read. Because they have forsaken me and have burned incense to other gods, that they might provoke me to anger with all the work of their hands, therefore my wrath will be kindled against this place, and it will not be quenched." (2 Kings 22:16–17)

But except for this one act of prophecy Chuldah leaves us no other record. It is most curious, because in her own time, as the one who authenticated the word of God, her stature as a prophet apparently exceeded that of Jeremiah.

Chuldah was not the only woman to claim prophetic gifts. Isaiah refers to an unnamed prophetess who bears a son and names him as directed by God, relayed through the prophet (Isa. 8:1–4). Both Nehemiah and Ezekiel mention false prophetesses like Noadiah as members of a group of pretenders and diviners, apparently of both sexes, who led Israel astray (Neh. 6:14; Ezek. 13). In addition, there were some women who practiced magic. After the death of Samuel, King Saul banished "the mediums and the wizards" (1 Sam. 28:3), but he appeals to the witch at Endor, who raises the spirit of Samuel from the dead at Saul's request, to advise him after he loses God's blessing (1 Sam. 28:7–19). And, as already remarked, the prophet Micah names Miriam along with Moses and Aaron as leaders of the Hebrews' exodus from Egypt (Mic. 6:4), even though God treats Miriam differently from Aaron when they both question his judgment.

The Wise Women: Their Autonomy and Anonymity

There are both named and unnamed "wise women" who intercede at critical points in King David's reign with beneficent consequences for the ruler and the community. However, despite their obvious importance, they either are defined by their relationship to men rather than God, or act without autonomy, or remain forever anonymous.

For example, there is Nabal's wife, Abigail, who saves her household and community from slaughter by David's troops when she directly approaches and mollifies the king after her husband refuses to pay him tribute. As David sees it, she also saves him from committing "blood-guiltiness," or murder. Finally summoned to her ultimate reward, Abigail becomes one of David's wives after God kills Nabal for his wickedness, and she is described as not only "of good understanding" and intelligent, but beautiful as well (1 Sam. 25). In short, her good judgment and heroic intervention are measured by her relationships with men, not God, and by the nature and status of those men.

Also, there are a few nameless "wise women," and their position relative to men is rather odd. At Joab's instigation, one of them intervenes with David and facilitates the reconciliation of the king and his beloved son Absalom (2 Sam. 14). But she does not act autonomously. She is told what to do and say by Joab, and acts at most as an intermediary between Joab, Absalom, and David:

> And Jo'ab sent to Teko'a, and fetched from there a wise woman, and said to her, "Pretend to be a mourner, and put on mourning garments; do not anoint yourself with oil, but behave like a woman who has been mourning many days for the dead; and go to the king, and speak thus to him." So Jo'ab put the words in her mouth. (2 Sam. 2–3)

The other "wise woman" prevents the destruction of an entire settlement by David's general Joab when she arranges instead for the death of the one guilty man who provoked some of the tribes to rebel against the king's authority (2 Sam. 20). However, like the woman who served as Joab's medium, she is not named. This seems most peculiar in a literary work that, in general, meticulously mentions everyone by name who was considered to have played a significant role in the history of Israel and, in particular, mentions the name, and that of his father and tribe, of the man who caused many of the Israelites to turn away from David: "a worthless fellow, whose name was Sheba, the son of Bichri, a Benjaminite" (2 Sam. 20:1). When Sheba flees to her city, and Joab encircles it and lays it under siege, and the woman saves the city by offering Joab Sheba's head (2 Sam. 20:15–22), she is identified merely as "a wise woman called from the city" (2 Sam. 20:16) and "the woman (who) went to all the people in her wisdom" (2 Sam. 20:22).

There are, of course, some notable exceptions to these anonymous women. One is the Queen of Sheba, who comes in pomp and splendor to see for herself whether Solomon's reputation for wisdom is deserved. While she undoubtedly interacts with Solomon on an equal basis and judges him, she is, after all, a foreign queen from an alien culture, which practiced other social customs (1 Kings 10:1–13). But there are some strong Hebrew women as well.

Deborah and Jael

Both Deborah, the prophetess, judge, and liberator of Israel, and Jael, who assumes a temporary though decisive role in a quasi-military capacity, figure in the early, chaotic period, characterized by lawlessness and warfare, in the book of Judges. There is no doubt that Deborah is an authentic judge and charismatic leader of Israel: "Now Deb'orah, a prophetess, the wife of Lap'pidoth, was judging Israel at that time. She used to sit under the palm of Deb'orah between Ramah and Bethel in the hill country of E'phraim; and the people of Israel came up to her for judgment" (Judg. 4:4–5).

She lived at a time when "the people of Israel again did what was evil in the sight of the Lord" (Judg. 4:1), and consequently the Canaanite king "oppressed the people of Israel cruelly for twenty years," "with nine hundred chariots of iron," so that "the people of Israel cried to the Lord for help" (Judg. 4:3). It is interesting to note that when she is first introduced, it is not only as prophetess and judge but also as the wife of Lapidoth. Needless to add, neither Yabin, the king of Canaan, nor Sisera, the captain of his army, nor Barak, the Israelite general who is also identified as "the son of Abin'o-am out of Kedesh-naphtali" (Judg. 4:6), is named as the husband of anyone.

Deborah transmits to Barak God's command to raise an army against the Canaanites, and she promises to deliver Sisera to him. Barak, in turn, fully acknowledges her power: "If you will go with me, I will go; but if you will not go with me, I will not go" (Judg. 4:8). Deborah's response is that the victory will be credited to a woman, not to the Israelite general: "I will surely go with you; nevertheless, the road on which you are going will not lead to your glory, for the Lord will sell Sis'era into the hand of a woman" (Judg. 4:9).

At the head of ten thousand men, Barak is accompanied by Deborah and aided by the Lord, who "routed Sisera and all his chariots and all his army before Barak at the edge of the sword" (Judg. 4:15). All the Canaanites are killed and Sisera escapes from the carnage on foot. He comes to the tent of "Jael the wife of Heber and Kenite" (Judg. 4:17) since Heber and the king of Canaan are at peace. She welcomes him, gives him a drink, lets him rest, and when he falls asleep she drives a nail through his head with a hammer and kills him. When Barak arrives in pursuit of Sisera, Jael shows him his corpse (Judg. 4:18–22). "So on that day God subdued Yabin the king of Canaan before the people of Israel" (Judg. 4:23).

In the song celebrating their victory, Deborah and Barak praise God, and she describes her role when depravity ruled in Israel, "when new gods were chosen, when war was in the gates" (Judg. 5:8): "Deborah arose as a mother in Israel" (Judg. 5:7). She "mothers" the nation but is not otherwise depicted as a biological mother. And, like Deborah, the slayer of the captain of the Canaanite host and the agent of divine wrath is identified first as a wife, and then her military prowess is hailed:

> "Most blessed of women be Ja'el,
> the wife of Heber the Ken'ite,
> of tent-dwelling women most blessed.
> He asked water and she gave him milk,
> she brought him curds in a lordly bowl.
> She put her hand to the tent peg
> and her right hand to the workmen's mallet;
> She struck Sis'era a blow, she crushed his head,
> she shattered and pierced his temple.
> He sank, he fell, he lay still at her feet;
> at her feet he sank, he fell;
> where he sank, there he fell dead."
>
> (Judg. 5:24–27)

There is no question that Deborah, as prophetess, judge, general, and liberator, and Jael, as fearless victor over Sisera, play rather unusual roles for women. In their assertiveness, acts of physical aggression, influence over the male leaders of Israel, and the subsequent course of historical events, one would have to compare them with foreign and idolatrous queens of Israel like Jezebel. Deborah and Jael are, in fact, prominent for their rarity as strong female leaders and soldiers of Israel, and for the benign results of their forceful leadership for the people of Israel.

The overwhelming majority of Israelite rulers were men. If there never was a queen like David, there was likewise never a female leader famous for her wisdom like Solomon (with countless husbands and male concubines), a female smasher of idolatrous worship like Josiah, a female prophet and judge like Moses, or a female soldier like Joshua. Most of the prophets—and (unlike Chuldah) certainly all those who wrote the books that were later canonized and whose views were therefore most influential and enduring—were men. Even on a much lesser scale, women were not seen as possessing a monopoly on magical powers. Wizards as well as witches were banished by Saul, and both are described as possessing "familiar spirits."

The Books of Women

Ruth

With the exception of the book of Ruth, which features a Moabite woman who, like the Queen of Sheba, is from an alien culture where females might well have played a larger part in social life and cult, the Old Testament and Apocryphal books titled with the names of women either confirm the absence of autonomous power exercised by women or show that power as almost entirely dependent upon their beauty and sexuality. Indeed, in some respects the book of Ruth stands virtually alone, for, as different from the others, the primary affectional relationships portrayed are between women, and the whole narrative hinges on female affiliation.

Ruth chooses to leave her own people and country because of her love for her mother-surrogate, Naomi, and the expression of that love is among the most personal and tender passages in the Old Testament about the *feelings* of people for each other. As her mother-in-law is about to leave Moab for her own land, Ruth says:

> "Entreat me not to leave you or to return from following you; for where you go I will go, and where you lodge I will lodge; your people shall be my people, and your God my God; where you die I will die, and there will I be buried. May the Lord do so to me and more also if even death parts me from you." (Ruth 1:16–17)

In comparison with this mother-daughter devotion, there is no special affection ascribed to Ruth's marriage to her first husband, Naomi's deceased son, or for her future husband, Boaz. In fact, Boaz initially treats Ruth kindly because he values her filial affection for his kinswoman Naomi.

Throughout, Ruth does what Naomi tells her to do. She works to support her, marries her kinsman Boaz to continue the name of Naomi's son, and presents Naomi with security and a grandson to nurse in her old age after she suffers the loss of her own husband and two sons:

Then the women said to Na'omi, "Blessed be the Lord, who has not left you this day without next of kin; and may his name be renowned in Israel! He shall be to you a restorer of life and a nourisher of your old age; for your daughter-in-law who loves you, who is more to you than seven sons, has borne him." Then Na'omi took the child and laid him in her bosom, and became his nurse. And the women of the neighborhood gave him a name, saying, "A son has been born to Na'omi." (Ruth 4:14–17)

Ruth provides for Naomi in her old age. Naomi, in turn, provides a husband for her daughter-in-law through the customs of her people, in this case levirate marriage. And Ruth is rewarded for her love for Naomi with status explicitly compared to that held by Leah and Rachel, "who together built up the house of Israel" (Ruth 4:11), for though she bears but one son, he is the grandfather of David (Ruth 4:17). Interestingly, the action in this book is initiated by women; the central result—the birth of David's ancestor—issues from the love of women for each other; and the witnesses and commentators are "the women of the neighborhood."

Esther

The book of Esther is quite different in both its content and message and expresses attitudes toward women from a later time, when they apparently were not as autonomous or as highly valued as persons. Although Esther is shown as the savior of the Jews during their exile, all the events in the story—and indeed her success in preventing the extermination of the Jews and enabling their revenge on their enemies—rest on the consequences of female insubordination to husbands and on Esther's beauty, sexuality, and obedience to her cousin and adoptive father, Mordecai. She is at the center of a network of relationships between men, and saves her people in ways acceptable to them.

The book opens with King Ahasuerus deposing his queen, Vashti, after she refuses to appear, at his command, to display her physical charms before him and his royal companions during a marathon drinking bout. The rationale for her fall from power is that Vashti's behavior might set a precedent for the insubordination of the other rulers' wives. Esther is rounded up along with all of the other beautiful young virgins so that a new queen may be chosen, and because of her beauty she supplants Vashti. Following Mordecai's directions, she conceals the fact that she is a Jew. Mordecai meanwhile discovers a plot against the king's life, conveys the information to Esther, and she informs the king that she had this from Mordecai.

Events are set into motion by a rivalry between men, from which Esther is excluded. Haman is elevated to a position of authority second only to the king, and Mordecai is the only one who refuses to pay him proper homage. Haman determines to rid himself of Mordecai and, along with him, all the rest of the Jews. Toward this end, he persuades the king to issue an edict ordering the murder of all the Jews throughout his vast empire.

Though she has nothing whatsoever to do with initiating it, Esther is forced at this point to enter the struggle between the two men, Mordecai and Haman. The former tells Esther that she must plead for her people before the king. When she shows some reluctance, Mordecai threatens her real father's line with extinction. He predicts that the Jews will be saved anyway (presumably by God), but that she will have only a temporary reprieve should she refuse. Under this compulsion, Esther once more obeys Mordecai. She risks her life by appearing before the king unsummoned and, once more, he is so struck by her beauty that he promises to grant her almost any request.

Esther proposes that the king and Haman banquet with her. When she is again asked for her petition, Esther tells the king that she and all her people face death because of Haman. In a fury, the king leaves the table and retreats to the garden to think about this piece of news. In his absence, Haman falls on Queen Esther's couch to beg for his life. The king returns and mistakes the scene for Haman attempting to force himself on the queen sexually. Once again trading with her sexuality, Esther does not contradict his misapprehension, and this seals Haman's fate. He is hanged from the gallows intended for Mordecai, and all the rest of his family is put to death as well. Also, partly because of his prior service to the king but especially because of his relationship to Esther, Mordecai is given a high place in the palace, and together they easily convince the king to cancel the order to exterminate the Jews and to grant them the right to dispose of their enemies.

The moral of the story seems fairly clear. If only they are beautiful enough and obey the orders of their closest male relatives, women can rise to any rank in society, violate accepted conventions, even royal ones, and accomplish almost anything, indeed turn aside royal decrees and save their people. Conversely, even queens like Vashti and Esther risk their positions and their lives if they are insubordinate to their royal husbands, or do not "find favor" in their eyes.

Judith

The book of Judith in the Apocrypha adds another dimension to the male perception of the power of female beauty and sexuality. The Assyrian King Nebuchadnezzar sends a tremendous army against all the peoples in Western Asia who refuse to surrender to his dominion and pay him tribute. His greatest general, Holofernes, conquers and plunders everything in the line of his march until he reaches Judea in Canaan, where he threatens the Hebrews and the new temple they had erected to God after their return from captivity. The Hebrews face more than 170,000 infantry and 12,000 cavalry with nothing to oppose the Assyrian onslaught but their faith in God and their control of the narrow mountain passes. When their water supply is cut off, their leaders in effect give God five days to save them or they will surrender.

At this juncture, pious, wise, rich, widowed, and beautiful Judith makes her appearance. She castigates the Hebrews for pretending to know God's intentions and for testing God when, in fact, the reverse was usually the case, and announces that she is "about to do a thing which will go down through all generations of our descendants," and that "the Lord will deliver Israel by my hand" (Jth. 8:32–33). After the elders leave, Judith prays to God and pleads that "through the deceit of my lips" their enemies might be crushed by "the hand of a woman" (Jth. 9:10–11).

Then she returns home, removes her widow's weeds, bathes and anoints herself, puts on her most gorgeous clothing and jewelry, "and made herself very beautiful, to entice the eyes of all men who might see her" (Jth. 10:4). When the elders of the city see her, they respond not to her piety or daring but to her physical appearance: they "noted how her face was altered and her clothing changed, they greatly admired her beauty, and said to her, 'May the God of our fathers grant you favor and fulfill your plans, that the people of Israel may glory and Jerusalem may be exalted.' And she worshipped God" (Jth. 10:7–8).

Judith and her maid descend to the Assyrian camp. The patrols, taken in by her beauty, believe her fabrication that she has left her people to avoid capture and her offer to show their commander how to capture the Hebrews without losing a life, and they escort her to the tent of Holofernes. While she waits for an audience with him, his men:

> marveled at her beauty, and admired the Israelites, judging them by her, and everyone said to his neighbor, "Who can despise these people, who have women like this among them? Surely not a man of them had better be left alive, for if we let them go they will be able to ensnare the whole world!" ... when Judith came into the presence of Holofernes and his servants, they all marveled at the beauty of her face. (Jth. 10:19, 23)

Judith tells Holofernes that his siege has forced the Hebrews to sin by eating things forbidden to them by God. She offers to stay with them, claims foreknowledge of when the Hebrews will transgress, predicts that on that day God will abandon the Israelites and hand them over to their enemies, and promises to lead Holofernes in triumph through Judea and place him on the throne in Jerusalem. Holofernes replies that God chose well to send a messenger like Judith to help the Assyrians defeat the Hebrews. He calls her as wise as she is beautiful, promises to adopt her God as his own if she keeps her word, and predicts that she will live in Nebuchadnezzar's palace and be famous throughout the world (Jth. 11:22–23).

Several days later, Holofernes is overcome with desire for her and has her brought to him during a feast for his slaves. He drinks a great deal, becomes intoxicated, and after everyone leaves Judith remains alone with him in his tent. While he is in a drunken stupor, she tells God that she is acting "for the exaltation of Jerusalem" (Jth. 13:14), and she cuts off his head. She and her maid return to the Israelites. Judith shows them the commander's head, tells them the whole story, and declares, "it was my face that tricked him to his destruction" (Jth. 14:16).

Holofernes' head is displayed on the parapets of Judea, and the mighty Assyrian invaders retreat in confusion. The Israelites attack, outflank, destroy, and plunder them, and Judith is honored as a heroine of Israel. She shares this honor with the other women, and in a song of thanksgiving to God, Judith says:

> But the Lord Almighty has foiled them by the hand of a woman.
> For their mighty one did not fall by the hands of the young men,
> nor did the sons of the Titans smite him,
> nor did tall giants set upon him;
> but Judith the daughter of Merari undid him
> with the beauty of her countenance. (Jth. 16:6–7)

After a period of worship and general rejoicing, the people return home. Judith refuses many offers of marriage and is revered to the end of her long life.

The Moral

Again, as in the case of Esther, a woman risks her life to save her people, and, although she acts on her own, Judith too is identified through her relations with men, as a widow and daughter. Like Esther, and unlike Deborah and Jael, her success depends on her physical beauty. She literally and single-handedly ravishes the Assyrian war machine to defeat. Only added to her beauty are many other virtues —piety, wisdom, wealth, courage. There is still another, for after the death of her husband she remains chaste and faithful to his memory, or the very paradigm of a monogamous wife.

And that is just the point. The great male heroes of Israel exhibit their courage and save their people by relying on God rather than their physical beauty and sexuality. While Esther and Judith are also courageous and pious, it is their beauty and sexuality alone which guarantee their triumph over the enemies of Israel. Furthermore, while Esther's obedience to her uncle and Judith's faithfulness to her deceased husband only serve to enhance their virtue, the virtue of men is not likewise defined by their obedience to women or their fidelity to wives, either living or dead. Moreover, among a people ever conscious of God's covenant with the patriarchs, in which the divine promise is to multiply greatly the seed of the Israelites until they become a great nation, what is strangely omitted from the stories of Esther and Judith are any allusions to their capacity for motherhood, as though heroism in women, in some fashion, precludes maternity. By implication, then, those women who saved their people by their heroism occupy a status only peripheral to the fulfillment of the divine covenant, since they are shown as contributing to the conservation rather than enlargement of Israel.

Virtue in Women, Virtue in Men

This nonmaternal motif is repeated in the concluding chapter of Proverbs, which describes a virtuous woman as wife not mother (Prov. 31:10–31). It is rather remarkable on several counts. Besides the self-description of Wisdom, Proverbs is addressed almost entirely to men. The final section describes the advantages accruing to men from the possession of a virtuous wife and delineates the meaning of virtue along sexual lines. While virtue in men is seen as achieved by the pursuit of wisdom, adherence to divine commandments, and avoidance of all the temptations to moral transgression—i.e., virtue is accessible to men across a fairly broad spectrum of behavior rooted in moral choices—the path to virtue for women is more restricted and flows out of their roles as wives.

Though her children are mentioned fleetingly, and she undoubtedly was expected to produce heirs for her husband, it seems significant that the virtuous wife is for the most part described and exalted primarily in her role as economic producer. And it is a mighty role indeed, for both the survival and prosperity of her husband and family depend on her economic labors. (Incidentally, this conforms to much of what is known about the major roles of most women in families in historic times. It appears that they contributed indispensable economic labor as household producers and managers of domestic industries essential to life, in addition to any other work they may have done. Their roles as mothers, while vital, were not seen as consuming all of their energies and intelligence by any means and may have been perceived as almost secondary once offspring were produced.)

In addition to working from the middle of one night to the middle of the next while her husband is "known in the gates, when he sits among the elders of the land," she is lauded for contributing to his "gain," "does him good and not harm, all the days of her life" (and nothing is said about his treatment of her), and is described as dispensing charity, showing fearlessness even in the face of "the times to come," or the last days, has good business sense, and works with "strength," "dignity," "wisdom" and "kindness." The last thing she would (or could) do, apparently, was "eat the bread of idleness."

She is "blessed" if she exhibits all these traits. Her "praise" for these monumental labors is given divine sanction by cleverly linking her prescribed role to her fear of God, or her domestic work is viewed as a sign of her piety and acceptance of the divine ordering of existence. And her reward is that "her works praise her in the gates" of the city, or win her approval from the men and "elders of the land" who congregate there.

Thus, her domain as virtuous woman or virtuous wife, for they are synonymous—the exercise of her judgment and authority, the concerns of all her waking hours (and they are many), the requirements of her virtue itself—is circumscribed by the material and physical world in which she productively labors. She certainly does not have time to sit "in the gates" with the male elders to dispute, praise, or blame, nor would she receive praise if she did. She herself becomes an *object* of praise or blame. She is rewarded by the favorable judgment of the men in the gates if she industriously fulfills her economic role, and presumably would be punished by the withdrawal of praise if she chose to occupy her time otherwise.

By way of contrast, the domain of men is the rest of the world. Their concerns revolve around how to achieve righteousness through following the teachings of wisdom, how to make difficult moral choices, and how to preserve themselves from moral corruption, sometimes embodied in Proverbs as sexual women.

The wife's labor for her husband and household is emphasized, with a curious silence about any feelings she might have as mother to her own children, although if she were barren it would be her greatest disability. In short, the physical world is where wives exercise their virtue, and the moral world becomes reserved for their fathers, husbands, and sons, who are released from the time-consuming domestic obligations of material and menial work by the exertions of their virtuous daughters, wives, and mothers. This division of labor on earth recalls the reason for the creation of humanity by divinities of the Sumerian and Babylonian pantheons. People were to perform all the physical and menial labor and thus relieve goddesses and gods of the necessity to do it themselves. But whereas in polytheistic creation-stories such work was assigned to persons irrespective of sex, in Proverbs it seems to fall within the sphere of women alone.

Gender and the Domain of Moral Judgment

Furthermore, a curious shift in focus may be noted. While goddesses were hardly viewed exclusively as cosmic mothers any more than gods were portrayed only as cosmic fathers, and both usually had other important functions as well, the ancient polytheistic reverence for femaleness, personified and deified as the source of life and fertility or seen as importantly involved in the creation and reproduction of life along with male divinities, gives way to the image of an asexual deity as the source of life, nature, and moral law. In the absence of any female involvement, the secular corollary of this image in Proverbs is a greater reverence shown to mortal women as economic producers than as producers of life, thereby discounting the one thing only women can do, and an assumption of the domain of moral judgment by men.

In like fashion, the ancient polytheistic reverence for femaleness in its chthonic aspect, in the form of goddesses receiving the dead back into the womb of the earth or as sitting in judgment of the dead along with male divinities, is supplanted by the biblical view of the final judgment of people after death, or at the end of human history, as presided over by a nominally asexual deity who is represented as making different moral judgments on the basis of sex in his interactions with the human community. And in the process of judging women, the measure of their righteousness or virtue might very well have depended on the extent to which they conformed to their sexually prescribed economic roles, or confined themselves to the business of the material world, as determined by God and interpreted by men.

Honor in Women, Honor in Men

However, the emphasis on the nonmaternal contributions of women is only one facet of a deep ambivalence toward appropriate roles for women, for simultaneous with the highest value assigned to their economic labor as virtuous wives was the premium that came to be placed on their roles as mothers or, more properly, reproducers. The concept of honor itself seems to have been different for women than men. For the latter, honor was often thought of as synonymous with the possession of property or wealth, which in ancient Israel belonged to men, and it was also equated with strength or valor.[1]

Deborah and Jael are among the strongest and most valorous women in the Old Testament. But they are really anachronisms from an older period, dating from a time before the almost total masculinization of ritual, which was marked by the interdiction of the "holy men" and "holy women" of the temple, the suppression of the cult of women mourning the dying god Tammuz, and the elimination of the sacred sexual cults appropriated from Canaanite worship (2 Kings 23:4–16, 19–20, 24; 2 Chron. 34:2–7). In other words, the honor of Deborah and Jael is described in the same way as that of men at a time when women still apparently played an important role in cult.

By the exilic and postexilic eras, close to when the Old Testament was set in its final form, the concept of honor for women had changed considerably and was seen as available to them only through marriage and motherhood. (This is especially ironic since, according to Jewish law, propagation is obligatory for the man but not for the woman.) In his seminal work on ancient Israel, for example, Pedersen writes:

> The honor of a woman is to bear a man's name through marriage. If she does not obtain this, she is dishonoured (*Isaiah,* 4:1). And her honour as a wife she only maintains by multiplying and continuing the name of her husband through posterity. As a mother the woman is honoured; childlessness is a shame which she can hardly survive. Only when Rachel gives birth to a son, is she able to say: God has taken away my shame (*Genesis,* 30:23). Hannah is so bowed down by her childlessness that she nearly dies with shame. The woman who gives birth to a son no longer needs to be afraid; she has fulfilled her task, her soul has acquired merit (*1 Samuel,* 4:20). Jerusalem is sometimes called a childless widow, when its state of deepest degradation is to be characterized. A childless widow is entirely destitute of honour and has no great hope of acquiring any. And still less honour has perhaps the woman who has been repudiated by her husband, because she could not fulfill her task of supplying him with children. . . . To bear a man's name and to increase it is the honour of the woman. The dishonoured virgin is bowed down with shame, because she has been taken by the man without his giving her a name. And the faithless wife degrades herself and sins against her own soul, because she has given it to her husband and takes her name from him, while at the same time giving herself to another, whose name she does not bear (cf. *Hosea,* 2:7)[2]

This notion of honor in women as deriving totally from their relationships with their husbands, in which the wives provide for them, is consistent with the portrait of the virtuous wife in Proverbs and of Sarah's relationship with Abraham. Its importance for understanding the roles of Old Testament women is that it establishes a sexual hierarchy of access to the divine. Women achieve their highest honor through their relationships with their husbands, by providing them with children. Their husbands, in turn, achieve their highest honor through their relationships with God, by participating in sacred rites.

Other Views of Women As Mothers, and Some Problems

The equation of honor with motherhood for women has prompted a number of recent writers to reinterpret or explain the respective roles of the sexes in the Old Testament from a somewhat new perspective, which challenges the more traditional belief that ancient Israel was overwhelmingly patriarchal in structure. These theories range from a contention that those sex roles were substantively complementary but equal, to an argument that women as mothers were regarded as superior to men, to an explanation of the restriction of women's most important roles to the domestic and reproductive spheres as having been necessitated by historical events rather than having originated in the biblical vision of the divine-human relationship. All of these speculations share a common assumption, namely that divine sanction of different roles assigned to people on the basis of their sex in no way alters or diminishes the concern for righteousness and justice attributed to God.

For instance, in an essay on the images of women in the Old Testament, Phyllis Bird maintains that the varying, sometimes ambiguous, even contradictory, portrayals of women, all drawn from the male point of view, may be joined by understanding woman's role, in relation to man, as "a helper, whose work as wife and mother is essential and complementary to his own. In a sense she completes him—but as one with a life and character of her own. She is his opposite and equal."[3]

Bird finds substantiation for this in her reading of the story of creation:

> While the two creation accounts of Genesis differ markedly in language, style, date and traditions employed, their statements about woman are essentially the same: woman is, along with man, the direct and intentional creation of God and the crown of his creation. Man and woman were made for each other. Together they constitute humankind, which is in its full and essential nature bisexual.[4]

Though Bird recognizes that "Israel rarely lived up to this vision,"[5] she believes that "male-dominated language and structures disguised to a considerable degree the actual power, freedom and respect of women in the society—respect based largely, though not solely, upon complementarity of roles."[6] And again, "Israel's best statements about woman recognize her as an equal with man, and with him jointly responsible to God and to cohumanity."[7]

However, Bird's own account of women's restricted and inferior roles in Israel, measured by economic criteria, legal status, and participation in cult, and the frequent depiction of women as adjuncts to men in a document written exclusively by men, focusing mostly on male activities in a male-dominant society,[8] are all difficult to reconcile with her description of the "power," "freedom," and "respect" supposedly accorded to women at the same time, or with her conclusion that the Old Testament considers women "equal" to men. Also, it seems somehow inappropriate to evaluate ancient Israel's statements as "best" or worst from the vantage of our own times, or to refer to its "vision" as if it were a thing apart from its concrete expression in the Bible.

God's *intentionality* in creating both man and woman says nothing about their creation in *equality,* and "helper" to man means just that. That "humankind" includes both sexes is of course self-evident, but woman was made for man; they were not "made for each other." In fact, the very notion of "complementarity" would seem to underscore the extent to which men's sphere in life was exclusionary of women.

This last is perhaps most significant because men's world of cult, war, honor, governance, moral choice, and proprietorship of the promised land, or the cluster of human activities that together formed the content of the divine-human covenant, were viewed as infinitely more important than the roles occupied by women. For if the latter's primary function and honor came to reside in "building up the houses" of their men, it must be seen that women as reproducers are shown in many biblical narratives as fairly interchangeable in perpetuating the male line—e.g., Hagar for Sarah, Lot's daughters for his wife, Leah for Rachel, the anonymous virgins of Jabeshgilead and Shiloh for the lost wives of the Benjaminites.

Moreover, motherhood conferred no special rights on women. In the midst of a difficult delivery just before Rachel was to die in childbirth, the midwife says to her: "Fear not: for now you will have another son" (Gen. 35:17). Rachel is deprived even of the right to name the son who is to cost her her life. As she lay dying, she called him Ben-oni, but his father named him Benjamin (Gen. 35:18), or "the son of my old age."

Likewise, the all-important initial division of the land of Canaan, promised by God under the covenant with Abraham to him and his posterity, involved only the adult males of the tribes that left Egypt with Moses. The latter and Eleazar, son of the priest Aaron, are instructed by God to take a census of Israel, including all those over twenty years of age, counted by membership in their "fathers' houses

. . . who are able to go forth to war" (Num. 26:2). This census excludes women, for the rest of the chapter enumerates all the *sons* of their fathers, and God orders the distribution of the land according to the size of the families of these sons (Num. 26:52–56).

Thus, women are included as settlers in the promised land or share in the fulfillment of the divine covenant not in a direct fashion but by virtue of their relationships to men as wives, mothers, and daughters. And though their roles as mothers must have been highly valued then, since the size of land allotments was proportionate to their fecundity, as reproducers they remain anonymous. Yet again, in a chapter that carefully names the men and their tribes, the anonymity of the women is telling and perhaps symbolic of their indirect relation to God.

Carol Meyers sees the movement toward constricting the roles of women to the domestic arena and motherhood as an outgrowth of the need to maintain the population level at a time when epidemics, high infant and maternal mortality, and a scarcity of women of childbearing age all precipitated a demographic crisis in Israel by the end of the Bronze Age.[9] John Otwell extends this thesis a bit further by arguing that the incorporation of woman's identity into that of her father or husband, who then represented the family unit in its dealings with the rest of the community, was more than compensated for by the mother's crucial role in providing for the survival of the group in the face of disease, famine, and constant warfare.[10]

Otwell surmises that God's promise to the Hebrews in the covenant, namely that they would survive as a people in exchange for the fidelity of Israel to his worship, made them see all new life as a consequence of divine intervention, or woman as reproducer was seen as:

> a primary locus of divine activity. Her fecundity was a basic evidence of divine care for Israel. Motherhood thus was not only a biological and sociological function. It was a sacred act of great magnitude which only the woman could perform. The very high esteem in which the mother was held was then described, especially as it is reflected in similes of God's care for Israel and of God's judgment upon Israel.
>
> No higher status could be given anyone than was given the mother in ancient Israel.[11]

There are several problems inherent in both of these approaches. With regard to the last, the obvious reality is that the survival of the group was guaranteed by the reproduction of women in all cultures, those which worshiped Yahweh and those which did not. Further, regardless of whether or not the Israelites attributed pregnancy to divine intervention, there is evidence that they also knew about more mundane causes and the participation of men in reproduction, e.g., as in the pregnancies of Hagar, Leah, Rachel, Tamar, Bathsheba, Ruth. In addition, women who were also mothers seem to have held higher positions in cult and public life in some of the polytheistic cultures surrounding Israel that shared the monotheistic belief in a divine source of fertility.

Therefore, factors other than a reverence for motherhood alone or a belief in divine intervention in the creation of new life were apparently responsible for the radical elevation of the importance of gender as the basis of largely segregated roles in the Old Testament. Moreover, women were not only indispensable as mothers but, as has been seen, also highly honored as economic producers. In any event, the fact that they were highly honored in either or both of these roles would hardly and in itself explain their subordination to men in cult, war, the family, and under the law.

Adverse social conditions due to military conflicts, plagues, and a high incidence of infant and maternal mortality were by no means unique to the end of the second millennium or to ancient Israel. Those same afflictions existed in many societies in varying degrees throughout recorded human history. Hence, one would have to look at complex political, social, economic, and ideological factors in addition to the need to replenish the population in order to explain why, for instance, women's roles were not as restricted in other times and places that had like population requirements.

To cite but two of many possible examples, the Homeric tradition dating from the late Bronze Age describes warrior societies with similar needs for population replacement within which some women—Klaitemnestra, Helen, the mothers of Nausicaa and Andromache—exercised considerable power and autonomy apart from their roles as mothers. Later, in ancient Sparta, the status of women as compared with men was quite high even while both sexes were required either to serve as warriors or to breed them for the state. Within the limits of motherhood, or the provision of an adequate supply of soldiers or reproducers of soldiers, Spartan women apparently enjoyed at least as much personal and sexual freedom as men, were not burdened with legal prescriptions of their inferiority, did not suffer cultic deprivations because of their sex, and lived in a culture where male rather than female infanticide was practiced. Indeed, before the demise of Sparta as a great city-state, and even in the midst of a critical decline in population, Spartan women not only seem to have enjoyed a fair amount of economic independence but also apparently had some control over their own reproduction.

In other words, as compared with polytheistic societies of approximately the same period, motherhood among the Israelites did not in itself always confer high status in social life or cult, and the emphasis on virtue or honor in women as contingent on the fulfillment of either their economic or maternal roles cannot be explained merely by the pressing need for a larger population. In contrast with the individualized representations of the great male leaders of Israel, the very interchangeability and anonymity of some of the women honored in their maternal roles reflect the lesser status accorded to those roles.

Attitudes toward Women under Divine Laws

Furthermore, it may be that it was precisely in their roles within the family—as wives and mothers, as sexual females, and in their normal biological functioning as reproducers of the social group—that women were treated most punitively, even as they were prized for their economic labors or came to be honored most for their motherhood; here the full force and depth of the ambivalence toward women becomes visible. Unlike the polytheistic attitude toward sexuality, and particularly female sexuality, as not only natural but also the source of social good, with rare exceptions like the *Song of Songs,* there is in the Bible a pervasively pejorative attitude toward sexual females that almost borders on the obsessive.

However, before examining the evidence for this, it should be reemphasized that a broad-scale comparison of the position of women under the civil laws of polytheistic societies and the biblical laws of the Pentateuch, presumably emanating from Yahweh, is neither intended nor appropriate here. Rather, within the very limited context of determining the extent to which ancient Israelite women were especially honored for their motherhood (as Otwell contends), or the extent to which wifehood and motherhood conferred complementary but equal status for women as compared to men (as Bird maintains), it is necessary to look at those biblical laws that directly bear on the status of women as wives and mothers. Since the capacity for motherhood rests on female sexuality and normal biological functions, it seems appropriate to consider biblical attitudes toward those aspects as well. Furthermore, it is important to recall that, unlike the civil statutes that governed relations between the sexes in polytheistic cultures, biblical laws were represented as universal moral laws of divine origin and therefore imply some assessment of women and men as moral beings as they participate in the divine covenant.

Under divine law, the differences between the rights of women and men seem to be predicated solely on sexual differences. The unifying thread running through women's legal status with regard to property rights, inheritance, influence within the family, control over their own bodies, access to divorce and the like, is the view of ancient Hebraic law, presented as divine commands, that women as members of their sex had fewer rights and less protection under those laws than men. The thrust of the law's concern is for the rights, honor, and welfare of men as husbands or fathers.

Woman As Wife

For example, women were at an enormous disadvantage within the type of monogamous relationship laid out for them by God. A jealous husband had inordinate power over his wife, whether she committed adultery or whether she did not (Num. 5:12–14). Not only was the procedure the same in either case, but there were no comparable rights for the wife who either knew her husband committed adultery or was jealous simply because she thought he had.

The divinely ordained trial by ordeal was used only for the wife. In a society that countenanced polygamy and, from the male perspective, an easy coexistence of wives and concubines within one man's household, it comes as no surprise that adultery committed by wives would be harshly punished. But there are several other elements in this test of female monogamy that seem so excessively punitive to married women that the latter can be seen only as victims.

On the most superficial level, of course, while wives could commit adultery that affected their own husbands, the latter could commit adultery that affected only other women's husbands. Far more vindictive was the divine edict that wives should be subjected to what must have been a fairly public and humiliating trial by ordeal, involving rather horrible and anxiety-producing rituals, literally executed by a male priest, not only for the commission of adultery but even if their husbands merely suspected it (Num. 5:11–30).

Perhaps the most revealing part of the process, in terms of what it denotes about the utterly powerless position of the woman relative to her husband in marriage, is the conclusion. If the wife was found guilty, her belly would swell, her thigh would rot and fall off, and she would become a curse among her people (Num. 5:27). However, whether the woman was found innocent or guilty, "the man shall be free from iniquity, but the woman shall bear her iniquity" (Num. 5:31). In addition, if she was found innocent, the wife's powerlessness was highlighted by the priestly promise that she would "conceive children" or be impregnated by the very husband who submitted her to that awful trial in the first place.

If there was little equality between wives and husbands under divine law, and if the woman was at the mercy of her husband's caprice while married, it was likewise his unilateral right to divorce her if "she finds no favor in his eyes because he has found some indecency in her" (Deut. 24:1). While one school of later rabbinic commentators translated "some indecency" to mean unchastity in the wife, another maintained that it signified any kind of indecency. In any case, the right to divorce, and very likely the determination of what was "indecent," appears clearly to have been only the husband's prerogative. There is no reference to any sort of protection for the wife in these circumstances, even from her own family. There is no reciprocal right of the wife to test the truth of her husband's allegations by subjecting him to a public and noxious trial by ordeal. In the context of married women's lack of power or autonomy in relation to their husbands under the law, it seems most probable that the husband might define anything not to his liking in his wife as "indecent."

Again, in light of the concern expressed by God in Deuteronomy for the "hired servant," "the poor man," "the sojourner," "the fatherless," and "the widow" (Deut. 24:12–22), and the divine admonitions to care for their needs and not oppress them, it seems at the least anomalous that the situation of married women was not seen as oppressive. But once more, the key question is, "oppressive to whom?" and it apparently was not so to the husbands or men who wrote the books.

It is likewise anomalous that one finds in our own century scholarly comments on biblical texts like the following:

> 'It is astonishing to find how many of the laws—especially in the greathearted Book of Deuteronomy—are expressly designed to protect the interests of the impoverished and defenceless members of society' (McFayden). 'No other system of jurisprudence in any country at any period is marked by such humanity in respect to the unfortunate' (Houghton). The stranger, fatherless, and widow should be treated with a generous perception of the peculiar difficulties of their lot. Care for them is characteristic of Jewish civilization generally, whether in ancient, medieval, or modern times.[12]

That married women—victims of trials by ordeal simply because "the spirit of jealousy" seized their husbands, like a fit, or subjected to instant divorce by their husbands who found them "indecent"—are in our own time excluded from the class of the "defenceless" and "unfortunate" would seem to indicate a strong tradition of continuity with the biblical view that women as wives could not be deprived, and certainly were not victimized, by their position under the law or under their husbands' "authority" (Num. 5:19–20). In fulfilling what was seen as their divinely ordained roles within the family as virtuous wives, women truly do not fall within the purview of divine sympathy for the unfortunate, and indeed earn praise for their performance in these roles.

To question the justice afforded women in their roles as virtuous wives might imply that God is less righteous to women than to men. Indeed, the former inhabit an existential space that is only marginal in its relation to those whose sufferings elicit God's compassion. It is the widow, not the wife, who must not be oppressed and whose special needs must be met, as though marriage itself in extraordinary fashion exempted women from oppression or having special unmet needs. And as members of a sex seen as somehow less moral than men, and never shown as experiencing the moral torments of a Job or an Abraham, from the vantage of male biblical writers even the pain of women is seen as somehow of lesser magnitude than that of men. Portrayed as preoccupied with the material and economically productive tasks in a religious universe dominated by moral issues, the lives of women as virtuous wives or mothers emerge as merely auxiliary to those large issues, and their suffering is both minimized and trivialized.

With the terrain of the rulers, prophets, sages, warriors, and priests largely off-limits to most biblical women, it is not too difficult to see why their more constricted roles in marriage as compared with those of their husbands—especially when these narrower confines were validated by divine commands—did not in themselves constitute pressing moral issues to the male authors of the Bible and to later biblical commentators. The nature of the relationship between God and his people is, moreover, clarified as one between males, when God says, after he had led the Israelites out of Egypt:

> "All the commandment which I command you this day you shall be careful to do, that you may live and multiply, and go in and possess the land which the Lord swore to give your fathers. . . . Know then in your heart that, as a man disciplines his son, the Lord your God disciplines you." (Deut. 8:1, 5)

The Chastity of Women

The masculine imagery that cloaks the relationship of God and Israel is enhanced by the manner in which disputes over the chastity of newly married women were settled by men. If a husband charged his wife with not being a virgin at marriage, her parents had the responsibility of displaying the proofs of her virginity (presumably bloody bed-coverings) to the male elders of the city. If the proof of her chastity was convincing, the elders "chastise" the husband and compel him to pay a monetary fine to the father, "because he has brought an evil name upon a virgin of Israel" (Deut. 22:19). The falsely accused wife must not only return to that loving husband who has publicly charged her with unchastity, and been whipped and fined on her account, but just as "he may not put her away all his days" (Deut. 22:19), so she must live all *her* days with a man who suspected her and was punished because of her.

If persuasive enough evidence of her prior virginity was not forthcoming, the alternative provided by God to this state of wedded bliss for the wife was:

> "then they shall bring out the young woman to the door of her father's house, and the men of her city shall stone her to death with stones, because she has wrought folly in Israel by playing the harlot in her father's house; so you shall purge the evil from the midst of you." (Deut. 22:21)

With the high value placed on the virginity and monogamy of women to assure legitimate heirs for men, the disparity in the punishment assigned by God for the false public accusation of the wife by the husband on the one hand, and the sexual activity of the betrothed woman on the other, is as striking as the two awful and only alternatives the wife was faced with, both stemming from her husband's initiative. She was consigned either to a lifelong marriage with a probably hostile husband or to death.

The central concern, it would seem, was for the honor of the husband and the father, since the latter was compensated for a false accusation. The woman occupied a peripheral status in the contest between the two men. Her future (or her lack of a future) was determined by its outcome, and for her either result must have been horrendous. Indeed, the position of the wife was utterly powerless and passive, while the husband, father, and the elders of the city contended among themselves to judge, exonerate, or condemn her. In sum, she became an *object* to be acted upon in a process of adjudication she neither helped to establish nor participated in. On another level, she almost served as the embodiment of the community's sin, not unlike the ancient use of scapegoats either animal or human. And her suffering served also as a potent warning to other women, and as a means of socializing them to compliance with male law.

Female Sexuality

When women move outside of the confines of monogamous marriage in a sexual way, as, of course, men like David and Solomon did, or attempt to escape the absolute power of husbands or fathers within the family and behave with some autonomy in terms of their sexuality, whether Hebrew or alien they are shown as either powerless, anonymous, or sexual predators. For example, the Egyptian Potiphar's wife (otherwise unnamed) tries unsuccessfully to seduce Joseph (Gen. 39:1–20). While she becomes the unwitting vehicle for his incarceration, subsequent interpretation of the Pharaoh's dream, and ascendance to high rank in the palace, she is in no way responsible for his talents. Joseph was interpreting his own dreams while he was still a shepherd with his brothers in Canaan, and it was one of the things that made his brothers hate him and sell him into slavery (Gen. 37:5–9). The woman is shown as sexually aggressive, dangerous to Joseph in a mindless sort of way, and a liar, but she is ultimately powerless to affect his destiny in any way. Lacking even a name to corroborate her existence as an individual, she is, in fact, objectified as a test of Joseph's virtue.

In the book of Proverbs, men are specifically warned against the danger of seduction by wicked women, particularly those who "belong" to other men, if they intend to live righteously. It is noteworthy that there are no comparable warnings to women to beware of seduction by married men, possibly because the advice and warnings are issued by Solomon to his "sons," more likely because the preservation of male righteousness took precedence over the righteousness of women. Female sexuality outside of monogamous marriage was viewed as a defilement of God's laws and a threat to men's virtue. Women are portrayed as sexual predators and men as their innocent victims, and their involvement with women who would sexually divert them from righteousness can only lead men to their death. While Wisdom as a feminine abstraction is revered, the imagery confined to real women is starkly misogynistic and reveals a deep fear of their sexuality.

The adulterous woman lurks in dark corners, ready to pounce on her innocent victims like the evil spirits of ancient Babylon. She is described as a "loose woman," an "adventuress" who flatters, cajoles, and seduces her "simple" young prey with "smooth words." She is "loud," "wayward," dressed as "a harlot," and "her feet do not stay at home"—the very opposite of a pliant, submissive wife. With her "seductive speech" she "persuades" and "compels" her young man to follow her, "as an ox goes to slaughter" (and this does not say much for the self-control or good sense of the young man). Beyond her adultery, the overarching images are of the woman as overtly sexual, sexually aggressive, and sexually predatory; of the young man as her victim; and of the inevitable association of female seductiveness and sexuality with death (Prov. 6:29, 7:4–13, 18–19, 21–23, 25–27).

Rape

It is perhaps in the narratives and laws that deal with the sexual assault of women that the clearest statement of their power relative to men may be found. While they do not differ substantively from the accounts of Lot's attitudes toward his daughters in Genesis or those of the Levite toward his concubine in Judges, their appearance in episodes of the settlement of the promised land under the divine covenant, in the behavior of the first great king of Israel, and in the body of divine laws in the Pentateuch, all enhance the force of their message about the lack of divine protection from unprovoked violence directed against women. Taken together, the sexual oppression of women, and the extent to which it was not recognized as especially oppressive by men, provide a sort of benchmark for measuring the elevation of gender in ancient Israel as a divinely mandated sign of power or powerlessness.

In fulfillment of the divine covenant, Jacob buys land and settles in Canaan. When his daughter Dinah is raped by Schechem, a Canaanite prince, her brothers Simeon and Levi avenge her by first pretending friendship with her rapist and his kin, and then by killing Schechem, his father, and all the men of their city after they are weakened by circumcision. They loot the city, capture the women and children, and remove Dinah from Schechem's house. Jacob's reaction to his sons' revenge for his daughter's rape articulates a new point of view, different from the strong sister-brother bond characteristic of many Near Eastern polytheistic myths, and in this new view the fate of the woman barely figures, except for her implicit inclusion as part of her father's "household." Jacob says to his sons: "You have brought trouble on me by making me odious to the inhabitants of the land, the Canaanites and the Per'izzites; my numbers are few, and if they gather themselves against me and attack me, I shall be destroyed, both I and my household" (Gen. 34:30). Simeon and Levi reply: "Should he treat our sister as a harlot?" (Gen. 34:31). In an interesting footnote to this dialogue, a modern biblical scholar remarks: "Jacob has been criticized for merely rebuking his sons because their actions might cause him personal danger, and not pointing out the heinous crime they had done in taking advantage of the helplessness of men with whom they had made a pact of friendship."[13] However, on his deathbed, Jacob curses his sons' "fierce anger" and "cruel wrath."

One can hardly distinguish here between the attitudes toward women in biblical times expressed by Jacob and the attitudes toward women in our own time expressed by biblical scholars. Is the rape of a woman not a "heinous crime," and was Dinah not also helpless? Do the friendships and pacts among men assume greater moral weight than sexual violence committed against women? Is the sense of outrage over the rape of Dinah insufficient provocation for her brothers' anger? Are the lives and integrity of women dispensable and subordinate to the alliances among men?

Likewise, when King David learns that his son Amnon had raped his sister Tamar, "he was very angry" (2 Sam. 13:21), but David did not punish the rapist. Fully two years later, when Amnon was killed by his brother Absalom to avenge the rape of their sister, Absalom fled from the city and remained away for three years, fearing reprisals from his father. And the intensity of David's longings for his absent son were far greater than his displeasure over the rape of his daughter (2 Sam. 13).

In the provision of penalties for adultery and rape commanded by God, it would seem that the greatest concern was shown for the men involved and the least for the women. There is scant reference to any reciprocity or equality of punishment for both sexes, and one can only conclude that the welfare of women was close to the bottom of the scale of religious and social priorities in ancient Israel.

Under divine law, if a man had intercourse with a married woman, the penalty for both was death. That was considered adultery, in both cases committed against the woman's husband. However, both the transgression and the penalties were different when an unmarried woman had intercourse with a married man. Since the latter had access to more than one wife as well as concubines (and, in any case, one's "property" did not require sexual fidelity, and only the woman had to be monogamous), a man could not, by definition, commit adultery in relation to a woman but only in relation to a woman's husband. Therefore, the punishment for such a sexual liaison, freely entered into by the woman and man, would probably have fallen on the woman alone, not for adultery but for harlotry.

If a man raped a betrothed virgin, the penalty for the woman and man did not depend on the crime but on its location. If it took place in the city where she could be heard, and she did not cry out, they were both to be put to death, he not for having raped the "bethrothed virgin," but "because he violated his neighbor's wife" (Deut. 22:23–24), and she, presumably, for having committed adultery, since a betrothal was considered sexually binding on a woman.

However, this law apparently ignored the violent nature of rape itself. Faced with probable punishment for his act of violence against the woman as "his neighbor's wife," the man might well have forcibly prevented her from making an "outcry," and she would still have been condemned and punished. That it is rape that is being discussed, and not a mutually congenial sexual act, is made clear in the very next verses. If the rape occurred outside the city where no one could hear her outcry, the man was to die and the betrothed virgin was to go free. She was to be absolved from sin and the legal consequences of sin (Deut. 22:25–27), even though she was not its perpetrator but its victim. Indeed, it is hard to comprehend what sin she was absolved from except that of coming to her betrothed husband as an unchaste woman.

If a man raped a virgin who was not betrothed, then he had to compensate her father with a money payment, marry her, and was forbidden to "put her away," or divorce her (Deut. 22:28–29). And yet again, the woman against whom the violence was committed was compelled to spend the rest of her life with the man who raped her. His good feelings toward her may be imagined. He was forced to pay her father and marry her; he could not divorce her; and the only one who benefitted from all of this was her father.

Even if it is argued that in those times a raped woman had a negligible chance of being married because of men's obsession with female chastity and monogamy, and that it likely would have been intolerable for the woman to remain unmarried all her life given the heavy social pressures against it, the compulsion of marriage between the raped and the rapist simply underscores the priority given the sexual preferences of men over the suffering of female victims. Ironically, a society pervaded by a religious outlook that mandated special consideration for the disadvantaged on humanitarian and moral grounds could not devise a more humane option for the raped woman than to swing the full weight of divine law behind her indissoluble union with her rapist.

If women were either seen as sexually predatory and wicked when not monogamous or suffered as victims of the sexual whims of men, even when they used their sexuality (perhaps their only weapon) in an attempt to compel male compliance with divine law, their position under that law was most precarious. In addition, a double standard of possible retribution based on sex reinforced the association of power with maleness and powerlessness with femaleness in ways that discouraged independent action by wronged women.

Judah and Tamar: The Double Sexual Standard

For instance, Judah refuses to permit his youngest son, Shelah, to perform levirate marriage with his daughter-in-law, Tamar, as required under the law, after she has lived as a widow, at Judah's direction, for many years after the deaths of her husband 'Er and his brother

Onan. Tamar sets into motion some interesting circumstances, which vividly illustrate how power was a component of male sexuality and powerlessness of female sexuality.

After the death of Judah's wife, Tamar learns that her father-in-law is going to attend a sheep-shearing in Tinmah. After years of enforced celibacy, she puts aside her widow's clothes and sits disguised at the crossroad along the way, "for she saw that Shelah was grown up, and she had not been given to him in marriage" (Gen. 38:14). Judah mistakes her for a prostitute, has intercourse with her, and promises to pay her with a kid from his flock. She asks for a pledge of his payment, and he gives her his signet, scarf, and staff. He later sends a servant to redeem his pledge, but she is gone, and Judah says: "Let her keep the things as her own, lest we be laughed at" (Gen. 38:23).

About three months later, he is told: "Tamar your daughter-in-law has played the harlot . . . she is with child by harlotry" (Gen. 38:24). As the male head of his family, Judah holds the power of life and death over its members. When Tamar is led out for punishment, she sends her father-in-law's pledges back to him, and tells him that their owner fathered her child. Judah acknowledges them as his own and says: "She is more righteous than I, inasmuch as I did not give her to my son Shelah." And he did not have intercourse with her again (Gen. 38:26).

The similarities and dissimilarities in their positions are rather glaring. They both lack spouses, i.e., there is no question of adultery in the usual sense. They both commit fornication. Her crime was harlotry, his disobedience to the levirate law. She faces death by burning because she was betrothed to Shelah as a child until he grew up and, as already mentioned, betrothal was considered as sexually binding on a woman as marriage. Tamar had no alternative but to present Judah's pledges, and her life was in his hands. Judah could acknowledge the pledges and not burn her, or alternatively not acknowledge the pledges and put her to death.

Further, he never does permit his son to "marry" her, or father a child in the name of his dead brother, for the twins Tamar bears are Judah's. And the latter's only punishment for breaking the law (for men could not be guilty of harlotry), is that he does not "know" Tamar again, although there were probably other prostitutes available. Judah does not have to relinquish his position as head of the clan because of his wrongdoing, and he and his descendants are assured of a place in the inheritance of Israel.

This double standard of punishment based on sex is fairly consistent. Queen Jezebel meets a horrible death because of her idolatry (1 Kings 21:23). However, when Moses is up on Mount Sinai receiving the Ten Commandments, the Hebrews ask Aaron to make them an image of the gods, and he complies with the Golden Calf (Exod. 32:1–5). The enormity of making a graven image of the divine may be estimated by its consequences. In retaliation, God tells the Levites to slaughter three thousand people, and he afflicts the Israelites with a plague as well (Exod. 33:26–35). But he treats his appointed male leaders differently. Aaron and his male descendants retain their power as priests of Israel, despite his idolatry.

Female Biology, Ritual Uncleanness, and Sin

The same double standard applied to the normal biological functioning of women and men. Divine law held that a menstruating woman was "impure" and "unclean," placing her in the same category with lepers, those who had "issues" from their bodies, semen or infectious ones, and those who touched the dead, all of whom were seen as sources of contamination and danger to the rest of the social group (Lev. 15). Thus, recurrently impure in her body, not from disease or sexual intercourse or contact with anything unclean, but simply from being born female, the woman became a source of "uncleanness" to men.

Though it has been maintained by some that this uncleanness applied only to the seven days around her menstrual period, there is some evidence that, in a more general sense, women were seen as more unclean than men. Apparently it was assumed that women were more likely to excite men sexually, or cause an "issue" of semen or uncleanness in men, than the reverse. Men were not considered a cause of uncleanness in women in quite the same way, since the notion of men sexually arousing women, if the latter were virtuous, apparently fell outside the pale of biblical conceptions of female sexuality; e.g., David is not shown as sexually arousing Bathsheba any more than Judah arouses Tamar or Amnon arouses Tamar. In other words, as different from men who might suffer from overt, predatory female sexuality, the danger to women's pursuit of righteousness lay in their own culpability rather than in male sexuality.

Another facet of the overriding ambivalence toward women was encompassed in their role as mother which, as has been seen, was to become their greatest and sometimes only source of honor. Although both women and men are told to be fruitful and multiply, after the part of the father in reproduction was known, it is only the mother who must make a sin-offering after childbirth as atonement to God. There is a later rabbinical explanation that every woman in childbirth vows never again to come near her husband in order to avoid the pain of delivery, and that her sin-offering at the birth of another child represents an atonement for abrogating her vow to God, not for childbirth itself. But since no vows made to God by women were binding unless they were endorsed by their fathers or husbands (Num. 30), it is unlikely that the latter would frequently endorse the permanent termination of their sexual pleasure. In addition, what does one do with all those women for whom childbirth is relatively fast and easy? Are they not also women and mothers?

Furthermore, there is something intrinsic in the birth of a female child that renders the mother more unclean and impure than the birth of a male child. She is unclean after childbirth, as when she menstruates, seven days for a male child but fourteen days for a female. She requires only thirty-three days of discharging to be "purified" after bearing a son, but sixty-six days after bearing a daughter (Lev. 12).

In what is presented as God's view, then, unlike men, women are impure in the flesh from birth by virtue of their sex, and sinful as a result of their sexuality, at the same time that they are most honored as mothers for the issue of their sexuality, which depends upon their normal menstruation. Obviously, the attitudes and rituals surrounding menstruation and childbirth are not only virtually lifelong but have nothing whatsoever to do with the circumstances a woman finds herself in or her moral qualities, because they are rooted in her biology. By contrast, men's "uncleanness" or, as we shall see, unfitness for participation in cultic rites, is only occasional in most instances, and may be cured or washed away. The uncleanness of women is seen as a part of their very nature, since it originates in their normal bodily processes. But, lacking the latter, they would be barren or most dishonored and vulnerable. It is perhaps this fixing of impurity and uncleanness in the body, joined to the economic roles of the virtuous wife, which most irrevocably marks women off as a sex—as at once more a part of the physical universe and more subject to it than men. These factors in effect keep women as a group out of "the gates" and, as shall be seen, out of the Sanctuary as well.

Was There a "Counterculture" in Israel?

Recently, a strong argument has been made that Old Testament attitudes toward women are neither as misogynistic as some have claimed, nor as ambivalent as claimed here, but rather represent a more complex theological development over time, which incorporates both positive and negative attitudes toward women in different periods and genres. Like Swidler's beliefs about the feminism of Jesus, this line of reasoning rests on the assumption that there is an original vision of sexual equality in the Bible, which, after a period of time, became skewed toward misogyny. Since this position has been so influential in the thinking of many who believe the Old Testament can be rescued from its worst misogynistic affect, and since it often includes some kind of reassessment of the creation account, historically so central to the Judeo-Christian understanding of appropriate roles for women and men in a divinely ordained universe, it seems important to consider a number of its major components.

Phyllis Trible's contributions in this area are not only representative of this process of reevaluation but appear to have laid some of the groundwork for looking at the Old Testament in new ways. In a brief but significant essay on women in the Old Testament,[14] for example, she argues that later interpretations may have overemphasized its accounts of unequal power relationships between women and men at the expense of other, nonsexist attitudes also found in that literature.

Trible describes the position of women in the Old Testament as shaped by two contending forces. Attitudes toward women and their status under the law were determined by the patriarchal society and religious system within which they lived. But in her view there was considerable opposition to both, arising out of that same patriarchal structure, which tended to modify them to some extent and allowed for the wider acknowledgment of women as full persons. After reviewing some of the familiar kinds of evidence for the subordination of Hebrew women within the family, in cult, and under the law, Trible goes on to cite what she sees as contrary evidence to illustrate this process of modification, found in some of the biblical genres that emerged at different times in the history of Israel.

Commencing with a list of the outstanding women, both native and foreign—e.g., Deborah, Jael, Chuldah, Noadiah, Ruth, Jezebel, the Queen of Sheba, Delilah, and the unnamed "wise women" of King David's reign—she then refers to "the extraordinary portrayal of wisdom itself as a woman closely associated with Yahweh (*Prov.* 8)." While Trible maintains that they alone did not change the patriarchal order, she nevertheless believes that they cannot be regarded as mere mavericks and exceptions, and that, in fact, they take on real importance in conjunction with what she terms biblical "evidence which directly challenges patriarchy," or what she calls the "counterculture."

Central to her argument for the existence of this countercultural trend is her rather novel reading of the second version of creation in Genesis:

> The patriarchal culture of Israel knew a counterculture. Perhaps its paradigm was the Yahwist story of creation (*Gen.* 2–3). Special among the literature of the ancient Near East in focusing upon the creation of woman, this narrative depicts sexuality as occurring simultaneously for

male and female (2:28). Moreover, the appearance of the woman is the climax of the whole story (cf. *Gen.* 1:27). While the animals were helpers for "the man," they were inferiors. By contrast, the woman is "a helper fit for him" (2:18). This phrase connotes the equality of woman with man, an equality that is stressed in various ways. Both man and woman owe their lives solely to Yahweh. When the Lord created woman, the deity first put the man to sleep so that he did not participate at her birth. Woman herself is not the "rib" of man, for that extracted bone required the creative work of Yahweh to become woman. The rib means solidarity and equality. Out of his ecstasy man discovered a partner in woman rather than a creature to dominate.

In *Gen.* 2 the man remains silent while Yahweh plans his existence. He speaks only in response to the birth of woman. Then he recedes again while woman emerges as the strong figure. In conversation with the serpent, she quotes God and adds her interpretation ("neither shall you touch it") to the divine prohibition (*Gen.* 3:2–3). She contemplates the forbidden fruit physically, aesthetically, and theologically (vs.6). This primal woman is intelligent, independent, and decisive, fully aware as theologian when she takes the fruit and eats. But her husband does not struggle with the prohibition. Not a decision maker, he follows his wife without question.

The divine judgments describe (they do not prescribe) the disastrous effects of disobedience. Specifically, the rule of man over woman is a perversion of creation, which stands in need of grace. Thereby the culture of Israel received a formidable critique in the theology of the Yahwist.[15]

Trible believes the existence of this counterculture may be deduced from the writings of other Old Testament theologians as well, and she quotes some passages from the prophets Hosea and Jeremiah, which, in her view, display an antipatriarchal bent: ". . . Jeremiah himself proclaims the overthrow of patriarchy: 'For the Lord has created a new thing on the earth: a woman protects a man' (31:22)."[16]

She then proceeds to discuss the Song of Songs as an exemplification of countercultural attitudes in its portrayal of the sexual autonomy of both the woman and man, with no hint of dominance, subordination, or the ownership of the woman by the man; the mutuality of their relationship, marked by the open and active expression of sexuality by the woman; and the release of the woman from any suggestion of uncleanness related to her bodily functions. In short, while noting the existence of a patriarchal society throughout Israel's long history, Trible contends there were substantial variations in attitudes at different times and, prior to the sixth century B.C.E., or in pre-exilic times, "a depatriarchalizing principle was prominently at work in Hebrew faith."[17]

It is in the exilic and postexilic periods, under what Trible sees as the influence of the priesthood, that she contends the consolidation of patriarchal attitudes in cult occurred, characterized by the identification of wickedness, sin, and impurity with women. But she maintains that this development represented a point of view that was at variance with what she obviously understands as the inclination of a substratum of religious faith in the Old Testament, namely that which accorded the status of full personhood to women as well as men:

> Gradually, then, in postexilic thinking an understanding of womanhood became dominant which moved toward misogyny: woman as an impure, subordinate, and inferior human creature.
>
> Nevertheless, that view did not replace altogether the dynamic thrust of OT faith. Though it came to expression in a patriarchal culture, that thrust challenged, corrected, and transcended the culture. Accordingly, OT faith undercuts all man-made structures and ideas to place both woman and man *sub specie aeternitatis.* [18]

One hardly knows where to begin with an argument of this sort, and perhaps it would be best to consider it sequentially. As Trible observes, there were doubtless a variety of views expressed by different authors at different times within the limits imposed by the patriarchal structure of ancient Israel described in the Old Testament. That is the "given" in any sensible approach. Moreover, as already observed, the Bible is rich in inconsistencies and contradictions throughout its many parts, probably due in part to the different times of its composition. But once having said that, its utility as proof of any particular position is only minimal, and it is finally the text that must be looked to for substantiation.

No amount of trotting out the accomplishments of strong women in the Old Testament can compensate for their rarity as compared with men. All such efforts list the same few, over and over. They include even those who were aliens (and therefore in their status atypical of Hebrew women, e.g., the Queen of Sheba, Ruth), or idolatrous (and therefore despised, e.g., Queen Jezebel, Delilah), or unnamed (and therefore significant for their anonymity, e.g., the "wise women" of King David's reign), or obviously revered in their own time (but about whom we know little else and from whom we have no written legacy, e.g., Chuldah), or apparently of some prominence in cultic life (but treated by God more punitively than male cultic leaders for the same transgression, e.g., Miriam).

Also, wisdom is most assuredly not a real woman, as Trible says, even though it is designated as feminine, and even though "she" briefly describes herself in human imagery (Prov. 9:1–6). Clearly, she is a personification of the path to righteousness for the sons of Solomon. Simply, her power is too boundless, her "life" too long, and God, too, sometimes uses "human" imagery to describe himself. Indeed, if one were to take literally her self-description in this chapter and elsewhere (e.g., chapter 8), one would almost have a female counterpart to God.

Trible's analysis of the second story of creation (Gen. 2, 3) is a moving statement for the equality of women and men, or possibly even the superiority of women in that particular episode, but it seems to be based more on desire than on reality. For example, she is right when she says, "this narrative depicts sexuality as occurring simultaneously for male and female," but it is hard to imagine anything other if the passage describes a heterosexual relationship. And she is right when she isolates it as "special . . . in focusing on the creation of women." But its meaning hinges on its purpose.

Again, simply because the woman is created last, it does not necessarily mean that her appearance is "the climax of the entire story." She may, indeed, have been necessary to the man, especially for procreation. But she may also have been an afterthought of God and, by analogy (in this case a rather foreboding one), the purpose of her creation might have been not unlike the purpose for which humanity was created in Sumerian and Babylonian myths, namely to serve divinities. However, in these last instances service to the divine meant the presence of both sexes in cult, thus guaranteeing the continuity of divine intervention in human history. When the image of the last-created woman is joined to that of wife, whose virtue is established by her material, economic service to her husband rather than God, it casts the purpose of her appearance in a somewhat different light.

While the animals may well have been created as both "helpers" for the man and inferior to him and the woman as only a "helper" to the man, if she is "fit for him," his existence is prior to hers in time and therefore provides the norm against which the fitness or unfitness of his human helper is measured. Hence, it is difficult to see how the description of woman as a helper fit for man connotes "the equality of woman with man" unless man is also described (and he is not) as a helper fit for woman.

The fact that "both man and woman owe their lives solely to Yahweh" hardly suggests their necessary equality either, since everyone/thing owes her/his/its existence to Yahweh. Likewise, when God puts the man to sleep during the woman's creation, it does not necessarily imply that the man does not participate in her birth. How much more closely can one participate than to have another being created out of part of one's body, asleep or awake?

The meaning of "The rib means solidarity and equality" is elusive. (In fact, as Samuel Noah Kramer pointed out, the image of the rib might well have come from the myth of Dilmun, the Sumerian paradise, when the goddess Ninhursag restores the failing god Enki by creating goddesses and gods to heal specific parts of his diseased body. According to Kramer, the goddess Ninti, "the lady of the rib," was created to heal Enki's ribs,[19] and thus the famous rib of Adam may have been intended as nothing more than a literary pun.) With regard to Trible's assertion that "Out of his ecstasy man discovered a partner in woman rather than a creature to dominate," one can only remark that it was God, not man, who established the nature of their relationship. And it is also uncertain and unclear that the man was all that ecstatic.

Furthermore, the scene between the woman and the serpent does not seem to demonstrate that the primal woman is "fully aware as theologian when she takes the fruit and eats." She may well have been "intelligent, independent, and decisive." However, as indicated earlier, hers could not have been a theological decision until after she ate the fruit, since before then she lacked knowledge of good and evil, and hence could not have known that disobedience to God and death were either sinful or evil. If anyone is a theologian, it is the serpent. And though Adam does indeed remain silent during the dialogue between the woman and the serpent, he too "takes the fruit and eats."

The meaning of this scene becomes clarified only by its consequences. It provokes God to place the woman in subordination to man, in a narrower range of roles than those suffered by Adam, and, perhaps only incidentally, it served as the basis for the centuries-long damnation of the nature of women as morally weaker and more vulnerable to sin than that of men by a host of poets, philosophers, and theologians.

Trible calls "the rule of man over woman . . . a perversion of creation, which stands in need of grace," but this is not only obscure; it is also textually unwarranted. Whatever it stands in need of, when God orders the subordination of the woman to the man as the aftermath of their creation, he does not term it a perversion but presents it rather neutrally, as a consequence of transgression. Nor does God indicate in any way that it is a temporary situation, or that its cessation is contingent on an act of divine grace. In any event, if it is a perversion, its author is neither the woman, the man, nor the serpent. Likewise, maintaining that "the culture of Israel received a formidable critique in the theology of the Yahwist" seems barely adequate as a summary of the chapters that establish a secular hierarchy based on sex, and evidence the treatment of the woman by God as though she possesses a lesser capacity for moral judgment than either Adam or the serpent, in the sense that God is not shown as directly linking the woman's transgression to her punishment, as he does with the man and the serpent.

The few passages quoted by Trible from the prophetic literature that use feminine, or ostensibly more benign, imagery are rather unconvincing when placed in their larger context. For example, she quotes Hosea as saying that Israel will call Yahweh "my husband" rather than "my master" and claims that this phrase is "echoing the harmony of woman and man before their corruption."[20] However, it is a bit difficult to locate precisely the harmony she refers to. Genesis is fairly silent on this matter, beyond the man's initial acknowledgment of the woman as his wife. From what is written elsewhere in the Old Testament about marriage relationships, they were a far more harmonious state for husbands than wives, given the former's almost absolute authority over the latter. Moreover, the use of the phrase "my husband" by *women* (as different from Hosea) might not automatically imply endearment.

As Trible notes, there is no question that the Song of Songs is in important respects quite different from many other parts of the Old Testament, most especially in its nonhierarchical picture of heterosexual love and its celebration of female and male sexuality. There are, of course, other rabbinical interpretations of its meaning. It has been held, for instance, that it symbolizes the union of bride and bridegroom, with Israel as the former and God as the latter, or that it may be understood as a representation of the consummation of God's love for Israel expressed in highly erotic language, in which Israel as the beloved is designated as feminine, recalling some of the imagery found in other books (e.g., Ezekiel).

But whatever the reasons for its inclusion in the final canon, and however its imagery was taken in those early times, the Song of Songs seems to fall short as an example of an authentic "counterculture" thrust in the Old Testament. It may or may not be a midrash on Gen. 2 and 3, as Trible speculates in an earlier article.[21] In its focus on love and sexual pleasure, it does not attend at all to any of the political and legal strictures placed on married and unmarried women alike. And since it bears only minimally on cultic practices, it does not touch on the belief in women's recurrent uncleanness in the body, which provided the basis for the association of sin with their normal biological functioning and for their periodic exclusion from worship in the Sanctuary.

Finally, it is hard to identify just what Trible means by "the dynamic thrust of OT faith," which, "Though it came to expression in a patriarchal culture . . . challenged, corrected, and transcended the culture . . . and undercuts all man-made structures and ideas to place both woman and man *sub specie aeternitatis.*" Again, there are the nagging questions, *whose* faith, and what do the different rewards and penalties for women and men tell us about the nature and content of that faith?

In the absence of any convincing evidence of powerful countercurrents in the Old Testament (as different from more or less benign attitudes toward women), what is left is the image of a single deity acting and reacting in the context of a patriarchal culture qua religion. And all of this contributes to a real dilemma in trying to disentangle the substance of "the faith" from the web of antiwoman biases apparent in Old Testament imagery, the content of the law, and the diminished status of women in cult. In short, the emergence of different attitudes toward women at different times is certainly a matter of interest and importance to students of the history of religion. But from the perspective of the worshipers of Yahweh, the Old Testament expresses deeply ambivalent images of women, who were at once fully incorporated into the community of believers under divine laws or grace, but were subjected to severe strictures placed on them in that community on account of their sex and sexuality.

The New Testament

On the surface, gender may seem more blatantly linked to power and powerlessness in the Old Testament than in the New. However, the opening of the latter, which places Jesus in a direct line of descent from Abraham through his earthly "father," even as his mother is about to deliver him in a Virgin Birth in order to enable his redemptive mission, sets the stage for a work that portrays women somewhat differently than in the Old Testament but that ultimately exhibits the same degree of ambivalence toward females as a sex.

As in the Old Testament, women appear in a variety of roles. In the course of Paul's proselytizing journeys, reference is made to the Jews of Antioch, who incite "the devout women of high standing" as well as "the leading men of the city" to persecute Paul and Barnabas (Acts 13:50). In Thessalonica, Paul and Silas convert "a great many of the devout Greeks and not a few of the leading women" (Acts 17:4). When they preach the message of Christ in Beroe'a, "Many of them therefore believed, with not a few Greek women of high standing as well as men" (Acts 17:12). When Paul is accused by the Jews of Jerusalem, the Roman governor Felix comes with his wife, Drusilla, to hear him preach (Acts 24:24–25), and two years later the new governor,

Festus, lays Paul's case before King Agrippa, who is accompanied by Bernice (Acts 25:13–14).

However, the inclusion by name of these prominent women would seem to reflect more upon the relatively high standing of some non-Semitic women in the various places visited (perhaps an indication of the greater freedom enjoyed then by upper-class women in Hellenistic Greece, Egypt, and Imperial Rome) than on any of the early Christian attitudes toward proper roles for women. More important, women as well as men were included in the process of conversion to Christianity.

The Anonymous Women

As already mentioned, women were among those who first identified the special mission of Jesus in his infancy, and who later were healed, baptized, and converted. Women both taught his message and prayed with the apostles after his death and resurrection. However, though some of these women were of obvious importance in the life of Jesus and in early Christianity, like their counterparts in the Old Testament, they too remain veiled in anonymity. Therefore, in effect they are remembered not so much for their individual spiritual gifts but almost as interchangeable prototypes of their sex.

For example, Philip has four unmarried daughters who prophesy (Acts 21:8–9). Jesus speaks to the unnamed Samaritan woman at the well (John 4:7–26), who returns to Samaria and repeats her conversation and conversion. "Many Samaritans from that city believed in him because of the woman's testimony" (John 4:39), and they go to hear the words of Jesus for themselves. Here, despite Jesus' dialogue with a woman and a Samaritan, on both counts as dramatic as it was remarkable, there is the uneasy suspicion that for his purpose *any* Samaritan woman would do.

In the last few emotion-charged days before his crucifixion, there are two instances when women enable him to reveal his mission and demonstrate the new kind of ethics he preached. In the first, when a woman of Bethany anoints him with expensive oil, to the indignation of his disciples, who believe it wasteful because it could have been sold in order to provide for the poor (Matt. 26:6–10), Jesus attributes foreknowledge or the gift of prophecy to her and says: "In pouring this ointment on my body she has done it to prepare me for burial" (Matt. 26:12). Then he calls her act beautiful and says she will be remembered for it all over the world, wherever his gospel is preached (Matt. 26:10, 13).

In the second instance, a sinning woman from the city weeps over him and anoints him while he dines with the Pharisees. The latter question whether Jesus is a genuine prophet, because he permits the woman to touch him despite her sinfulness, and he relates a parable to illustrate his new ethic, namely that her love for him and faith in him made her worthy of divine forgiveness (Luke 8:36–50). And in each case the woman who, in her love and faith, provides Jesus with an opportunity to defy the traditional wisdom and morality and replace them with his own, remains eternally anonymous.

Gender-Based Distinctions in Relations to the Divine

There is no question that Jesus introduces a number of radical ideas about the proper roles of women and men in relation to each other and to the divine, for in many places faith in him and his teachings rather than submission to Mosaic law is stressed as the way to salvation. Nevertheless, there are other aspects of early Christian attitudes toward sex roles and the relation of gender to power and powerlessness that seem to have made as much of a distinction on the basis of sex as any of the biblical selections examined from the Old Testament. At times these distinctions were overt, at other times implicit and more subtle, but their cumulative effect was to move men more closely than women into the orbit of Jesus' mission, and to place women still again in a more peripheral relation to divinity than men. These sexual distinctions appear in the Gospels, in Jesus' relations with women and men, and in the views and roles of his apostles and disciples.

On its simplest level, there is a strong implicit identification of godliness with maleness. Jesus is male, repeatedly described as the son of his father, and he rests his mission on this attachment even while he publicly repudiates his biological mother (Mark 3:33–35), and even in the absence of a heavenly mother. This seems especially significant because it occurred at a time when, as seen earlier, Hebrew women came to be honored most for their motherhood. It might appear that Jesus was opening up roles other than motherhood as sources of honor for women, except that he addresses any woman in the crowd who believes in his message as his mother. Moreover, Mary was identified as the unique instrument for the fulfillment of the divine purpose, but even in this role she is shown in the New Testament as playing only a minimal part in the mission of her son, *except* as his biological mother. Thus, while her motherhood was essential to her son's destiny, it was simultaneously rejected by Jesus as of any special importance in relation to him. In other words, Mary is portrayed with the most profound ambivalence.

Undoubtedly, women appear in various roles in the New Testament, but those who stand closest to Jesus are men. By way of example, many of the New Testament narratives describe how Jesus reveals his identity, mission, compassion, and power through supernatural signs and wonders. He heals wherever he goes, resurrects the dead, and feeds thousands with loaves and fishes (Mark 8:1–21; Luke 7:12–16, 9:10–17; John 6:1–14). It therefore seems most indicative of his purpose that his power to heal, reflective of his origin and ability to convert the unbelievers, was passed along by Jesus to his male apostles and followers but not to his mother or female disciples:

> And he called the twelve together and gave them power and authority over all demons and to cure diseases, and he sent them out to preach the kingdom of God and to heal. . . . And they departed and went through the villages, preaching the gospel and healing everywhere. (Luke 9:1–2,6)

That these divine endowments were regarded as authentic and were used effectively in winning people over to Jesus may be seen, for example, in the instance of Paul healing a man in Lystra who had been crippled from birth (Acts 14:8–10), when the response of the onlookers is: "The gods have come down to us in the likeness of men!" (Acts 14:11). Likewise, Peter heals a paralyzed man with the result that: "all the residents of Lydda and Sharon saw him, and they turned to the Lord" (Acts 9:33–35). In contrast to males, who share in the divine power to heal and convert, the female disciple Dorcas "was full of good works and acts of charity" (Acts 9:36). Or, recalling the ambiguities surrounding the ability of childbearing women to devote themselves totally to the life of the spirit because of their necessary preoccupation with material labor, some of the men who follow Jesus are shown as more closely affiliated with the divine and the process of spiritual conversion, while the woman who follows Jesus is shown as dispensing her charity and good works in the material world. Along these lines, Paul envisions a hierarchy on earth as decreed by God: "And God has appointed in the church first apostles, second prophets, third teachers, then healers, helpers, administrators, speakers in various kinds of tongues" (1 Cor. 12:28). And men were among the most prominent and numerous of the apostles, prophets, teachers, and healers.

Jesus accommodates this male-centered view during the Last Supper, when he promises his male apostles residence in the kingdom of heaven, where they will judge Israel: "You are those who have continued with me in my trials; and I assign to you, as my Father assigned to me, a kingdom, that you may eat and drink at my table in my kingdom, and sit on thrones judging the twelve tribes of Israel" (Luke 22:28–30).

Indeed, it would appear that part of the appeal by Jesus to abandon exclusive obedience to the teachings of the Torah in favor of his own was directed primarily to men. For example, as expressed by John:

And the Word became flesh and dwelt among us, full of grace and truth: we have beheld his glory, glory as the only Son from the Father. . . . And from his fullness have we all received, grace upon grace. For the law was given through Moses: grace and truth came through Jesus Christ. No one has ever seen God; the only Son, who is in the bosom of the Father, he has made him known. (John 1:14–18)

Since most Hebrew women of those times were not taught Torah and seemed to occupy a more marginal place than men in cult, it is likely that their decisions with regard to following the lead of Jesus rather than adhering to the Old Testament may have been based on less weighty moral and spiritual considerations than those confronting men.

The Ritual Uncleanness of Women

In the New Testament, both the transcendent importance attached to faith in Jesus and love for one's neighbor, as compared with mere observance of Mosaic law (John 1:17–18), and Paul's elimination of the hitherto mandatory requirement of circumcision for male gentile converts to Christianity (Rom. 2:25–29; 1 Cor. 7:18–20) would seem, by implication, to have lifted the onus of ritual uncleanness and sinfulness from menstruant and childbearing women. But the persuasiveness of this argument is weakened somewhat by those instances in the narratives in which people are physically liberated from the jurisdiction and punishment of the law through the compassion and grace of Jesus.

There is a suggestion of symbolic conformity to Old Testament doctrines of "cleanness," not too surprising since Jesus sometimes preached in and around synagogues. Hence at times he and, through him, his apostles chose to demonstrate the power of faith in him by healing members of *precisely* those groups whose physical imperfections or afflictions formerly excluded them from worship under Mosaic law. Among them were those who were unclean because of their bodily issues, the leper and the hemorrhaging woman. Indeed, the Hebrew emphasis on ritual cleanness may explain, in part, one of the underlying motives for the repeated call by Jesus and others to abandon the treasures and pleasures of the earthly life for the greater ones of the spiritual, since even those who experienced bodily secretions as a result of sexual intercourse were rendered temporarily unclean or unfit for participation in sacred rites for a while afterward.

In short, Jesus healed or made clean those who had been isolated or kept apart because of their physical conditions and thus restored them to full membership in the religious community. Moreover, though the sanctity of Mosaic law was superseded by the doctrine of redemption through faith in Christ (John 1:17–18), in the New Testament there is no explicit rejection of the uncleanness and sin associated with menstruant and childbearing women under the law comparable to the exemption of male gentile converts from mandatory circumcision.

While it may be speculated that the last was possibly a mere political move designed to win more converts and make the church truly catholic, it may also be argued that in not specifically lifting the cultic burden of blood taboos from women they remained as an implicit residue, and this might have stemmed from the fact that women were not thought of as important a group to convert as men. After all, at least among the Hebrews, it was the men who controlled the power, wealth, dispensations of rewards and punishments under the law, and cult.

But whatever the reasons for the disparate attitudes toward women and men in terms of cultic requirements for physical marks of holiness or cleanness, or however one understands Paul's long discussion of why circumcision for men is merely an external or less important sign of dedication to God than faith (*Rom.* 2:25–29, 3, 4:1–12), while he maintains absolute silence about the ritual uncleanness of women in their normal biological functioning, those episodes which seem to address themselves explicitly to the former exclusion of various groups from sacred rites because of what was perceived as their physical imperfections or uncleanness did not refer to women, unless they also were lepers or bled for twelve years. The special status accorded to all women, in which they were periodically forbidden a role in cult *only* because of their biology, could not be implicitly or explicitly addressed. Since they suffered from no disease, they could not be healed through faith in Jesus.

The Paradox of the Adulterous Woman

Also, though the views of Jesus about permanence in marriage and equal responsibilities and rights for men and women in cases of divorce and adultery introduced among the Semitic peoples of his time some radical notions of reciprocity and equality in relations between the sexes in this life (Mark 10:6–12; Luke 16:18), at times he seems morally at ease with more traditional distinctions made along sexual lines. For example, there is a passage that is often cited to illustrate the compassion of Jesus, his special love for sinners and the downtrodden, his insistence that justice be dispensed in an even-handed manner, and the inclusion of all persons within the shelter of his way, or the universality of his message. This episode deals with his treatment of the adulterous woman.

What she was indulging in—the nature of her "sin," as it were—was sexual activity outside of monogamous marriage, in violation of the law. While Jesus, with his new ethics of responsibility for adultery irrespective of sex, says to the men who would stone her, "Let him who is without sin among you be the first to throw a stone at her" (John 8:7), their "sin" might or might not have been of a sexual nature. It is interesting that no man is pardoned by Jesus for his overt sexuality even though the woman obviously could not have committed adultery without a male partner.

Hence, though Jesus clearly breaks with Mosaic tradition in his treatment of the woman, when he also tells her "do not sin again" (John 8:11) and does not so admonish her partner in sin, he focuses more attention on female than male sexuality as sinful. Indeed, since the New Testament was written by men, it would seem that female sexuality might have been one of the things many of them had to struggle with, not unlike Jerome and Augustine later on, when they turned their backs on the joys of this world in order to attain the more perfect ones of the spiritual world.

The Traditional Roles of Women

In addition to those women already discussed, who anoint his body prior to the crucifixion (Matt. 26:6–13; Luke 8:36–50), or fulfill roles conventional for women throughout the ancient Near East (and later elsewhere) by assuming the care of the dying and the dead, whatever the Christian overlay in those scenes, in other places and times women are shown as "ministering" to Jesus and physically caring for him in very traditional ways (Matt. 26:6–13, 27:55; Mark 1:31, 14:3–9, 15:40–41; Luke 5:39, 7:37–39, 44–48, 8:1–3). Silas's mother-in-law serves Jesus and his disciples after he heals her (Mark 1:30–31, Luke 4:38–39). Many women follow Jesus from Galilee, "ministering to him," among them Mary Magdalene and Mary, the mother of James and Joseph (Matt. 27:55; Mark 16:40–41). Other women who had been healed and cured travel with him and the apostles and "provided for them out of their means" (Luke 8:1–3). While none of these acts of love is necessarily related to sex, again Jesus does not tell men to share in the cooking so that women have time to share in the life of the spirit. He does not specifically say anywhere that women are not unclean or impure in the body because they menstruate. He does not speak against the need for a sin-offering or purification of only the mother after childbirth.

And he does isolate only women for compassion before the end of time, when he says: ". . . in the days of vengeance, to fulfill all that is written. Alas for those who are with child and for those who give suck in those days!" (Luke 21:22–23). In other words, when he predicts that Jerusalem will be destroyed by the gentiles, in a time of great chaos, confusion, and destruction, it is strange that he does not also sorrow for the probable difficulties of the elderly, infirm, and crippled who might not easily escape from the city, but only for the women with children. *And it is possibly because he knows that the full responsibility for the children will be theirs, or other women's.*

Ambivalence toward Women

The full force of the early Christian ambivalence toward women may be inferred from gospel accounts of the life of Jesus and from the letters written by those men who were closest to him. At the same time that Jesus himself frequently treats women as equals, he is also shown as accepting traditional roles for women based on social inequalities between the sexes. The failure of Jesus to identify as a high moral issue the sex-segregated roles of his time, in which women's preoccupations fell largely and of necessity within the province of material concerns so that men could devote themselves more to moral and spiritual concerns, thus places the well-known misogynistic dicta from the New Testament in context as part of the negative aspect of this pervasive ambivalence.

Therefore, while the equality of all persons in Christ stands (Gal. 3:28), in the secular world other relationships coexist and are indeed sanctioned. Thus man is the image and glory of God and woman is the glory of man; woman was created from man, not the reverse; woman is to keep silent in churches and be subordinate and subject in every-thing to her husband (1 Cor. 11:7–9, 14:33–36; Eph. 6:33). Men are to love their wives and the latter are to respect their husbands (Eph. 6:22). Women are not to teach or have authority over men; "Adam was not deceived, but the woman was deceived and became a transgressor. Yet woman will be saved through bearing children" (1 Tim. 2:11–15). Women are urged to be submissive to their husbands, "as Sarah obeyed Abraham, calling him lord" (1 Pet. 3:6), and women are "the weaker sex" (1 Pet. 3:7). And in a reference to the destruction of Sodom and Gomorrah as examples of the results of ungodliness, there is a eulogy of righteous Lot—who offered up his daughters for rape to protect the male strangers in his house (2 Pet. 2:7–8).

These sentiments have been explained away as having been necessitated by sociological, historical, and theological circumstances—the disruptiveness of some women in the congregation at Corinth, the need for order, the threat of gnosticism, the influence on Paul of the first-century Jewish milieu, the realization that the end-times were not indeed at hand, even by the possibility that not all of the Pauline writings are from the hand of Paul.[22] Historically, all of this may be so. However, these prescriptions about women also constitute part of the canon, along with the compassion and inclusion of all persons who have faith in Christ taught by the primitive church. And these passages may, as well, represent an amplification and transformation of the pejorative attitudes that formed part of the deep ambivalence expressed toward women as a sex in the Old Testament as they passed through the prism of the first-century outlook and environment of Jesus, and of those males who were most closely affiliated with him.

Sex Roles in Polytheistic and Biblical Texts

As compared with polytheistic religions, then, in parts of the Bible prescribed roles seemed to be more closely grounded in gender. There is a greater emphasis on the association of power, autonomy, and influence with maleness than with femaleness, an emphasis explicit in the Old Testament, more implicit in the New. Simultaneously, like men, women were considered as part of the religious community, sometimes even portrayed in central roles. Consequently, biblical attitudes toward femininity came to be characterized by a profound and pervasive ambivalence, which was relatively absent from polytheism.

This tended to be reflected in attitudes toward sexuality, and particularly female sexuality, which not only came to be seen in its reproductive aspect as essential to the survival of the social group, but also apparently elicited some male fear and anxiety. As different from most polytheistic attitudes toward female sexuality, which in general seem to have celebrated it as natural and beneficent in its results for the community, a number of biblical passages appear to view it as dangerous to the pursuit of righteousness by men, and mark women off as inherently "unclean" because of their normal sexual functioning.

In the Bible, there is a decisive shift away from the polytheistic view of divine maternity and paternity as indispensable to life and the fertility of nature, toward a belief in the supreme importance of an asexual god as creator. In the absence of a feminine involvement in the all-important act of creation, a view emerged of the lesser importance of women on earth, who labored as economic producers even as they bore the children, and even if their offspring was referred to as the son of God, while men inhabited the more important sphere of moral and spiritual concerns.

Both testaments introduced, in a systemic way, the concept of a secular hierarchy based on sex, in which power and powerlessness became associated with gender; virtue and honor came to mean different things for each sex; and men came to be seen in their secular roles as the more authentic spokesmen for the divine, at the same time that women were portrayed in a variety of roles in the community of believers and were both honored and valued in some of them. In short, it was both the monotheistic elevation of the importance of gender as the basis of power and the ambivalence exhibited toward women as a sex that were most alien, in many respects, to the vision and practices of polytheistic religions in the ancient Near East.

CHAPTER 7

The Relation of Gender
to Participation in Cult:
Biblical Imperatives and Models

MUCH of the recent controversy over the ordination of women has been grounded in differing interpretations of relevant sections of the Bible as well as later biblical commentaries and the historic practices of Judaism and Christianity. With regard to the Bible, the same passages not infrequently serve as the basis for widely divergent conclusions depending, for example, on how much weight is given to the historical and sociological contexts out of which these passages emerged; the particular interpretations of the nature and order of creation in Genesis and what they might signify; the probable intention and meaning assigned to the Pauline statements on the silence of women in churches and the deference of women to their husbands; the various concepts of the term "ministry" itself; and the more general problem of determining precisely what represents divine law as different from human preference and tradition. Perhaps the salient impression yielded from these extensive discussions of Scripture is the inconclusiveness of the evidence for both supporters and opponents of the ordination of women.

It may be that part of the difficulty stems from those portions of the biblical narratives which exhibit the same profound ambivalence toward women as participants and leaders in cult as was apparent in some of the passages that describe divine-human interactions or that establish appropriate sex roles within those interactions in the religious community. As has been seen, the greater responsibility of women for performing economically productive labor and providing for the very material care of the young and the greater preoccupation of men with moral and spiritual concerns—in the context of religions centered on those very concerns—in themselves established different positions for women and men in cult. In addition to those discussed earlier, there are still other biblical narratives that bear on the involvement and status of women in the ritual life of the community. Despite the many ways in which women are shown as essential to the fulfillment of the divine covenant, and despite the many roles they play in both testaments, as different from the outlook prevalent in polytheistic religions, women in the Bible are ultimately portrayed as less important than men in cult. But even their lesser importance is surrounded with ambiguities.

Some Sources of Ambivalence
toward Women in Cult

There are three powerful indications that God intended women to participate fully in cult. In the Old Testament, women as well as men are subjected to divine punishments in this world for transgressions of divine commandments. In the New Testament, divine compassion and grace are extended, less differentially with regard to gender, to women as well as men. In both testaments, final judgment is a prospect faced by all people. At the same time, greater power, autonomy, and influence in the human community are linked with maleness rather than with femaleness. Above all, there is a linkage of negative and even sinful connotations with women's normal biological functioning, or of ritual impurity and "uncleanness" with female sexuality and its issue. And there is a strong suggestion that women are somehow viewed as dispensable to cultic life.

This ambivalence seems to derive, in part, from the representation of the single deity as operantly male in some of the narratives. However, as argued earlier, its deeper source would appear to lie in the emergence of gender itself as a far more fundamental, value-laden epistemological category in biblical than in polytheistic texts, underpinning many of the portrayals of the divine and the network of divine-human affiliations. In a literature whose doctrines rest so heavily on the moral and spiritual accountability of the individual and the community to the divine, distinctions drawn along sexual lines, in which women are shown as suffering somewhat lesser moral and spiritual capacities than men, would seem to have located women as a sex in a position of existential marginality and "otherness" in many of their interactions with divinity. In short, these kinds of descriptions of women's proper place in the community of believers would seem to imply not only a different but a diminished status for them in cult as compared to men.

Male Primacy in the Old Testament

In the Old Testament, the belief in the "naturalness" of greater male than female participation in cult was represented as sanctified by divine law and embodied in the secular community by the creation of a male priesthood. Descending through the sons of Aaron, it probably marked the symbolic consecration of the firstborn male children to God after they were spared in Egypt prior to the exodus, and it was reflected and reinforced by the male leadership of the tribes of Israel. The virtual monopoly of cultic leadership by men from the time of Moses on was accompanied by an attitude toward most women as not only subordinate to men but even sometimes dangerous to their dedication to righteousness, while there is no comparable portrayal of men's danger to women.

Indeed, the correlation of ritual uncleanness with female sexuality was seen as overridingly important. For instance, three months after Moses leads the Israelites out of Egypt, God establishes a covenant with them, establishing them as a nation. He tells the Hebrews: "you shall be my own possession among all peoples" (Exod. 19:5) and designates them as "a kingdom of priests and a holy nation" (Exod. 19:6). Before he gives Moses the Ten Commandments, God tells him that he will descend in a "thick cloud" and speak to him before all the people so they will believe in Moses and his divinely inspired laws forever. Moses sanctifies the Hebrews for this solemn and sacramental occasion and instructs them to wash their clothes, or purify themselves (Exod. 19:9–10). However, this message relayed from God is directed toward only the *male* Israelites. In preparation for the Lord's coming, Moses says to them: "Be ready by the third day: *do not go near a woman*" (Exod. 19:15—italics mine).

The rituals surrounding sacerdotal offices in ancient Israel most especially stressed the necessity for cleanness or purity, in people and even in every physical element involved in worship and sacrifice (Lev. 22:3, 6, 7, 9; Num. 19, 20). Therefore, from the time of Solomon until the destruction of the temple in Jerusalem in 70 c.e., when holiness rested on purity, women, as already seen, were recurrently excluded from access to the sanctuary at regular intervals during their entire adulthood, since menstruation and childbirth rendered them unclean, or unsuitable for full participation in sacred rites, or "unholy."

In addition, women shared with men the intermittent states of uncleanness resulting from sexual activity or disease, which also barred them from worship (Lev. 22:3–7; Num. 19:20–22; Deut. 23:10). But these states were the result of choice, were sporadic or sometimes amenable to cure, and in any case were not as deeply rooted in the inevitable bodily processes of either sex. In other words, the normal physiological functions of *only* women made them unclean or unholy. They remained in that condition for a longer time than men, or were excluded from participation in cultic rites more often and for longer periods of time than men, and this exclusion was based solely on their sex.

In fact, as different from men, women were seen as threatening God's sanctuary with periodic defilement by their mere physical presence for about as long as they lived. The gravity of this threat, once holiness came to be centered in the temple at Jerusalem, may be gauged by the following assessment by Pedersen:

> All depended on holiness, therefore an infringement of it was always so dangerous a transgression that the sinner must be exterminated. This applied not only to the person who desecrated Yahweh's name and made his holiness unclean by a non-Israelitish cult (*Lev.* 20, 1ff.); but also to any one who entered the sanctuary or touched the sacred things in an unclean state (*Lev.* 22, 3:9; *Num.* 19, 20).[1]

From early times, the "maintainers" of the religious community of Israel were the priests, prophets, and chieftains, whose roles were sometimes interchangeable and overlapping. All of them were to be pervaded by holiness. For a considerable period, this latter requirement virtually closed off access to commanding positions in cult for women. If the power of the priest, as servant of the temple, resided in his ability to obtain guidance for Israel from Yahweh through oracles,[2] that power became automatically denied to all women, since they were regularly prohibited from entering the Sanctuary or handling the sacred objects because of their recurrent uncleanness (Lev. 23:3, 6, 7; Num. 19, 20).

Most frequently, women are not pictured as pure for their own sakes, but are almost objectified and used as points of reference to ascertain the purity of those men who played crucial roles in cultic life. For instance, there was a requirement of absolute purity for Israelite warriors, superseding that required for the community at large. One of the ways for them to attain this state of purity was to abstain from sexual intercourse with women, as when King David and his men kept away from women "as always" while on an expedition, and therefore were permitted by the priest to eat "holy" bread (1 Sam. 21:3–6).

In like fashion, in order to sustain his purity, a priest of Israel was forbidden to "take" a harlot, a "profaned" woman, or a divorced woman, "for he is holy unto his God" (Lev. 21:7), and those three states were typically dishonorable ones for women. Indeed, there are no really comparable states of purity for women that are defined by their abstinence from sexual intercourse with men or by prohibitions of marriages with promiscuous or divorced men. Promiscuity and divorce did not dishonor men, nor were women perceived as capable of "taking" a man, except to endanger his righteousness if she were betrothed or married. There is only slight reference to the holiness of women, and purity or holiness was possible for men only if they refrained from sexual contact either with all women or with "dishonored" women.

Male Primacy in the New Testament

In the New Testament, the restrictions placed on women by the law with respect to their participation in cult are, of course, not repeated. However, the New Testament's silence on the subject of ritual uncleanness in women on account of their biology is not very promising when considered alongside the elimination of mandatory circumcision for men as a sign of special dedication to God. Moreover, if early Christian worship was accessible to women as well as men, its two basic rituals, Baptism and the Eucharist, are replete with masculine references.

Baptism was initially associated with John, and both the Eucharist and the Lord's Supper commemorate and celebrate stages in the life and redemptive mission of the son of God, whose paternity was understood by his followers as the source of Jesus' power and truth. Certainly the main actors and authors of the New Testament are male, as are those who stand closest to Jesus as active agents of his ministry. Though women, as we have seen, do minister to Jesus in a physical way, and are shown as active in the episodes of his life and in the spread of his teachings after his death, he chooses his own closest disciples. And though women undoubtedly participated in early Christian cult, as in the Old Testament, the most significant leadership positions are occupied by men.

Though many women are named in the New Testament, with the exception of a handful like Dorcas and Priscilla, it is not entirely clear from the text what their roles were in the early church. Also, there are no individual portrayals of strong women like Deborah who assume positions of cultic leadership among the early Christians or initiate any really momentous doctrinal issues or ritual practices. While this is purely speculative to be sure, one sometimes suspects from the emphasis placed on conversion, or the need for early Christianity to greatly multiply its followers if it were to survive as more than a small Jewish sect, that there may have been a hidden, if unconscious, agenda with regard to women.

If the appeals to follow the spiritual life seem to have been more consonant with the lives of men and older women, it may be that younger women were valued for quite other activities, namely their ability to bear Christian babies. Just as Jesus did not address the social inequalities of the sexes within marriage in his own time, so Paul's doctrine of equality for all persons in Christ in Gal. 3:28 did not seem necessarily applicable to this world. Indeed, the very next verse reiterates God's covenant with Abraham, not Sarah or Hagar. Hence, while the issue of women as leaders of the religious community is not raised, the model of leadership is predominantly male.

Unquestionably, there are great differences in content and outlook between the Old Testament and the New. However, there are a number of fundamental continuities and shared views as well. For example, there are many references in the New Testament back to the Old, to the writings of some of the prophets and the story of creation, and it seems anything but arbitrary that the New Testament opens with the tracing of Joseph's ancestry back to Abraham. Further, there is the same general concern in both testaments for the oppressed, although it seems to shift somewhat from the moral responsibility of the community to provide them with material support in the Old, to the mitigation of suffering by divine grace in the New. These shared views are substantial in yet another area, and that is the attitude toward men as far more irreplaceable and indispensable to the perpetuation of cult than women.

The Dispensability of Women in Cult: The Old Testament

In the Old Testament, actual human sacrifice as practiced by Hebrews is only rarely mentioned, though child-sacrifice is vigorously condemned by many of the prophets. If one compares the fate of Abraham's son, Isaac, and Jephthah's daughter, who is not even dignified by a name of her own but is described only as her father's daughter and a virgin (with no allusion to her mother), what becomes starkly evident is the depth of Old Testament distinctions based on sex, and how much more importance is attached to males than to females in ancient Israelite religion.

Both Isaac and Jephthah's daughter are demanded as human sacrifices by God, in the instance of Isaac because God was testing the strength of Abraham's faith, in the instance of Jephthah's daughter because her father wanted to win his war with the Ammonites and made a vow to God: "If thou wilt give the Ammonites into my hand, then whoever comes forth from the doors of my house to meet me, when I return victorious from the Ammonites, shall be the Lord's, and I will offer him up for a burnt offering" (Judg. 11:30).

Jephthah is victorious, and his daughter comes out to meet him "with timbrels and with dances" (Judg. 11:34), obviously overjoyed to see him. He is greatly distressed, but is also almost accusatory in his first words to her, as if *she* were responsible for his awful oath and her impending death. He says: "Alas, my daughter! *you have brought me very low, and you have become the cause of great trouble to me*; for I have opened my mouth to the Lord, and I cannot take back my vow" (Judg. 11:35 —italics mine).

With fitting docility, and primary concern for Jephthah's triumph and welfare, his daughter replies: "My father, if you have opened your mouth to the Lord, do to me according to what has gone forth from your mouth, now that the Lord has avenged you on your enemies, on the Ammonites" (Judg. 11:36). Her only request is that she be permitted two months respite to wander in the mountains with her companions, not to mourn her imminent death, but to "bewail my virginity" (Judg. 11:37).

At the end of that time she returns to her father, "who did with her according to his vow which he had made. She had never known a man" (Judg. 11:39). There is no mention of Jephthah's grief over her sacrifice, no mention of any possible conflict between his feelings for his daughter and his vow to God, but only: "And it became a custom in Israel that the daughters of Israel went year by year to lament the daughter of Jephthah the Gileadite four days in the year" (Judg. 11:39–40).

Several things ought to be noted here. There are other accounts of Hebrew kings, for instance Ahaz and Manasseh, who burned their sons as offerings to God (2 Kings 16:3, 21:6). But they are both described as idolaters and abominable in the sight of God. While Jephthah is no Abraham, he is sought out by the male elders to lead the Gileadites in their war against the Ammonites (Judg. 11:4–11). Jephthah responds to their request when he speaks "all his words before the Lord at Mizpah" (Judg. 11:11). He is portrayed as wise and statesmanlike when he communicates with the Ammonites and attempts to avert a war by establishing the legitimacy of Gilead's claim to the land (Judg. 11:12–27). He is backed by God in his struggle—"the spirit of the Lord came upon Jephthah" (Judg. 11:29)—and he therefore fights a holy war. After his daughter's death, he judges Israel for six years, until his own (Judg. 12:7), and, at least by the time of Moses, the administration of justice apparently was regarded as a religious rather than a civil function.[3]

In sum, unlike Ahaz and Manasseh, Jephthah is not pictured as evil, defiling the Lord and the land or reverting to other religious practices, but is shown instead as a divinely sanctioned leader and judge of Israel, functioning in a cultic role. And his sacrifice of his daughter to God passes almost without comment, except from the other daughters and virgins of Israel.

Furthermore, Abraham's son is named, but Jephthah's daughter is identified only as a virgin. It goes without saying that the issue of Isaac's virginity, or lack of it, is not an issue and is irrelevant. Isaac questions his father about the nature of the sacrifice to be offered when he sees the fire and the wood (Gen. 22:7), but Jephthah's daughter never questions anything about the pact between God and her father, to be paid for with her life. While an animal is used as a surrogate sacrifice for Isaac at the very last moment, Jephthah's daughter is herself sacrificed, even though two months are available in which to locate (or plead for) a substitute.

In these episodes, Isaac was viewed as indispensable to God's intention to multiply greatly the seed of Abraham through the male line, but apparently Jephthah's daughter was seen as dispensable and replaceable in the light of that intention, since any virgin could fulfill that purpose. Well might the daughters of Israel have engaged in annual lamentations over her death, for her anonymity, virginity, and importance *only* as the instrument of sealing her father's vow to God may as easily have defined their own subordinate status in life and in cult.

Again, it should be pointed out that the book of Judges recounts the events of a chaotic time of instability and warfare, when Israel is often shown as sinning. But yet again, there is the portrayal of God's complicity in both the victory of Jephthah and the sacrifice of his daughter, and Jephthah was rewarded for his actions by becoming a judge of Israel. What emerges from these narratives, then, is the characterization of God as far more concerned about the survival of males like Abraham, Isaac, and Jephthah, and the retention of the land won from the Ammonites for the use of their religious community, than for the survival of females because of their importance in cult. For if women were in short supply to guarantee the proliferation of Abraham's seed, they could always be replenished by anonymous virgins captured by force, as in Jabeshgilead or Shiloh.

The Enigma of Mary in the New Testament

In the New Testament, despite much evidence for the inclusion of women as followers of Jesus, and the apparent sense of ease with which women as well as men were employed to spread his word after his death and resurrection, the same motif of women's marginal role in early cult reappears. The paramount example has to do with the lack of prominence of the mother of Jesus. Extending far beyond the surfeit of designations of Jesus as the Son of man (John 6:27), not woman, or the Son of His Father, or the Son of God, is his fairly consistent treatment of Mary as unimportant.

In one view, Jesus' transformation of water into wine during his attendance at the marriage at Cana had profound sacramental significance because it helped to establish the basis for the Eucharist.[4] But in this foreshadowing, symbolic setting, when Mary simply tells Jesus that the wine is gone, his response is: "O woman, what have you to do with me? My hour has not yet come" (John 2:4). And typical of her passivity and belief in him, Mary tells the servants: "Do whatever he tells you" (John 2:5).

It has been maintained by some that the reason Jesus spoke to Mary in this way at that particular juncture in his life is that she did not yet understand the full meaning of what was happening. For instance, Oscar Cullmann writes:

> Since Jesus' mother cannot yet grasp this sense of the miracle, he says to her . . . 'Woman what have I to do with thee.'[5] That would then mean: you still share the Jewish conception of glorification. My Messiahship is given me by God, my hour is not yet come, when water shall be turned into wine, namely the hour of my death, *when on the Cross the foundation will be laid for the Eucharist*. The wine is a pointer to the wine of the Lord's Supper, i.e., the blood, which Christ shed for the forgiveness of sins.[6]

All of this may be true. Perhaps Mary did not yet comprehend the true nature of his mission, or the connection of the miracle at Cana with the stages of his life in their full sacramental meaning. But it is frequently the case that neither did his apostles or many others he came into contact with, and Jesus responds to them in a variety of ways —with patience, anger, instruction, and allusions to events yet to come, of which they can have no foreknowledge. It is rare that he tells *anyone* he has nothing to do with them, since his mission embraces all people. However, it is precisely the kind of language he uses to his mother, as different from other people, which is the crux of the matter, regardless of which translation is looked at, viz., "what have you to do with me?" or "what have I to do with thee?"

For what is finally so unsettling is that Mary, as his mother, is absolutely indispensable to his redemptive mission. While Jesus is identified by others, over and over, as the Son of his Father, it cannot be overemphasized that the accomplishment of his destiny as the saviour of humanity was made to depend upon his suffering, death, and resurrection in the *flesh,* or his filial relation to Mary. From the perspective of early Christian worship, his mission was seen as resting on the fact that, at one and the same time, he was to be the risen Christ present in a spiritual sense to his body, the Christian Church, during its celebration of the Lord's Supper and, projected backward, the mortal son of Mary as well, who was to be crucified and resurrected in the body. Indeed, the magnitude of the sacramental ramifications of his mortality, or his "coming" as the son of Mary, is consistent with the internal evidence in Scripture as well as later interpretations.

The centrality of Mary's role is attested in later times under a wide variety of historical circumstances. She quickly attained great prominence in Eastern Christian worship. Indeed, some of the most misogynistic of the early Church Fathers attached such importance to her act of maternity that they not only exalted her as an ideal but actually believed that by her Virgin Birth alone she enabled the redemption of all other women, in their views, all the daughters of Eve. Some claim that she was used as a bridge in the conversion of the Northern European polytheistic tribes to Christianity, by an association of Mary with their own goddesses, at a time when the notion of a masculinized deity that excluded the feminine was too alien. By the late Middle Ages, people in Western Europe built magnificent cathedrals and sanctuaries in her honor, and medieval troops went into battle and faced death shouting, "In the name of Our Lady."

During this time, she was seen as the gentle intermediary for human sinners, who interceded on their behalf with what was seen as an essentially abstract and judgmental male God, and as a counterforce to the open corruption and worldliness rampant among male officials of the church, even in the highest places. For instance, Jacob Burckhardt tells us that during the Italian Renaissance, when disillusionment with this process of clerical secularization seems to have been widespread, every peasant hut in Italy was adorned with a picture of Mary, not Jesus. And in our own time, the Catholic church has promulgated the doctrine of the assumption of Mary to the side of God and Christ.

But in the New Testament itself, it is almost unaccountable how Mary fades into near-invisibility during the ministry of Jesus. In his public repudiation of her *specifically* as his earthly mother in favor of his heavenly father, her role seems to be reduced by him to utter insignificance. In such a climate of opinion, it is not surprising that, despite the fact that Joseph plays no part in the Virgin Birth, Philip identifies Jesus in the following manner: "We have found him of whom Moses in the law and also the prophets wrote, Jesus of Nazareth, *the son of Joseph*" (John 1:45—italics mine). And if even Mary was viewed by Jesus, his apostles, and disciples as fairly inconsequential, what does this say about the importance of all other women as participants in cult?

The Lesser Importance of Women in Cult: Ambivalence toward Women

Throughout both testaments, men seem to appear in the foreground of the religious community as the more powerful authorities on divine law, more frequent judges of human behavior, and more authentic spokesmen for divinity. Women recede, either fixed forever by their periodic (and normal) "impurity" in the body to a position of lesser participation than men in cult, or seen as dispensable to cult, or discounted in their normal bodily functions even when their maternity was of utmost importance in the development of cult. By an emphasis on women's physical nature, and an assessment of them as either unclean or only minimally important, the biblical image of women's involvement in cultic rituals emerges as seemingly more trivial, restricted, and marginal than that of men.

This view of women as generally more dispensable and less important than men in assuring the continuity and victory of monotheism over competing religions in its environment is augmented by the relative absence of biblical women from positions of leadership in the ritual life of the community. While there is no absolute prohibition of the latter, even if the priests of Israel and the apostles of Jesus are male, there is also an overwhelming preponderance of men who serve both their God and their people as elders, judges, prophets, rulers, warriors, priests, apostles, proselytizers, and saviors, in short, as leaders in the many-faceted existence of the cult. Women like Deborah, Jael, Chuldah, Dorcas, and Priscilla may appear as possible female counterparts, but their rarity in comparison to the number of men in parallel roles, and the lack of evidence for female authorship of any part of the Bible, suggest the probability that women's contributions and influence in the development and maintenance of biblical doctrines and sacred rites were fairly scant.

It may be argued that there was, in fact, no male prophet like Moses who spoke "mouth to mouth" with God, just as there was no male savior like Jesus, and that both were unique. However, this contention does not speak to the fact that both were conceived of as male in the body, and therefore most likely acted on the imaginations of people in ways that were quite different from either the personification of Wisdom as female, or the portrayal of Mary's major importance in cult as the physical mother of Jesus.

Unlike Wisdom, both Moses and Jesus are incontestably mortal. They are born, struggle, suffer, get angry, show love, are wise, and die as men. Unlike Mary, the range of their activities and impact, either as judge and transmitter of the law, or as embodiment of divinity and transmitter of the New Covenant, extend far beyond the ramifications of physical fatherhood. There are many areas of possible identification with these two unique males available for men, and far fewer available for women. For example, when Moses is overburdened with his labor as a judge of Israel, he delegates much of this responsibility to other men (Exod. 18:13–26). Likewise, throughout the Gospels, Jesus is assisted primarily by male apostles in the dissemination of his message.

In terms of their involvement in the sacred rituals of the community, in the absence of many strong female role models in the Bible, the choices for women seem to have been different and more restricted than those for men. They might aspire to emulate Mary in her motherhood, for lack of any other particularly distinctive feature about her in the New Testament. They might proclaim themselves prophets like Chuldah and Noadiah, but the prophetic literature was all written by men. They might try to be as earthshakingly beautiful as Esther and Judith, or as devoted to their mothers-in-law as Ruth.

If Deborah and Jael were to serve as models, one would first have to be a wife, though the wife who was held in highest esteem was hardly considered virtuous because she was a judge or soldier of Israel. The most powerful female presence was Wisdom. But the very eternity of Wisdom, her function at the center of human righteousness, kingship, and history—and the fact that she was not depicted as a mortal woman but was rather an agent of God and a product of men's minds—removed her to an impassable distance from women's real lives, and rendered her a far less likely model for real women. Truly, there are few women immortalized as leaders in cult.

It would appear, then, that the same kind of ambivalence toward women expressed elsewhere in biblical literature is found in those passages which allude to their participation in cult. Particularly conspicuous in both testaments is the relative absence of women from leadership roles in the cultic life of the community. Since these roles were sometimes filled by men whose holiness and virtue were hardly unblemished—men like Aaron, David, Solomon, and Judas Iscariot—one can only conclude that the criterion used to exclude most women of possibly equal or greater righteousness from the most influential religious positions might have been their sex alone. Apparently those qualities seen as required for cultic leadership were viewed by early proponents of monotheism as not present in women to the same degree as they were in men, even as the former were an integral part of the community of believers.

EPILOGUE

FROM the third through the first millennium, it appears that a dramatic modification in religious beliefs about the importance of gender accompanied the passage from polytheism to monotheism in the ancient Near East.

In the polytheistic view, gender was considered comparatively insignificant to the exercise of divine power, in the sense that communities of worshipers endowed deities of both sexes with great powers. This may be seen in the not infrequent sharing, in rough equivalence, of the same or similar broad and indispensable attributes by goddesses and gods. Furthermore, in many cultures throughout this area, there was a long history of active participation by both women and men in many aspects of both popular and official cult. Persons of both sexes occupied even the highest priestly positions, with all they entailed in the way of landholding, retinues, and commercial privileges.

Polytheistic myths exhibit a nonjudgmental, even favorable attitude toward active sexuality in the divine sphere, and in particular female sexuality, which was seen as assuring the orderly and prosperous functioning of human society. While both goddesses and gods, in the performance of their varied functions, were portrayed as guarantors of continued fertility—e.g., Hathor and Osiris, Gaia and Zeus, Anath and Baal, Inanna and Enki—it was the active sexuality of Isis that enabled her impregnation with Horus from the body of the dead king Osiris. Her sexuality thus guaranteed the stability of royal succession in Egypt, as each pharaoh "became" the living incarnation of Horus. Likewise, it was the active sexuality of Inanna/Ishtar in Mesopotamia, expressed in the Sacred Marriage rite, that was seen as guaranteeing the fertility of the land and the stability of secular rule.

These attitudes toward female sexuality spilled over into expansive attitudes toward priestesses, who were valued as avatars of the providential goddesses, and were marked by a more general lack of fear, stated negatively, and a celebration, stated positively, of female bodily functions. Childbirth and maternity were portrayed as good and nonlimiting in the active lives of goddesses. Outside of some of the Semitic cultures like Canaan, as late as the second millennium there were apparently no special taboos associated with childbirth more than with any other mortal conditions requiring purification. In addition, the afterlife came to be administered by deities of both sexes. Generally, polytheistic myths portrayed sex roles in both the divine and earthly spheres as less restrictive and rigid than those familiar to us from biblical literature, and they were characterized by an orientation that seems to have been fairly inclusive of all persons, regardless of gender.

As different from what is found in polytheistic myths, parts of the Bible represent men in a very special and closer relation to God than women. Men wrote the Bible from a male perspective, reflecting the values of their own times. This may be seen in the representation in the Old Testament of the usual dominance of men in cult, war, governance, family life, social structure, and as transmitters of divine commandments, and in the representation in the New Testament of a male embodiment of divine purpose, accomplished through the closest affiliation of Jesus and his male apostles.

Yet the God of monotheism is shown as one who differs from polytheistic deities in the extent of his overriding concern for justice, compassion, and righteousness in this world, and his promise of final judgment for all persons based on adherence to his moral laws or of personal redemption based on faith in the teachings of Jesus.

However, within the context of this moral and spiritual universe, biblical attitudes toward women demonstrate a pervasive ambivalence and fear. Women are without question included as part of the community of believers, but not in positions of cultic leadership as often as men. In the Old Testament, like men, women are subject to divine punishment for transgression, but they are sometimes punished differently for the same transgression, apparently on the basis of their sex alone. And in a religious view that values the moral and spiritual commitment of the individual, women are shown as somehow possessing lesser moral and spiritual capacities than men. Moreover, in both testaments, as opposed to men, women are frequently shown as more tied to the material than to the moral and spiritual concerns of this life.

Above all, portions of biblical literature exhibit a profound ambivalence toward and fear of female sexuality and normal bodily functions. Even as they are essential to "build up" the men's houses, women are variously shown as sexually dangerous to men's pursuit of righteousness, excluded as "unclean" and unfit for participation in cultic rites because they are normal females in the body, or seen as dispensable in cult. Even when a woman physically gives birth to Jesus, and thereby enables the accomplishment of his redemptive mission, she is shown to be of relatively slight importance in early cult. In sum, biblical writings exhibit a significance attached to gender that was relatively absent in polytheistic literature.

For a very long time, both polytheistic and monotheistic societies in the ancient Near East seem to have been structured, from our modern perspective, around a remarkable degree of interpenetration of conceptions of the "divine" and organization of the "secular" in many facets of their lives. In historic times, Western culture appears to have been characterized, among other things, by a gradual but important disentanglement of religious beliefs and practices from the daily organization and functioning of secular society. This process of secularization has been long and complicated, marked by an uneven pace and by periods of religious ascendance and decline. It has by no means diminished the influence of religion on thought and life, but the nature of that influence has changed.

Some time ago, Max Weber pointed out that the advent of Protestantism did not cause the rise of capitalism, nor was the latter responsible for the wave of Protestant dissent. But the ethical components of Protestantism—its emphasis on the return of individuals to the content of the Bible as the basis of a well-ordered life, and the Calvinist doctrine of the Elect—proved particularly congenial to the spirit of capitalism, namely its emphasis on individual enterprise, self-reliance, rationality in planning and keeping accounts in business, and financial success as a sign of individual worth.

Conversely, the spirit of capitalism, with the high premium it placed on individual work and accomplishment and its rewards of earthly prosperity and power, was particularly compatible with the Protestant belief in individual access to the divine without the necessary mediation of an ecclesiastical hierarchy. And while Protestantism and early capitalism did not stand in a causal relationship to one another, the ethic of the one and the spirit of the other lent mutual support and encouragement, and each provided a congenial ground for the flowering of the other.

In like fashion, biblical attitudes toward femininity and masculinity did not cause real secular hierarchies based on sex, expressed in political, legal, economic, and social restrictions placed on women. But in the past two thousand years, the general elevation of gender itself as a matter of considerable religious significance in biblical texts, and the latter's expression in some of its narratives of a deep ambivalence toward and fear of women, were very likely congruous in spirit with those Western societies that viewed women as subordinate and, in different periods, believed that women's lives ought to be more narrowly circumscribed than those of men. Indeed, secular beliefs about women's irrationality, unimportance, dispensability, moral weakness, seductiveness, and the like, expressed in philosophy, literature, and psychology, could find ample illustration and confirmation in parts of the Bible.

It seems that women were not uniformly subordinated to men throughout Western history. At times, different classes of women exercised a considerable amount of economic and political power, even if not always autonomously—e.g., the great Lady Abbesses in western Europe from the fifth to the twelfth century, and women traders and guild members in England and France in the thirteenth. But while women of every class made indispensable economic contributions to the survival and prosperity of the social group through their labor within and sometimes outside of their families, the gradual hardening of beliefs about the nature of women as inferior to men must have found some biblical attitudes particularly apt.

Conversely, secular attitudes about the inferiority and necessary subordination of women to their husbands in marriage, even while they were so visibly essential and productive economically, must have seemed felicitous and reinforcing to that part of the Judeo-Christian tradition which was grounded in the deep ambivalence toward women found in some passages of the Bible. But it was perhaps above all the enormous significance attached to gender itself as related to individual worth and importance, and an exaggeration of the significance of the differences between the sexes, found alike in parts of biblical literature and in the ethos of historic, and especially more recent, Western cultures, that made each so congenial to the other, and enabled each to provide for the other a fertile ground in which to flourish.

It may be, then, that among the most radically new ideas advanced by the biblical vision of divine-human relationships was the concept of worth, autonomy, and power as inextricably linked to gender, and the polarization of feminine and masculine in apprehensions of the divine and prescriptions for the organization of the human community. In contrast with the more androgynous attitudes prevalent in ancient Near Eastern polytheistic religions, out of which this vision emerged, to transform over time the religious consciousness of the West, biblical views on the seminal importance of gender have helped to shape and legitimize subsequent social ideologies about the "nature" of women and men. Grounded in profoundly ambivalent attitudes toward women as a sex and an inordinate fear of female sexuality found in parts of the Bible, these views have contributed to a legacy that has been destructive to the humanity of both sexes. Women have been burdened psychologically by a long history of deeply unsettling, mystifying, mixed messages about themselves. Simultaneously and not infrequently, men have been burdened by a distorted perception of reality when they have used these views to help justify spurious, wildly vacillating, or extreme beliefs about women and about themselves.

NOTES

Introduction

1. Joan Kelly-Gadol, "The Social Relation of the Sexes: Methodological Implications of Women's History," *Signs: Journal of Women in Culture and Society,* Summer 1976, vol. 1, no. 4, p. 809.

2. Phyllis Trible, "Depatriarchalizing in Biblical Interpretation," *Journal of the American Academy of Religion,* XLI/1, March 1973, pp. 30–48, and Trible, "Nature of God in the OT," in Keith Crim, Lloyd Bailey, Sr., Victor Paul Furnish, Emory Stevens Bucke, eds., *The Interpreter's Dictionary of the Bible: Supplementary Volume* (Nashville, Tenn.: Abingdon Press, 1976), pp. 963–66; Rosemary Radford Ruether, "Misogynism and Virginal Feminism in the Fathers of the Church," in Rosemary Radford Ruether, ed., *Religion and Sexism: Images of Woman in the Jewish and Christian Traditions* (New York: Simon and Schuster, 1974), pp. 117–47; Mary Daly, *The Church and the Second Sex* (New York: Harper & Row, 1975).

3. Trible, "Women in the OT," in Crim, et al., *The Interpreter's Dictionary, Supplementary Volume,* pp. 963–66.

4. Ruether, "Misogynism and Virginal Feminism in the Fathers of the Church," p. 179.

5. See, for example, M. Z. Rosaldo, "The Use and Abuse of Anthropology: Reflections on Feminism and Cross-cultural Understanding," *Signs: Journal of Women in Culture and Society,* Spring 1980, vol. 5, no. 3, pp. 389–417.

6. See, for example, Sarah Pomeroy, *Goddesses, Whores, Wives, and Slaves: Women in Classical Antiquity* (New York: Schocken Books, 1976), pp. 52–56, 35–42; Lina Eckenstein, *Woman Under Monasticism* (Cambridge: Cambridge University Press, 1896); A. Abram, "Women Traders in Medieval London," *Economic Journal* (London), no. 26, 1916, pp. 276–85; Diane Hughes, "Domestic Ideals and Social Behavior: Evidence from Medieval Genoa," in Charles E. Rosenberg, ed., *The Family in History* (Philadelphia: University of Pennsylvania Press, 1978), pp. 115–43.

7. See, for example, Elizabeth Gould Davis, *The First Sex* (New York: G. P. Putnam's Sons, 1971); Merlin Stone, *When God Was A Woman* (New York: The Dial Press, 1976).

8. See, for example, Naomi R. Goldenberg, *The Changing of the Gods: Feminism and the End of Traditional Religions* (Boston: Beacon Press, 1979).

9. Elizabeth Fisher, *Woman's Creation: Sexual Evolution and the Shaping of Society* (New York: Anchor Press/Doubleday, 1979), pp. 286–89.

10. See, for example, Erich Neumann, *The Great Mother: An Analysis of the Archetype,* trans. Ralph Manheim, Bollingen Series XLVII (New York: Pantheon Books, 1955); Joan Chamberlain Engelsman, *The Feminine Dimension of the Divine* (Philadelphia: The Westminster Press, 1979).

Chapter 1: Laying the Groundwork

1. Simone de Beauvoir, *The Second Sex* (New York: Bantam Books, 1961), pp. xiv–xx.

2. Aristotle, *Generation of Animals,* trans. A. L. Peck, Loeb Classical Library (Cambridge, Mass.: Harvard University Press, 1943), pp. 103, 133, 395–96, 401–403, 406, cited in Susan G. Bell, ed., *Women: From the Greeks to the French Revolution* (Belmont, Cal.: Wadsworth Publishing Co., 1973), p. 18.

3. Bell, *Women: From the Greeks to the French Revolution,* pp. 38–39.

4. Katherine M. Rogers, *The Troublesome Helpmate: A History of Misogyny in Literature* (Seattle: University of Washington Press, 1966), pp. 56–99; Eileen Power, "The Position of Women," in C. G. Crump and E. F. Jacobs, eds., *The Legacy of the Middle Ages* (New York: Oxford University Press, 1926), pp. 403–33.

5. H. C. Lea, *A History of the Inquisition of the Middle Ages,* 3 vols. (New York: Russell, 2d printing, 1959), III, pp. 513–19.

6. See, for example, Sarah Pomeroy, *Goddesses, Whores, Wives, and Slaves* (New York: Schocken Books, 1976), pp. 120–89.

7. Margaret Murray, *The Witch Cult in Western Europe* (New York: Oxford University Press, 1921).

8. Giovanni Pettinato, "The Royal Archives of Tell Mardikh-Ebla," *The Biblical Archaeologist,* vol. 39, no. 2, May 1976, pp. 44–52; Paolo Matthiae, "Ebla in the Late Early Syrian Period: the Royal Palace and the State Archives," *The Biblical Archaeologist,* vol. 39, no. 3, September 1976, pp. 94–113.

9. Samuel Noah Kramer, *Sumerian Mythology: A Study of Spiritual and Literary Achievement in the Third Millennium B.C.,* rev. ed. (Philadelphia: University of Pennsylvania Press, 1972), pp. 28–29.

10. Pettinato, "The Royal Archives of Tell Mardikh-Ebla"; Matthiae, "Ebla in the Late Early Syrian Period."

11. See, for example, an interview in *The Denver Post,* June 18, 1976, p. 6BB, with Dr. David Noel Freedman, a University of Michigan biblical archaeologist, and then president of the Society of Biblical Literature. Freedman said of Ebla, "Previous reports and rumors do not begin to indicate the true dimensions of the discovery and its importance for ancient Near Eastern and Biblical studies . . . a new chapter in the history of the Near East has been opened and it will not be closed for some time. . . . the new discoveries should tell us much about the background and origin of the people who later became Israel." The mythological, cultic, and ritual texts (e.g., incantations, spells) found on a number of the tablets should, Freedman said, "provide us with the

background information on the religion which the Israelites opposed so vehe-mently and nevertheless absorbed and adopted to some extent. . . . If the patriarchs and their descendants did not actually live in Ebla, they clearly belonged to the same cultural tradition and came from the area in which that tradition survived and exerted a powerful influence."

12. Thorkild Jacobsen, *The Treasures of Darkness: A History of Mesopotamian Religion* (New Haven: Yale University Press, 1976).

13. See, for example, Elaine Pagels, *The Gnostic Gospels* (New York: Random House, 1979).

14. James H. Charlesworth, *The Pseudepigrapha and Modern Research,* Spetuagint and Cognate Studies of the Society of Biblical Literature, no. 7 (Missoula, Mont.: The Scholars' Press, 1976).

15. See, for example, Department on Faith and Order and Department on Cooperation of Men and Women in Church, Family and Society, World Council of Churches, *Concerning the Ordination of Women* (Geneva, 1964).

16. See, for example, Kate Millett, *Sexual Politics* (New York: Doubleday & Co., 1970), pp. 51–54; Mary Daly, *The Church and the Second Sex* (New York: Harper & Row, 1975); Naomi R. Goldenberg, *The Changing of the Gods: Feminism and the End of Traditional Religions* (Boston: Beacon Press, 1979).

17. See, for example, Phyllis Trible, "Depatriarchalizing in Biblical Inter-pretation," *Journal of the American Academy of Religion* XLI/1, March 1973, pp. 30–48; Constance F. Parvey, "The Theology and Leadership of Women in the New Testament," in Rosemary Radford Ruether, ed., *Religion and Sexism: Images of Woman in the Jewish and Christian Traditions* (New York: Simon and Schuster, 1974), pp. 117–47; Leonard Swidler, "Is Sexism a Sign of Decadence in Reli-gion?" in Judith Plaskow and Joan Arnold Romero, eds., *Women and Religion,* rev. ed. (Missoula, Mont.: The Scholars' Press and the American Academy of Religion, 1974), pp. 167–75; Evelyn and Frank Stagg, *Woman in the World of Jesus* (Philadelphia: The Westminster Press, 1978); Carol Meyers, "The Roots of Restriction: Women in Early Israel," in *Biblical Archaeologist,* September 1978, pp. 91–103.

18. See, for example, John H. Otwell, *And Sarah Laughed: The Status of Woman in the Old Testament* (Philadelphia: The Westminster Press, 1977), pp. 49–66; Phyllis Bird, "Images of Women in the Old Testament," in Ruether, *Religion and Sexism,* p. 71; E. and F. Stagg, *Women in the World of Jesus,* pp. 162–258.

19. See, for example, Elaine H. Pagels, "What Became of God the Mother? Conflicting Images of God in Early Christianity," *Signs: Journal of Women in Culture and Society,* Winter 1976, vol. 2, no. 2, pp. 292–303; Elisabeth Schüssler Fiorenza, "Interpreting Patriarchal Traditions," and Joanna Dewey, "Images of Women," in Letty M. Russell, ed., *The Liberating Word* (Philadel-phia: The Westminster Press, 1976), pp. 39–81; Rosemary Radford Ruether, *Mary—The Feminine Face of the Church* (Philadelphia: The Westminster Press, 1977).

20. See, for example, Judith Hauptman, "Images of Women in the Tal-mud," Rosemary Radford Ruether, "Misogynism and Virginal Feminism in the Fathers of the Church," and Eleanor Commo McLaughlin, "Equality of Souls, Inequality of Sexes: Woman in Medieval Theology," in Ruether, *Reli-gion and Sexism,* pp. 184–212, 150–83, 213–66.

21. Winsome Munro, "Patriarchy and Charismatic Community in 'Paul,' " in Plaskow and Romero, *Women and Religion,* pp. 189–98.

22. See, for example, Trible, "Women in the OT," in Keith Crim, et al., *The Interpreter's Dictionary of the Bible: Supplementary Volume,* (Nashville: Abingdon Press, 1976), p. 965.

23. I am indebted to Rosemary Radford Ruether for pointing out to me the asymmetry between polytheistic and biblical texts, and also for a number of other valuable criticisms that helped to sharpen my focus.

Chapter 2: Gender and the Nature of the Divine: The Polytheistic View

1. For good discussions of this theory, which links the nature of polytheistic beliefs to the natural environment, see, for example, H. and H. A. Frankfort, John A. Wilson, Thorkild Jacobsen, *Before Philosophy: The Intellectual Adventure of Ancient Man,* 1st printing, 1946 (Middlesex, England: Penguin Books, Ltd., 1963), pp. 137–39, 216, 237–41; E. O. James, *The Ancient Gods* (New York: G. P. Putnam's Sons, 1960), pp. 200–207; Henri Frankfort, *Kingship and the Gods: A Study of Near Eastern Religion as the Integration of Society and Nature,* 1st printing, 1948 (Chicago: University of Chicago Press, 1971); Thorkild Jacobsen, *The Treasures of Darkness: A History of Mesopotamian Religion* (New Haven: Yale University Press, 1976), pp. 25–27, 36–37, 43–44.

2. See, for example, the Sixth Dynasty tomb inscription of Nefer-Seshem-Re in Miriam Lichtheim, ed., *Ancient Egyptian Literature: A Book of Readings* (Berkeley: University of California Press, 1973), p. 17; R. O. Faulkner, *The Ancient Eygptian Coffin Texts,* 3 vols. (Warminster, England: Aris and Phillips, Ltd., 1973).

3. Samuel Noah Kramer, "Lamentation Over the Destruction of Sumer and Ur," in James B. Pritchard, ed., *Ancient Near Eastern Texts Relating to the Old Testament,* 3d ed. with supplement (Princeton: Princeton University Press, 1969), pp. 612–19. (Hereafter referred to as *ANET.*)

4. Ibid., p. 617.

5. Ibid.

6. Samuel Noah Kramer, *Sumerian Mythology: A Study of Spiritual and Literary Achievement in the Third Millennium B.C.,* rev. ed. (Philadelphia: University of Pennsylvania Press, 1972), pp. 68–73.

7. See, for example, "The Baal and 'Anat Cycle," in Cyrus H. Gordon, *Ugaritic Literature: A Comprehensive Translation of the Poetic and Prose Texts* (Rome: Pontificium Institutum Biblicum, 1949), pp. 9–56.

8. See, for example, Sabatino Moscati, *The Face of the Ancient Orient* (Chicago: Anchor Books, 1962), pp. 203–33.

9. Dimitri Baranki, *Phoenicia and the Phoenicians* (Beirut: KHAYATS, 1961), p. 69.

10. Cyrus H. Gordon, *Ugarit and Minoan Crete* (New York: W. W. Norton, 1966), pp. 18–19.

11. Ibid., pp. 100–20.

12. Ibid., pp. 28, 151–53.

13. Samuel Noah Kramer, *The Sacred Marriage Rite* (Bloomington: Indiana University Press, 1969), pp. 85–106.

14. Siegfried Morenz, *Egyptian Religion,* trans. Ann E. Keep (Ithaca: Cornell University Press, 1973), pp. 6–15.

15. Morris Jastrow, *Aspects of Religious Belief and Practice in Babylonia and Assyria,* 1st printing, 1911 (New York: Benjamin Blom, 1971), p. 20.

16. See, for example, Sir E. A. Wallis Budge, *From Fetish to God in Ancient Egypt,* 1st printing, 1934 (New York: Benjamin Blom, 1972), pp. 3–18, and Budge, *Egyptian Religion,* 1st printing, 1900 (New York: University Books, 1959), passim, especially pp. 17–60.

17. For an almost classic rendition of this view from a Jungian perspective, see Esther Harding, *Woman's Mysteries Ancient and Modern: A Psychological Interpretation of the Feminine Principle as Portrayed in Myth, Story and Dream* (New York: Putnam, 1972).

18. Albrecht Goetze, "Egyptian and Hittite Treaties," in Pritchard, *ANET,* 'God List, Blessings and Curses of the Treaty Between Suppiluliumas and Kurtiwaza,' p. 205.

19. John A. Wilson, "Egyptian Myths, Tales, and Mortuary Texts," in Pritchard, *ANET,* 'The Assignment of Functions to Thoth,' pp. 8–9.

20. See, for example, Lichtheim, *Ancient Egyptian Literature,* "Unas Pyramid Texts: Utterance 245," pp. 32–33; "Teti Pyramid Texts: Utterance 350," p. 41; "Pepi I Pyramid Texts: Utterance 446," p. 46.

21. See, for example, E. O. James, *The Cult of the Mother Goddess* (London: Thames and Hudson, 1959); James, *The Ancient Gods,* pp. 46–49, 77, 106; James, *Prehistoric Religion: A Study in Prehistoric Archaeology* (New York: Barnes & Noble, 1957), pp. 153–54; Robert Graves, *The Greek Myths,* 2 vols. (Baltimore: Penguin Books, 1955), I, pp. 27–28; Ilse Seibert, *Women in the Ancient Near East,* trans. Marianne Herzfeld (New York: Abner Schram, 1974), pp. 11, 12, and illustrated plates of excavated statues, pp. 1–3, 15, 31, 39, 41, 47, 50, 53, 79, 86, 91.

22. Kramer, *Sumerian Mythology,* p. 23.

23. See, for example, James Mellaart, *Catal Hüyük: A Neolithic Town in Anatolia* (New York: McGraw-Hill, 1967), p. 23.

24. Jacobsen, *The Treasures of Darkness,* p. 7.

25. Ibid.

26. Ibid., p. 8.

27. Ibid., pp. 95, 137, 249, n. 89.

28. L. W. King, *Babylonian Religion and Mythology,* 1st printing, 1899 (New York: AMS Press, 1976), p. 85.

29. Charles Gordon Cumming, *The Assyrian and Hebrew Hymns of Praise,* 1st printing, 1934 (New York: AMS Press, 1966), "Hymn to Marduk No. 9," p. 145.

30. Ibid., "Hymn to Sin No. 5."

31. See passages from texts in Budge, *From Fetish to God in Ancient Egypt,* especially pp. 141–42, 171, 199.

32. Lichtheim, *Ancient Egyptian Literature,* "Ptah the supreme god," p. 54.

33. See, for example, Moscati, *The Face of the Ancient Orient,* p. 314.

34. Samuel Noah Kramer, "Sumerian Miscellaneous Texts," in James B. Pritchard, ed., *The Ancient Near East: Supplementary Texts and Pictures Relating to the Old Testament* (Princeton: Princeton University Press, 1969), 'The Curse of Agade: The Ekur Avenged,' pp. 647–51.

35. Jorgen Laessoe, *People of Ancient Assyria: Their Inscriptions and Correspondence,* trans. F. S. Leigh-Browne (London: Routledge & Kegan Paul, 1963), p. 24.

36. Ibid., p. 99.

37. Ibid., p. 105.

38. Ibid.

39. Ibid., pp. 117–22; Goetze, "Hittite Treaties," in Pritchard, *ANET*, pp. 205–206; Erica Reiner, "Akkadian Treaties from Syria and Assyria," in Pritchard, *ANET*, pp. 531–41.

40. James Henry Breasted, *A History of Egypt from the Earliest Times to the Persian Conquest* (New York: Charles Scribner's Sons, 1916), p. 62.

41. Edmund I. Gordon, *Sumerian Proverbs: A Glimpse of Everyday Life in Ancient Mesopotamia* (Philadelphia: The University Museum, University of Pennsylvania, 1959), p. 45, #1.7.

42. L. W. King, *The Seven Tablets of Creation II* (London, 1902), pls. 75–84, lines 42–50, cited in Jacobsen, *Treasures of Darkness*, p. 148.

43. Ibid., lines 67–78.

44. Ibid., obv. 58, rev. 8.

45. Jacquetta Hawkes and Sir Leonard Woolley, *Pre-History and the Beginnings of Civilization* (New York: Harper & Row, 1963), p. 711.

46. Morenz, *Egyptian Religion*, pp. 108–109.

47. Faulkner, *The Ancient Egyptian Coffin Texts*, I, p. 183, #316.

48. I.e., humble.

49. John A. Wilson, "Egyptian Hymns and Prayers," in Pritchard, *ANET*, 'Gratitude For a God's Mercy,' p. 380.

50. Ibid., 'A Hymn to Amon-Re,' p. 365.

51. Ibid., p. 366.

52. Ibid., p. 367.

53. Ibid., 'A Penitential Hymn To A Goddess,' p. 381.

54. Samuel Noah Kramer, *The Sumerians: Their History, Culture, and Character* (Chicago: University of Chicago Press, 1963), p. 124.

55. Ibid., p. 125.

56. Ibid., p. 159.

57. Enheduanna, *The Exaltation of Inanna*, trans. William W. Hallo and J. J. A. Van Dijk (New Haven: Yale University Press, 1968), p. 17, lines 21–23.

58. Cumming, *The Assyrian and Hebrew Hymns of Praise*, p. 71.

59. Ibid., p. 150.

60. Ibid., p. 128, "Hymn to Sin No. 5."

61. Ibid., p. 142, "Hymn to Marduk No. 7."

62. Ibid., p. 140, "Hymn to Marduk No. 12."

63. Ibid., p. 85.

64. Ibid., p. 150, "Hymn to Ishtar No. 2."

65. Ibid., p. 151, "Hymn to Ishtar No. 3."

66. Gordon, *Ugarit and Minoan Crete*, p. 68, and Gordon, *Ugaritic Literature*, Text 51:11, p. 29.

67. G. R. Driver, *Canaanite Myths and Legends*, 1st printing, 1956 (Edinburgh: T. & T. Clark, 1971), "Keret," p. 43.

68. U. Cassuto, *The Goddess Anath: Canaanite Epics of the Patriarchal Age*, trans. Israel Abrahams (Jerusalem: The Magnes Press, Hebrew University, 1971), p. 167, Tablet VI AB, line R. See also the discussion of El's moral qualities in Ulf Oldenburg, *The Conflict Between El and Ba 'al in Canaanite Religion* (Leiden, Netherlands: E. J. Brill, 1969), pp. 21, 173.

69. Driver, *Canaanite Myths and Legends*, "Aqhat," pp. 55–57.

70. King, *Babylonian Religion and Mythology*, p. 83.

71. Lichtheim, *Ancient Egyptian Literature*, pp. 58–80.

72. Ibid., p. 24.

73. E. A. Wallis Budge, *The Decrees of Memphis and Canopus: The Rosetta Stone,* 3 vols. (London: Kegan Paul, Trench, Trübner & Co., Ltd., 1904), I, pp. 117–18.

74. John A. Wilson, "Egypt: The Values of Life," in Frankfort, et al., *Before Philosophy,* p. 117.

75. Ibid., pp. 117–18.

Chapter 3: Sex Roles and the Relation of Power to Gender: Polytheistic Texts

1. Kramer, *Sumerian Mythology,* p. 39; Ferris J. Stephens, "Sumero-Akkadian Hymns and Prayers" in Pritchard, *ANET,* 'Prayer of Lamentation to Ishtar,' pp. 383–85; Thorkild Jacobsen, "Toward the Image of Tammuz," in William L. Moran, ed., *Toward the Image of Tammuz and Other Essays on Mesopotamian History and Culture* (Cambridge: Harvard University Press, 1970), pp. 73–101; Rudolf Anthes, "Mythology in Ancient Egypt," in Samuel Noah Kramer, *Mythologies of the Ancient World* (New York: Anchor Books, 1969), pp. 33–43; John A. Wilson, "Egyptian Myths, Tales and Mortuary Texts" in Pritchard, *ANET,* 'The Contest of Horus and Seth For the Rule,' pp. 14–17; Graves, *The Greek Myths,* I, p. 93; Emily James Putnam, *The Lady: Studies of Certain Significant Phases of Her History,* 1st printing, 1910 (Chicago: University of Chicago Press, 1970), pp. 72–74.

2. Driver, *Canaanite Myths and Legends,* "Baal" II, vi, line 46, p. 101; Hesiod, *Theogony,* trans. Richard Lattimore, 1st printing, 1959 (Ann Arbor: University of Michigan Press, 1970), lines 105–87.

3. Hesiod, *Theogony,* lines 155–82.

4. Ibid., lines 459–79.

5. Ibid., lines 494–95.

6. Ibid., lines 479–506.

7. H. L. Ginsburg, "Ugaritic Myths, Epics, and Legends," in Pritchard, *ANET,* 'Poems About Baal and Anath," pp. 132–33, 140.

8. See, for example, James, *The Ancient Gods,* p. 87.

9. *The Epic of Gilgamesh,* trans. N. K. Sandars (Middlesex, England: Penguin Books, Ltd., 1960), p. 83.

10. Budge, *Egyptian Religion,* p. 78.

11. Frankfort, *Kingship and the Gods,* p. 289.

12. Inscription cited in Budge, *From Fetish to God,* p. 202.

13. Enheduanna, *The Exaltation of Inanna,* trans. William W. Hallo and J. J. A. Van Dijk (New Haven: Yale University Press, 1968).

14. Samuel Noah Kramer, "Sumerian Hymns," in Pritchard, *ANET,* Introduction to 'Hymnal Prayer of Enheduanna: The Adoration of Inanna in Ur,' p. 579.

15. Enheduanna, *The Exaltation of Inanna,* p. 15.

16. Ibid., p. 50.

17. Samuel Noah Kramer, "Sumerian Myths and Epic Tales," in Pritchard, *ANET,* 'Inanna's Descent to the Nether World,' p. 53.

18. Ibid.

19. Ibid., p. 55.

20. Ibid.

21. Enheduanna, *The Exaltation of Inanna,* p. 15.

22. Ibid., p. 17.

23. Ibid., p. 19.
24. Ibid., p. 21.
25. Ibid., p. 31.
26. Ibid., p. 33.
27. Stephens, "Sumero-Akkadian Hymns and Prayers," in Pritchard, *ANET,* pp. 383–5.
28. Wilson, "Egyptian Myths, Tales and Mortuary Texts," in Pritchard, *ANET,* 'Deliverance of Mankind from Destruction,' p. 101; Anthes, "Mythology in Ancient Egypt," p. 18, and Cyrus Gordon, "Canaanite Mythology," in Kramer, *Mythologies of the Ancient World,* p. 197.
29. Gordon, "Canaanite Mythology," p. 197.
30. Ibid.
31. Ibid., p. 198.
32. Ibid.
33. Ibid., p. 199.
34. Ibid.
35. Ibid., p. 212.
36. Ibid., p. 213.
37. Ibid., p. 210.
38. Ibid., p. 204.
39. Ibid.
40. Ibid.
41. Ibid., p. 213.
42. Ibid., p. 208.
43. Ibid.
44. Frankfort, *Kingship and the Gods,* p. 31. "Two lands" means Upper and Lower Egypt.
45. Ibid., p. 32.
46. Budge, *Egyptian Religion,* p. 90.
47. See, for example, Frankfort, *Kingship and the Gods,* pp. 34–35.
48. See, for example, *The Golden Ass of Apuleius,* trans. Robert Graves (New York: Pocket Books, 1952), pp. 238–39.
49. See, for example, Martin P. Nilsson, *A History of Greek Religion,* 1st printing, 1925 (New York: W. W. Norton, 1964), pp. 79, 133; W. K. C. Guthrie, *The Greeks and Their Gods,* 1st printing, 1950 (Boston: Beacon Press, 1961), pp. 37–49.
50. See, for example, John Pinsent, *Greek Mythology* (London: Paul Hamlin, 1969), pp. 32, 60.
51. Ibid., pp. 58, 191; Graves, *The Greek Myths,* I, pp. 103–11.
52. Wilson, "Egyptian Myths, Tales, and Mortuary Texts," in Pritchard, *ANET,* 'The Contest of Horus and Seth For the Rule,' pp. 14–17.
53. Sandars, *The Epic of Gilgamesh,* p. 8.
54. Ibid., p. 105.
55. Ibid.
56. Ibid., pp. 107–108.
57. Ibid., p. 109.
58. Kramer, "Sumerian Hymns," in Pritchard, *ANET,* 'Hymn to Enlil, the All-Beneficent," pp. 573–76.
59. See the discussion of "Inanna's Descent to the Nether World" on pp. 82–87.

60. Kramer, "Sumerian Hymns," in Pritchard, *ANET,* 'Hymn to Enlil, the All-Beneficent,' p. 575.

61. Ibid., pp. 575-76.

62. Ibid., p. 575.

63. Ibid., pp. 576–77.

64. Kramer, *Sumerian Mythology,* pp. 64–68.

65. Ibid., p. 66.

66. Ibid., p. 68.

67. Gordon, "Canaanite Mythology," pp. 211, 213.

68. Budge, *From Fetish to God,* p. 280.

69. Introduction to Chapter CXXV in the *Book of the Dead: The Papyrus of Ani,* trans. Sir Wallis Budge, 1st printing, 1895 (New York: Dover Publications, 1967); Budge, *Egyptian Religion,* pp. 152–53.

70. See, for example, the appendix to the text of Plate IV in *Book of the Dead,* p. 261, and Anthes, "Mythology in Ancient Egypt," in Kramer, *Mythologies of the Ancient World,* pp. 59–60.

71. See, for example, Budge, *Egyptian Religion,* p. 124.

72. Ibid., p. 112.

73. Ibid., p. 111.

74. Budge, *The Book of the Dead,* Plate III, figures 1, 2, 3, p. 256.

75. Wilson, "Egyptian Myths, Tales, and Mortuary Texts," in Pritchard, *ANET,* 'The Theology of Memphis,' pp. 4–5. Note the similarity to the Old Testament association of speech with creation.

76. Budge, *Egyptian Religion,* pp. 162–69.

77. Ibid., pp. 121, 195.

78. Ibid., p. 122, and Anthes, "Mythology in Ancient Egypt," pp. 77, 79.

79. Anthes, "Mythology in Ancient Egypt," p. 84.

80. Wilson, "Egyptian Myths, Tales, and Mortuary Texts," in Pritchard, *ANET,* 'The God and His Unknown Name of Power,' pp. 12–14.

81. Ibid., p. 12.

82. Ibid., p. 13.

83. Ibid.

84. This is the point at which the substitution of any Egyptian's name for that of Rā might take place.

85. Wilson, "Egyptian Myths, Tales, and Mortuary Texts," in Pritchard, *ANET,* pp. 13–14.

86. Kramer, "Sumerian Myths and Epic Tales," in Pritchard, *ANET,* 'Enki and Ninhursag: A Paradise Myth,' pp. 37–40.

87. Ibid., p. 38, lines 1–30.

88. Ibid., p. 40, lines 218–19.

89. Ibid., line 220.

90. Ibid., line 250; pp. 40–41, lines 251–68. Also, see p. 37, n. 10.

91. Ibid., p. 39, lines 67–69.

92. Ibid., p. 37, n. 5.

93. The name of the goddess Nintu, "the mother of the land," is here used interchangeably with Ninhursag. Both are Sumerian mother-goddesses.

94. Kramer, "Sumerian Myths and Epic Tales," in Pritchard, *ANET,* 'Enki and Ninhursag: A Paradise Myth,' p. 39, lines 67–69.

95. Gen. 3:16.

96. Lev. 12:6–8.

97. Thorkild Jacobsen, "Mesopotamia: The Cosmos as a State," in Frankfort et al., *Before Philosophy,* pp. 158–59.

98. Many sources might be cited here. See, for example, C. Kerényi, *Eleusis: Archetypal Image of Mother and Daughter,* trans. Ralph Manheim (New York: Bollingen Foundation, 1967), pp. 18–25; Martin P. Nilsson, *The Mycenean Origin of Greek Mythology,* 1st printing, 1932 (New York: W. W. Norton, 1963); Robert Graves, *The Greek Myths,* 2 vols., cited above; Jane Ellen Harrison, *Mythology* and *Themis,* cited above; W. K. C. Guthrie, *The Greeks and Their Gods,* 1st printing, 1950 (Boston: Beacon Press, 1961).

99. Oskar Seyffert, *Dictionary of Classical Antiquities,* 1st printing, 1882, revised and edited by Henry Nettleship and J. E. Sandys (Cleveland: Meridian Books, 1969), p. 80.

100. See, for example, Pomeroy, *Goddesses, Whores, Wives, and Slaves,* pp. 75–76.

101. Hesiod, *Theogony,* p. 176, line 887.

102. Ibid., p. 177, lines 894–900.

103. Ibid., p. 180, lines 925–29.

104. See, for example, James, *The Ancient Gods,* p. 81.

105. Speiser, "Akkadian Myths and Epics," in Pritchard, *ANET,* 'Nergal and Ereshkigal,' pp. 103–104.

106. Ibid., p. 104, lines 82–88.

107. A. K. Grayson, "Akkadian Myths and Epics," in Pritchard, *ANET* (additions), pp. 507–12.

108. Ibid., p. 511 (v), lines 2–6.

109. Ibid., lines 7–10.

110. Ibid., lines 55–59. Erra is another name for Nergal.

111. Ibid. (v), lines 47–48.

112. Ibid. (vi), lines 47–48.

113. Budge, *Egyptian Religion,* pp. 166–67.

114. See, for example, Graves, *The Greek Myths,* I, pp. 44–45, 57; Pomeroy, *Goddesses, Whores, Wives, and Slaves,* p. 6.

115. Wilson, "Egyptian Myths, Tales, and Mortuary Texts," in Pritchard, *ANET,* 'The Theology of Memphis,' p. 5, n. 53.

116. See, for example, James, *The Ancient Gods,* pp. 84–85.

117. Wilson, "Egyptian Myths, Tales, and Mortuary Texts," in Pritchard, *ANET,* 'The Repulsing of the Dragon and the Creation,' (xxvii I), p. 6.

118. Ibid., 'The Theology of Memphis,' p. 5.

119. Kramer, "Sumerian Myths and Epic Tales," in Pritchard, *ANET,* 'Inanna's Descent to the Nether World,' pp. 52–57.

120. Ibid., p. 55, line 165.

121. Kramer, *Sumerian Mythology,* p. 31.

122. Or Nanna or Enki.

123. Kramer, "Sumerian Myths and Epic Tales," in Pritchard, *ANET,* 'Inanna's Descent to the Nether World,' pp. 53–54, lines 43–48.

124. Ibid., p. 53, n. 18.

125. Sandars, *The Epic of Gilgamesh,* pp. 68–82.

126. Ibid., p. 85.

127. Kramer, "Sumerian Myths and Epic Tales," in Pritchard, *ANET,* 'Inanna's Descent to the Nether World,' p. 54, line 8.

128. Ibid., line 57.

129. Ibid., lines 65–67.

130. Kramer, *Sumerian Mythology,* pp. 43–47.

131. Ibid., pp. 59–62.

132. Ibid., p. 60.

133. Ibid., pp. 62–63.

134. Ibid., p. 63.

135. Ibid.

136. Kramer, "Sumerian Myths and Epic Tales," in Pritchard, *ANET,* 'Inanna's Descent to the Nether World,' p. 56, lines 190, 204.

137. Ibid., pp. 56–57, lines 276–328.

138. Ibid., p. 52, n. 6.

139. Speiser, "Akkadian Myths and Epics," in Pritchard, *ANET,* 'Descent of Ishtar to the Nether World,' pp. 106–109.

140. Ibid., p. 108, lines 6–20, (reverse side of tablet).

141. Stephens, "Sumero-Akkadian Hymns and Prayers," in Pritchard, *ANET,* p. 383.

142. Ibid., pp. 383–85.

143. Sandars, *The Epic of Gilgamesh,* p. 85.

144. See, for example, Apuleius, *The Golden Ass: Being the Metamorphoses of Lucius Apuleius,* trans. W. Adlington, revised by S. Gaselle, 1st printing, 1915 (Cambridge: The Loeb Classical Library, Harvard University Press, 1947), Book XI, pp. 539–51; James, *The Ancient Gods,* pp. 85–87, 296–300; Pomeroy, *Goddesses, Whores, Wives, and Slaves,* pp. 216–26.

145. Sandars, *The Epic of Gilgamesh,* p. 21.

146. Ibid., p. 64.

147. Ibid., p. 86.

148. Ibid., p. 63.

149. Ibid., pp. 65–66.

Chapter 4: The Relation of Gender to Participation in Cult: Polytheistic Practice

1. Mellaart, *Catal Hüyük: A Neolithic Town in Anatolia* (New York: McGraw-Hill, 1967), pp. 23, 180–81, 184.

2. Ibid., pp. 24, 201–202.

3. Stylianos Alexiou, *Minoan Civilization,* trans. Cressida Riley (Heraklion, Greece: Spyros Alexiou Sons, 1969), p. 72.

4. Ibid., pp. 74–75.

5. Ibid., pp. 97, 105, 111–12. See also Leonard Von Matt, Stylianos Alexiou, Nikolaos Platon, Hanni Guanella, *Ancient Crete,* trans. D. J. S. Rhomson (London: Thames and Hudson, 1968), pp. 44, 118, 122.

6. Sir Flinders Petrie, *Religious Life in Ancient Egypt,* 1st printing, 1924 (New York: Cooper Square Publishers, 1972), pp. 45–47.

7. E. A. Wallis Budge, *The Gods of the Egyptians or Studies in Egyptian Mythology,* 1st printing, 1904 (New York: Dover Publications, 1969), 2 vols., I, p. 101.

8. Ibid., I, p. 93.

9. Petrie, *Religious Life in Ancient Egypt,* p. 51; Budge, *The Gods of the Egyptians,* I, p. 453; Alfred Wiedemann, *Religion of the Ancient Egyptians* (New York: G. H. Putnam's Sons, 1897), p. 10.

10. Budge, *The Gods of the Egyptians,* I, p. 422.

11. Ibid., I, pp. 444–49.

12. Frankfort, *Kingship and the Gods,* pp. 188–90.

13. James, *The Ancient Gods,* pp. 115–16.

14. Frankfort, *Kingship and the Gods,* pp. 79–88.

15. Ibid., pp. 123–39.

16. See, for example, Morenz, *Egyptian Religion,* pp. 183–212.

17. See, for example, James Henry Breasted, *A History of Egypt From the Earliest Times to the Persian Conquest* (New York: Charles Scribner's Sons, 1916), p. 70; James, *The Ancient Gods,* p. 170; Budge, *The Gods of the Egyptians,* I, pp. 233–34.

18. See, for example, Jacquetta Hawkes, *The First Great Civilizations: Life in Mesopotamia, the Indus Valley, and Egypt* (New York: Alfred A. Knopf, 1973), p. 401; James Henry Breasted, *Ancient Times: A History of the Early World,* 1st printing, 1916 (Boston: Ginn & Co., 2d rev. ed., 1944), pp. 70–80; Budge, *The Gods of the Egyptians,* I, p. 166.

19. E. A. Wallis Budge, *The Liturgy of Funerary Offerings,* Books on Egypt and Chaldaea, vol. XXV (London: Kegan Paul, Trench, Trübner & Co., Ltd., 1909), pp. vii–x.

20. Ibid., p. 18.

21. Ibid., pp. 83–84.

22. Ibid., pp. 92–93.

23. Déveria, *Catalogue des Manuscrits Egyptiens* (Paris, 1881, p. 171), quoted by Budge, *The Liturgy of Funerary Offerings,* p. 41.

24. Budge, *Egyptian Religion,* p. 163.

25. Budge, *The Gods of the Egyptians,* II, p. 205.

26. See, for example, ibid., p. 216.

27. E. A. Wallis Budge, *Book of the Dead: The Papyrus of Ani,* 1st printing, 1895 (New York: Dover Publications, 1967), p. 245.

28. Ibid., p. 323.

29. E. A. Wallis Budge, *The Mummy: Chapters on Egyptian Funereal Archaeology* (New York: Biblio and Tannen, 2d ed., 1964), pp. 170–72.

30. For a fairly recent expression of this view see, for example, Hawkes, *The First Great Civilizations,* pp. 398–405.

31. Budge, *Book of the Dead,* pp. 263–64, 269, 271; Budge, *The Mummy,* pp. 167, 169.

32. Hawkes, *The First Great Civilizations,* p. 404.

33. *Cambridge Ancient History,* 3d ed. (Cambridge: Cambridge University Press, 1973), vol. II, part I, pp. 327–28. (Hereafter referred to as *CAH.*)

34. James H. Breasted, *Ancient Records of Egypt: Historical Documents From the Earliest Times to the Persian Conquest,* 1st printing, 1906 (New York: Russell & Russell, 1962), 4 vols., IV, p. 257.

35. Ibid., p. 314.

36. E. A. Wallis Budge, *A Short History of the Egyptian People* (London: J. M. Dent & Sons, 1914), p. 201.

37. Breasted, *Ancient Records of Egypt,* IV, p. 373.

38. Ibid., IV, p. 375.

39. Ibid., IV, pp. 477–89.

40. These probably represented Upper and Lower Egypt, and symbolized her dominion over the whole country.

41. Breasted, *Ancient Records of Egypt,* IV, pp. 505–506.

42. See, for example, Jane Ellen Harrison, *Prolegomena to the Study of Greek Religion,* 2d ed. (Cambridge: Cambridge University Press, 1908), pp. 120–50.

43. See, for example, Kerényi, *Eleusis,* pp. 55–57, 59, 61, 64, 75, 79, 80, 110, 117, 149; Sterling Dow and Robert F. Healey, S. J., *A Sacred Calendar of Eleusis,* Harvard Theological Studies XXI (Cambridge: Harvard University Press, 1965), pp. 22, 24–25, 27, 30–31, 34–37, 41; R. E. Witt, *Isis in the Graeco-Roman World* (Ithaca: Cornell University Press, 1971), pp. 22–23, 33, 66, 71, 86–87, 89–99, 241–42; Pomeroy, *Goddesses, Whores, Wives, and Slaves,* pp. 217–26.

44. H. W. Parke, *Greek Oracles* (London: Hutchinson & Co., Ltd., 1967), p. 31; Peter Hoyle, *Delphi* (London: Cassell & Co., Ltd., 1967), pp. 74, 84, 87.

45. Walther Hinz, *The Lost World of Elam,* trans. Jennifer Barnes (New York: New York University Press, 1973), pp. 41–67, 91, 101–10.

46. Samuel Noah Kramer, "Poets and Psalmists: Goddesses and Theologians; Literary, Religious and Anthropological Aspects of the Legacy of Sumer," in Denise Schmandt-Besserat, ed., *The Legacy of Sumer,* Bibliotheca Mesopotamica: Primary sources and interpretive analyses for the study of Mesopotamian civilization and its influences from late prehistory to the end of the cuneiform tradition, ed. Giorgio Buccellati, Vol. IV (Malibu: Undena Publications, 1976), p. 12.

47. Ibid., p. 14.

48. Ibid., pp. 12–16.

49. Ibid., p. 13.

50. Enheduanna, *The Exaltation of Inanna,* pp. 1–11.

51. See, for example, L. Delaporte, *Mesopotamia: The Babylonian and Assyrian Civilization,* trans. V. Gordon Childe, 1st printing, 1925 (New York: Barnes & Noble, 1970), p. 157; Morris Jastrow, *The Civilization of Babylonia and Assyria,* 1st printing, 1915 (New York: Benjamin Blom, 1971), pp. 317, 338, 340–41, 346; Seibert, *Women in the Ancient Near East,* p. 31.

52. Georges Dossin and André Finet, *Archives Royales de Mari: Correspondence Féminine* (Paris: Librairie Orientaliste Paul Geuthner, 1978), letters #1, 3, 15, 22, 23, 31, 40, 50, 55; Bernard Frank Batto, *Studies on Women at Mari* (Baltimore: The Johns Hopkins University Press, 1974), pp. 79–139.

53. Batto, *Studies on Women at Mari,* pp. 64–72.

54. Dossin and Finet, *Archives Royales de Mari,* letter #50, trans. Kelley Eskridge. The "lock of hair" and the "fringe of the coat" sent to the king apparently were common types of "proof" of the authenticity of oracles.

55. Batto, *Studies on Women at Mari,* p. 122.

56. Ibid., p. 125.

57. See, for example, Rivkah Harris, *Journal of the Economic and Social History of the Orient,* 9, 1966, pp. 308–309; Batto, *Studies on Women at Mari,* p. 5.

58. See, for example, Delaporte, *Mesopotamia,* p. 310.

59. A. Leo Oppenheim, *Ancient Mesopotamia: Portrait of a Dead Civilization* (Chicago: University of Chicago Press, 1964), p. 100.

60. Albrecht Goetze, "Hittite Rituals, Incantations, and Description of Festivals," in Pritchard, *ANET,* pp. 346–51.

61. Ibid., pp. 347, 351–61.

62. John A. Wilson, "Oracles and Prophecies," in Pritchard, *ANET,* pp. 444–46.

63. Robert H. Pfeiffer, "Oracles and Prophecies," in Pritchard, *ANET,* pp. 449–50.

64. Hoyle, *Delphi,* pp. 37, 91–95; Parke, *Greek Oracles,* p. 31.

65. H. W. F. Saggs, *The Greatness That Was Babylon: A Sketch of the Ancient Civilization of the Tigris-Euphrates Valley* (New York: Mentor Books, 1962), p. 332.

66. Julian Morgenstern, "The Doctrine of Sin in the Babylonian Religion," in *Mitteilungen der Voerderasiatischen Gesellschaft* (Berlin: Wolf Peiser Verlag, 1905), p. 3.

67. See, for example, Jastrow, *Civilization of Babylonia and Assyria,* pp. 127, 272.

68. Morgenstern, "The Doctrine of Sin in the Babylonian Religion," pp. 23–25, 126–31.

69. R. Campbell Thompson, *The Devils and Evil Spirits of Babylonia, Being Babylonian and Assyrian Incantations Against the Demons, Ghouls, Vampires, Hobgoblins, Ghosts, and Kindred Evil Spirits, Which Attack Mankind,* trans. from the original cuneiform texts, Luzac's Semitic Text and Translation Series Vols. XIV, XV (London: Luzac & Co., 1903), 2 vols., I, Tablet V, Col. V, lines 30–44, p. 77.

70. Ibid., p. xliii.

71. Ibid., p. xxxvi.

72. Ibid., p. xxxii.

73. Morgenstern, "The Doctrine of Sin in the Babylonian Religion," p. 5.

74. Ibid., p. 57.

75. Ibid., p. 44.

76. See, for example, Morris Jastrow, *Aspects of Religious Belief and Practice in Babylonia and Assyria,* 1st printing, 1911 (New York: Benjamin Blom, 1971), p. 313; Georges Contenau, *Everyday Life in Babylon and Assyria,* 1st printing, 1954 (London: Edward Arnold, Ltd., 1964), p. 285; Hoyle, *Delphi,* p. 35; Harrison, *Prolegomena,* pp. 151, 154, 162.

77. Jacobsen, "Toward the Image of Tammuz," in Moran, *Toward the Image of Tammuz and Other Essays,* p. 82.

78. Kramer, *The Sacred Marriage Rite,* p. 59.

79. Ibid.

80. Ibid.

81. Ibid.

82. Ibid., p. 62.

83. Ibid., pp. 63–64.

84. Ibid., p. 64.

85. Oppenheim, *Ancient Mesopotamia,* p. 205.

86. Kramer, *The Sacred Marriage Rite,* p. 119.

87. Ibid., p. 122.

88. Jacobsen, "Toward the Image of Tammuz," in Moran, *Toward the Image of Tammuz and Other Essays,* pp. 73–101.

89. See, for example, Hawkes, *The First Great Civilizations,* p. 403; Petrie, *Religious Life in Ancient Egypt,* pp. 52–53.

90. See, for example, Walter Addison Jayne, *The Healing Gods of Ancient Civilizations,* 1st printing, 1925 (New York: University Books, 1962), p. 123.

91. *CAH,* vol. I, part 2, pp. 715–18.

92. *CAH,* vol. II, part 1, pp. 205–206; Maurice H. Farbridge, *Studies in Biblical and Semitic Symbolism* 1st printing, 1923 (New York: Ktav Publishing House, 1970), p. 255; Seibert, *Women in the Ancient Near East,* pp. 38–40.

93. Delaporte, *Mesopotamia,* p. 158; John Gray, *The Canaanites* (New York: Frederick A. Praeger, 1964), p. 136; Seibert, *Women in the Ancient Near East,* pp. 38–40.

94. *CAH,* vol. III, pp. 106–107; Seibert, *Women in the Ancient Near East,* p. 40.

95. Seibert, *Women in the Ancient Near East,* p. 52.

96. Ibid., p. 40.

97. George E. Mylonas, *Eleusis and the Eleusinian Mysteries* (Princeton: Princeton University Press, 1961), pp. 230–32.

98. Gray, *The Canaanites,* pp. 112–13, 115.

Chapter 5: Gender and the Nature of the Divine: The Biblical View

1. Phyllis Trible, "Nature of God in the OT," in Keith Crim, Lloyd Richard Bailey, Sr., Victor Paul Furnish, Emory Stevens Bucke, eds., *The Interpreter's Dictionary of the Bible: Supplementary Volume* (Nashville, Tenn.: Abingdon Press, 1976), pp. 963–66.

2. For example, the inference one might draw from Judges is that Yahweh is not always able to prevent Israel from reverting to idolatry, just as, at the beginning of Job, it is not clear that God knows with certainty about the outcome of Job's trials.

3. While female circumcision is practiced among Muslims today, and indeed has been practiced for a very long time in some cultures, its nature and purpose are quite different from those of the male circumcision required by God in the Old Testament. In most instances, it has no cultic significance. It is, in fact, a clitoridectomy, in which the clitoris is surgically excised in order to render women incapable of enjoying sex, or sexually passive. Its purpose may be to fulfill a cultural ideal of passive female sexuality or to insure the woman's monogamy. But in any event, male circumcision among the ancient Hebrews is not comparable to female circumcision.

4. See, for example, John H. Otwell, *And Sarah Laughed: The Status of Woman in the Old Testament* (Philadelphia: The Westminster Press, 1977), pp. 55, 143.

5. J. H. Hertz, ed., *Pentateuch and Haftorahs: Hebrew Text, English Translations and Commentary* (London: Soncino Press, 1972), p. 592, n. 1.

6. Ibid., p. 493, n. 25.

7. Fiorenza, "Interpreting Patriarchal Traditions," and Dewey, "Images of Women," in Letty M. Russell, ed., *The Liberating Word* (Philadelphia: The Westminster Press, 1977), pp. 49–51, 63–65.

8. William Foxwell Albright, *Archaeology and the Religion of Israel* (Baltimore: Johns Hopkins University Press, 1956), p. 175.

9. Moscati, *The Face of the Ancient Orient,* p. 253.

10. William Foxwell Albright, *Yahweh and the Gods of Canaan: A Historical Analysis of Two Contrasting Faiths* (New York: Doubleday & Co., 1968), p. 181.

11. Nahum M. Sarna, *Understanding Genesis: The Heritage of Biblical Israel* (New York: Schocken Books, 1974), p. 145.

12. Ibid., pp. 145–46.

13. Ibid., pp. 146–47.

14. Ibid., pp. 97–133, 154–63.

15. Rosemary Radford Ruether, *Mary—The Feminine Face of the Church* (Philadelphia: The Westminster Press, 1977), pp. 33–34.

16. Ibid., p. 33.

17. Leonard Swidler, "Is Sexism a Sign of Decadence in Religion?" in Judith Plaskow and Joan Arnold Romero, eds., *Women and Religion* (Missoula: The Scholars' Press and the American Academy of Religion, 1974), pp. 167–75.

18. Ibid., p. 168.

19. Constance F. Parvey, "The Theology and Leadership of Women in the New Testament," in Rosemary Radford Ruether, ed., *Religion and Sexism* (New York: Simon and Schuster, 1974), p. 128.

20. Krister Stendahl, "Enrichment or Threat? When the Eves Come Marching In," in Alice Hageman, ed., *Sexist Religion and Women in the Church: No More Silence!* (New York: Association Press, 1974), p. 120.

21. Swidler, "Is Sexism a Sign of Decadence in Religion?" p. 171.

Chapter 6: Sex Roles and the Relation of Power to Gender: Biblical Narratives

1. Johs. Pederson, *Israel: Its Life and Culture,* 1st printing, 1940 (London: Geoffrey Cumberlege, Oxford University Press, 1963), 4 vols., vols. 1–2, pp. 228–30.

2. Ibid., pp. 231–32.

3. Phyllis Bird, "Images of Women in the Old Testament," in Ruether, *Religion and Sexism,* p. 71.

4. Ibid., p. 72.

5. Ibid., p. 77.

6. Ibid., p. 76.

7. Ibid., p. 77.

8. Ibid., pp. 41–42, 48–55.

9. Carol Meyers, "The Roots of Restriction: Women in Early Israel," *Biblical Archaeologist,* September 1978, pp. 91–103.

10. Otwell, *And Sarah Laughed,* pp. 65–66.

11. Ibid., p. 66.

12. J. H. Hertz, ed., *Pentateuch & Haftorahs* (London: Soncino Press, 1972), note to Deut. 24:17–18, p. 852.

13. Phyllis Trible, "Women in the OT," in Crim et. al., *The Interpreter's Dictionary of the Bible: Supplementary Volume,* 1976, pp. 963–66.

14. Ibid., p. 965.

15. Ibid.

16. Ibid.

17. Ibid.

18. Ibid., p. 966.

19. Kramer, "Sumerian Myths and Epic Tales," in Pritchard, *ANET,* p. 41.

20. Trible, "Women in the OT," p. 965.

21. Trible, "Depatriarchalizing in Biblical Interpretation," *Journal of the American Academy of Religion,* XLI/I, March 1973, pp. 42–47.

22. See, for example, Constance F. Parvey, "The Theology and Leadership of Women in the New Testament," in Ruether, *Religion and Sexism,* pp. 117–49; Evelyn and Frank Stagg, *Woman in the World of Jesus,* (Philadelphia: The

Westminster Press, 1978), pp. 162–204; Munro, "Patriarchy and Charismatic Community in 'Paul,' " in Plaskow and Romero, *Women and Religion,* pp. 189–98.

Chapter 7: The Relation of Gender to Participation in Cult: Biblical Imperatives and Models

1. Johs. Pedersen, *Israel: Its Life and Culture* (London: Oxford University Press, 1963), vols. 3–4, p. 282.
2. Ibid., pp. 156–58.
3. H. H. Rowley, *From Joseph to Joshua: Biblical Traditions in the Light of Archaeology* (London: Oxford University Press, 1970), p. 151.
4. See, for example, Oscar Cullmann, *Early Christian Worship,* trans. A. Steward Todd and James B. Torrance (London: SCM Press, Ltd., 1969), pp. 66–71.
5. Note the variant translation in the R.S.V.
6. Cullmann, *Early Christian Worship,* p. 69.

Index